worship:

praying the sacraments

Peter E. **fink**, SJ

The Pastoral Press
Washington, DC

Acknowledgments

Chapter One originally appeared under the title "The Church as Sacrament and the Sacramental Life of the Church" in *Vatican II: The Unfinished Agenda*, ed., L. Richard and others (Mahweh, NJ: The Paulist Press, 1987). Chapter Two originally appeared under the title "Towards a Liturgical Theology" in *Worship* 47 (December 1973). Chapter Three, "Three Languages of Christian Sacraments," originally appeared under the same title in *Worship* 52 (November 1978). The material in Chapter Four originally appeared under the title "Sacramental Theology after Vatican II" in *The New Dictionary of Sacramental Worship*, ed., Peter E. Fink (Collegeville: The Liturgical Press, 1990). Chapter Five was originally delivered as an oral presentation in 1981 at a regional Jewish-Christian dialogue in Boston. It complemented a similar presentation on "The Significance of the Meal in Judaism." The material in Chapter Six originally appeared in *Worship* 58 (January 1984). Chapter Seven first appeared under the title "Investigating the Sacrament of Penance: An Experiment in Sacramental Theology" in *Worship* 54 (May 1980). Chapter Eight originally appeared in *Worship* 56 (November 1982). Chapter Nine is an edited combination of material that originally appeared in two publications. The first section originally appeared as "Liturgical Prayer and Spiritual Growth" in *Worship* 55 (September 1981); the second section appeared as "Liturgy and Spirituality: A Timely Intersection" in *Liturgy and Spirituality in Context*, ed., E. Bernstein (Collegeville: The Liturgical Press, 1990). The material in Chapter Ten was first published in *Worship* 58 (November 1984). It was originally delivered as the first part of three presentations at the "Theology for the 80s Seminar" at the St. Paul Seminary (now part of the University of St. Thomas) in St. Paul, Minnesota, in April 1984. Chapter Eleven originally appeared in *Worship* 59 (March 1985). Chapter Twelve is the third part of the presentations at the "Theology for the 80s Seminar" and first was published in *Worship* 59 (September 1985). We thank the publishers for permission to use again this material.

Unless otherwise noted, all citations from Vatican II documents are taken from *Vatican Council II: The Conciliar and Post-Conciliar Documents*, ed., Austin Flannery (Collegeville: The Liturgical Press).

ISBN: 0-912405-86-4

The Pastoral Press
225 Sheridan Street, N.W.
Washington, D.C. 20011
(202) 723-1254

The Pastoral Press is the publications division of the National Association of Pastoral Musicians, a membership organization of musicians and clergy dedicated to fostering the art of musical liturgy.

Printed in the United States of America

Dedicated

in

loving memory

to

Joseph Cavallo

1944-1990

brother priest

and

loyal friend

"Through Christ and in Christ

the riddles of sorrow and death

grow meaningful."

(Gaudium et Spes 22)

Contents

Introduction

THE BEST WAY I CAN THINK OF TO INTRODUCE THE ESSAYS WHICH
are collected in this volume is to tell a story. It is a story in
two parts. The first part dates to my years in graduate studies
at Emory University when I was asked to make a presentation
to the local parish liturgy committee. One of the women in
the parish, who knew me well, was surprised. "I didn't know
you knew anything about liturgy," she said, "I thought your
field was sacraments." The second part of the story followed a
few years later after I had begun to teach at Weston School of
Theology where I had been hired by the Pastoral Department
to teach liturgy. After several requests on my part that I teach
some of the basic courses in sacraments, someone murmured:
"Why does he want to teach sacraments? We hired him to
teach liturgy."

The story reflects a long history in which the worship of the
church was studied under two distinct and non-overlapping
headings. Liturgy was studied as liturgical history, as "rubrics," and, in the wake of the Vatican Council's liturgical reform, as liturgical implementation and praxis. Sacraments, on
the other hand, were explored by the dogmaticians in whose
hands the term *sacrament* was little more than an abstract theological concept. The study of liturgy blithely ignored any doctrinal depth to its subject, and the doctrinal study of sacraments failed to take any serious note of the fact that its subject

had a liturgical face. This unfortunate separation caused Walter Burghardt, in a 1973 address to the newly formed North American Academy of Liturgy, to lament a double loss: the loss to theology when the liturgy of the church is not taken seriously, and the loss to liturgy when so few liturgists were profound theologians.

The story also presents the challenge which, more than anything else, has been the primary passion of my own professional life, that is, to weave together in a single pattern of study the many faces of the church at prayer. This includes the doctrinal, the pastoral, the historical, the biblical, a concern for the intricacies of sacramental effectiveness, and an equal concern for the intricacies of successful liturgical celebration.

The essays gathered in this volume represent a journey of almost twenty years in which this challenge has taken flesh. Its guiding premise, schooled in the language of *Sacrosanctum Concilium*, is that the sacraments of the church *are* the liturgy of the church and that the systematic reflections of sacramental theologians are nothing else but efforts to explore the faith of the church as it arises and finds expression in its own liturgical celebrations. In the early years of the 1990s this premise is taken for granted as the term *liturgical theology* has arisen to name this unified approach to the church's worship. In 1973, when the earliest essay in this collection was published, and when Walter Burghardt issued his double lament, this premise was the distant hope of a very few.

In the same issue of *Worship* which presented my own "Towards a Liturgical Theology," included here as "Sacraments in a Human Church," John Gallen gave forth a challenge of a different kind. He called for the discovery or rediscovery of liturgy as *prayer* as the greatest need of the current liturgical reform. His challenge remains to the point. For many reasons it became for me the second passion of my professional life, to weave together not only sacramental doctrine and liturgical action, but the dimension of Christian spirituality as well. The reflecting church, the believing church, and the praying church all come together when the liturgy of the church is set in motion. In the classic movement of Anselm (*fides quaerens intellectum*) faith expressed in liturgical action seeks to be understood by reflective theology. And in a less classic, but no less important, movement (*intellectus quaerens fidem*), reflective theology seeks a return to faith through the medium of liturgical prayer.

The three parts of this triptych guide the structure of this volume. The first part gives strongest focus to reflective theology; the second, to the act of worship; the third, to the patterns and process of prayer. In each part, however, all three are in fact operative, for no one of them can successfully be examined except in light of the other two. The unity of the church at prayer must be preserved. The distinct focus of the three parts is nonetheless proper, for each face of the church's worship requires its own due attention. I hope the reader will discern the unity that underlies the three.

Part of the challenge of an emerging liturgical theology which this volume represents is the discovery and appropriation of a language with which to frame proper questions and pursue useful answers. I have, in the course of the journey, found many intellectual heroes and heroines. Three in particular deserve to be introduced along with the volume they have helped to produce. Paul Ricoeur, who in his own work on the structure and behavior of symbols combines a strong sense of the transcendent rooted in his Calvinist background with an equally strong sense of the immanent rooted in his love of Gabriel Marcel, particularly his theology of the incarnate body, provides a language that is uniquely apt to address the symbolic nature of Christian worship. A brother Jesuit, William Lynch, complements this with keen insight into the creative power of the human imagination and thus opens the tradition of sacramental effectiveness (*ex opere operato*), which Vatican II linked to the signifying power of sacraments (SC 7), to deeper and more fruitful understanding. Finally, the Scottish philosopher John Macmurray, who explored the realm of the personal and the interpersonal, offers a language that opens fresh windows on the relational nature of grace and prayer as well as the dynamics that must unfold in initiation, reconciliation, and eucharistic communion. To all three, none of whom did I have the privilege of knowing personally, I am deeply indebted.

There is another dimension to the journey which needs to be acknowledged because of its influence on the insights and explorations which unfold in this volume. Most liturgical theologians approach the worship of the church from the experiential base of a single ecclesial tradition. They may study other traditions as well, but they remain outsiders to all except their own. In addition to my own native tradition of Latin Roman Catholicism, I have been privileged to serve as priest in the West Syrian Maronite Church for almost ten years. Personally and professionally the experience has been invaluable. Humorously I say it keeps me honest; it certainly keeps me ecumenical. I can no longer explore Christian worship through Western eyes only. Nor can I enter into sacramental faith and prayer without holding together the affections of both East and West. I am most grateful to Monsignor Joseph Lahoud and the people of Our Lady of the Cedars of Lebanon parish in Boston for having granted me this rare and valued privilege.

Of course, any teacher is taught by his or her students, both those who cheer and those who frown. Many of the explorations in this volume passed first through the cheers and frowns of my students at Weston School of Theology in Cambridge, and to both the cheerers and the frowners I am grateful. The former give me motive to go on, and the latter keep me honest in the going.

Finally, I am most grateful to Virgil Funk for his invitation to gather these various essays into a single volume, and to Larry Johnson whose own efforts and graciousness made the going so smooth. And I am grateful to Michael Marx of *Worship* where the bulk of these essays first appeared in print. His eagerness and encouragement to a once young author hold a much treasured place in my heart.

Sacraments:
Theology and Practice

1

The Sacramental Life of the Church

ON 3 DECEMBER 1963 THE CONSTITUTION ON THE SACRED LITURGY (*Sacrosanctum Concilium*) was promulgated by Paul VI, the first official document to come forth from Vatican Council II. In its opening paragraph it stated the council's fourfold aim:

> . . . to impart an ever-increasing vigor to the Christian life of the faithful; to adapt more closely to the needs of our age those institutions which are subject to change; to foster whatever can promote union among all who believe in Christ; and, to strengthen whatever can help to call all mankind into the Church's fold. (SC 1)

In light of these goals, the constitution called for "reform and promotion of the liturgy," and set in motion a program of liturgical renewal which continues to unfold in the life of the church.

The most obvious and tangible result of this program of renewal has been the new ways of worship set forth in the revised rites for the eucharist and the other sacraments of the church. These represent, in many ways, a dramatic and radical change from the patterns of liturgical prayer established by the reform that followed the Council of Trent. Prayer in the vernacular, the recovery of the word as integral to the liturgy, the recognition and reinstatement of a variety of true liturgical ministers and ministries, the restoration of ancient liturgical texts, and the creation of new and original forms of prayer are but a few of the developments that have served to reshape the way in which Catholic Christians of the West worship in liturgical assembly.

Less obvious, perhaps, though no less dramatic and radical, is the understanding of sacrament that the Constitution on the Sacred Liturgy set forth, and which the new liturgical texts themselves embody. Theology before Vatican II had for centuries viewed sacraments somewhat objectively, as sacred signs and vehicles of grace, holy things that are administered to and received by the many through the ministry of a few. Each was defined in terms of its own special grace, and each was named a sacrament *of* the church insofar as the church was the custodian and dispenser of the mysteries of Christ. Each was considered to be on a par with the others, though some special note was always given to the eucharist, and little was said of the intrinsic relationship that exists among them. The 1917 Code of Canon Law treated the sacraments under the heading *de rebus* (on things), and, in accord with the decision first formulated at the Second Council of Lyons (1274), and solidly reaffirmed at the Councils of Florence (1439) and Trent (1547), there were considered to be exactly seven sacraments, no more and no less. The term *sacrament* was not used to identify anything else.

In contrast to this theological tradition, Vatican II recaptured and endorsed the understanding that sacraments are *liturgical acts*, the action prayer of the church gathered in assembly. This is true not only of the eucharist, where its application is somewhat easy to grasp, but also of the other sacraments where the role of the gathered assembly as integral to their enactment has been much less immediately evident. The revised Code of Canon Law now speaks of the sacraments under a different heading, namely, "The Office of Sanctifying in the Church," and the Constitution on the Sacred Liturgy gives a richer meaning to the statement that the sacraments are sacraments of the church. Each sacrament in its own way expresses and manifests "the mystery of Christ and the real nature of the true Church" (SC 2).

In addition, the sacraments are presented as ordered to the eucharist, which is itself primary. Lines of relationship are drawn, as, for example, with the initiation sacraments of baptism and confirmation leading to and completed by the eucharist. And in accord with certain theological developments in the middle twentieth century, notably those of Karl Rahner and Edward Schillebeeckx, the term sacrament is employed in both the Constitution on the Sacred Liturgy and the Dogmatic Constitution on the Church (*Lumen Gentium*) to name the very reality of the church itself and its relationship to the risen Christ. In Vatican II the term "sacrament" has clearly undergone development and transformation.

In this brief chapter I would like to explore some of the main lines of this development in understanding which Vatican II brought to the sacraments, a shift which now allows us to speak of the church as sacrament of Christ, and of the traditional seven sacraments as constituting the sacramental life of this sacramental church. I will sketch this development under six headings: (1) the church as sacrament of Christ; (2) sacraments as liturgical acts; (3) sacraments as signifying acts; (4) sacraments as expressive of the mystery of Christ; (5) the sacramental life of the Christian; and (6) the sacramental life of the church.

THE CHURCH AS SACRAMENT OF CHRIST

The Dogmatic Constitution on the Church speaks of the church as being "in the nature of sacrament—a sign and instrument, that is, of communion with God and of unity among all men" (LG 1). It seeks here to identify the intimate relationship between the church and the risen Christ. In like manner the Constitution on the Sacred Liturgy names the church "sacrament" in its very coming to be: ". . . it was from the side of Christ as he slept the sleep of death upon the cross that there came forth the 'wondrous sacrament of the whole Church'" (SC 5). As Christ is the sacrament of God in history, namely, God's visible manifestation, tangible presence, and embodied saving grace, in like manner the church is Christ's own sacrament in history until he shall come again. This extension of the word sacrament to the church is crucial both to Vatican II's theology of sacraments and to the ritual revisions which have come about as a result of its mandate for liturgical reform.

By naming the church *sacrament* the council expanded the

meaning of the term well beyond its familiar application to the liturgical acts of baptism, confirmation, eucharist, anointing of the sick, reconciliation of sinners, orders, and marriage. It is not as though an eighth sacrament were being named in addition to the traditional seven. Church as sacrament is more fundamental. It is a statement of the church's identity and mission, and one which serves to link the traditional seven to the church precisely in terms of its identity and mission.

The sacramentality of the church is central to the theology of Vatican II, and the extension of the word to name the church serves to illuminate both the reality of the church and the true sacramentality of the traditional seven liturgical acts. The liturgy is the outstanding means by which the faithful can "express in their lives and manifest to others the mystery of Christ and the real nature of the true Church" (SC 2). The truth of the church is that it is an expression, a visible manifestation, of the risen Christ and an effective agent of Christ's own saving work. The truth of the seven sacraments is that they visibly portray and effectively enact this deepest truth of the church itself. The church in assembly expresses its identity and carries out its mission as the sacrament of Christ whenever it baptizes, confirms, celebrates the eucharist, anoints the sick, reconciles the sinner, consecrates ordained ministers, or blesses married love.

As applied to the church, therefore, the term "sacrament" is descriptive. It names something essential to the church's mission and ministry, namely, that this community of believers is both the manifestation and effective agent of Christ's own presence and ongoing saving work. When the church gathers in assembly to carry out this mission and ministry through the medium of its ritual actions, it embodies, makes present, and effectively continues the saving work of Christ. These ritual actions are called sacraments precisely for this reason. They are not independent of the sacramentality of the church. They are the sacraments of the church precisely because they bring the church's sacramentality to expression.

SACRAMENTS AS LITURGICAL ACTS

With the primary sacrament of Christ identified as the

church, and more concretely the church gathered in liturgical assembly, the Constitution on the Sacred Liturgy proceeds to speak of sacraments as *liturgy*, that is, actions of the church in liturgical assembly. Immediately the understanding and imagination are invited to expand beyond the traditional and more restricted focus on matter, form, minister, and recipient alone, and to call into view, as the primary focus for each sacrament, the whole assembly and its total liturgical action. This is a remarkable enough recovery for the eucharist, which had for centuries been viewed as the act of the priest, with the people in passive attendance. It is truly astonishing with regard to baptism, or reconciliation, or orders, or even marriage, when an assembly, if one was gathered at all, was gathered exclusively to watch the sacrament take place.

It is clear from the constitution that the normative enactment of each sacrament is that which is done by the church in assembly: ". . . rites which are meant to be celebrated in common, with the faithful present and participating, should as far as possible be celebrated in that way rather than by an individual and quasi-privately" (SC 27). Because sacraments are actions of the church, it is important that everyone act: "In the restoration and promotion of the sacred liturgy the full and active participation by all the people is the aim to be considered before all else" (SC 14). And because the enacted ritual is itself the living expression of the sacrament, the ritual text and directives must foster, not hinder, this participation by all: "When the liturgical books are being revised, the people's parts must be carefully indicated by the rubrics" (SC 31), and "The rites should be . . . within the people's powers of comprehension, and normally not require much explanation" (SC 34).

A note should be made here about one of the more obscure yet vitally important tenets of scholastic sacramental theology. Sacraments are effective enactments of the saving work of Christ, and they achieve their effect in the very doing of them (*ex opere operato*). The two essential pieces of this tradition required that: (1) the ritual be done according to the mind of the church ("do what the church intends"), and (2) that people be open to what is done ("put no obstacle in the way"). As long as the focus remained on sacrament as thing, administered by a special minister, and received by the faithful, it was almost impossible to avoid the accusation that sacraments behaved like magic. Once the full and active participation of all the people is restored as essential to sacramental action, however, the puzzlement yields to something quite simple and obvious. People are affected by what they do, and what they do determines the effect. Provided they are open to what they are doing in sacraments, the entire assembly will be affected accordingly. What faith adds to the equation is that these effects, through the gracious action of God in Christ, are themselves redemption.

SACRAMENTS AS SIGNIFYING ACTS

Drawing on the insight of Augustine that when someone baptizes it is Christ who baptizes, scholastic theology secured for Catholic faith the effectiveness of sacraments. Christ himself, present in the act, is the source of all sacramental effectiveness. What the Scholastics mentioned, but did not develop, however, was the mode of this effectiveness: how sacraments work. The Constitution on the Sacred Liturgy brought forward this neglected dimension of sacramental effectiveness by remembering and reaffirming that sacraments achieve their effect "by signifying." Signifying is a specific way of making something happen, and proper signification is crucial if sacraments are to be properly effective.

This is made clear in the strong insistence throughout the Constitution on the Sacred Liturgy that the liturgical texts and rites express more clearly the holy things which they signify and signify more fully and accurately the holy realities they contain. If the preconciliar church was content to affirm that sacraments effect what they signify, the postconciliar church has added a complementary concern: that sacraments signify all we believe they effect. The relationship between what sacraments accomplish, namely, Christ's saving work, and the signifiers that constitute sacraments as such is clearly and boldly set out: the liturgy "involves the presentation of man's sanctification under the guise of signs perceptible by the senses and its accomplishment in ways appropriate to each of these signs" (SC 7).

Sacramental actions involve the participants in the truth of Jesus Christ, and in their own deepest truth as that is revealed in and by him. Whether we stand in thanksgiving around the table of sacrifice and partake of Jesus' own offering, the Father's embrace and consecration of Jesus, and the fellowship in the Spirit which Jesus has brought about, or enact that same truth specifically in the face of sin, or sickness, or service, or love, or those whom we initiate into our midst, in sacraments we are drawn into Christ's own truth. Our imaginations become shaped by the truths of Christ. Our affections take on the affections of Christ. And the behavior we enact together is Christ's own behavior toward God (*Abba*) and toward those he names as friends. The power of our sacraments is that they make an appeal to our consciousness, to our affections, and to our behavior, in order that, in the words of Paul, we "put on Christ." This appeal is made in the face of all other ways of imagining, all other ways of affection and behavior, that are rooted, not in Christ, but rather in our own sinfulness. What we do in sacraments places us in Christ's own way of being, and therefore calls us to conversion from our sins, and to transformation into Christ.

Doing what the church intends places us in Christ's own truth. Putting no obstacle in the way renders us vulnerable to his power to transform us. And our act of consent, Amen, enabled by Christ's own power within us, an act which is so essential to the completion of our sacraments, is nothing less than our surrender into his own gracious ways. Sacraments achieve their effect by signifying, and their signifying power works to transform us into Christ, into Christ's way of being, Christ's way of praying, Christ's way of acting, Christ's way of loving, healing, forgiving, serving.

It is important to remember that signifying, where sacraments are concerned, is not a purely cognitive act. This would be true if Vatican II had not reversed the medieval understanding of liturgy as "sacred drama" observed by the assembly as if by an audience. The catechetical method known as allegory which medieval theology spawned does rely on the cognitive precisely because it is a catechesis for watchers. In the wake of Vatican II, however, there are no watchers in sacraments, only doers, and the catechesis proper to doers, mystagogy, is intended to illuminate not only what one sees, but more deeply what one experiences with all of the senses. The awareness to which sacraments aim to lead the participants is not the "I understand" or "I see" of a cognitive appeal, but rather the "Amen," the surrender, of the whole person to the fullness of that in which we are engaged.

SACRAMENTS AS EXPRESSIVE OF THE MYSTERY OF CHRIST

The rituals of our sacraments, including the prayers, the gestures, and the material elements such as food, water, and oil, allow those who enact the sacraments to express the mystery of Christ (SC 2). This mystery of Christ is the truth of Jesus' own life, lived in obedient love toward the Father and in embracing love toward all creation. It is the truth expressed in the familiar hymn which Paul incorporated into his Letter to the Philippians: ". . . he humbled himself and became obedient unto death, even death on a cross. Therefore God has highly exalted him . . ." (Phil 2:8-9). This truth is presented with its challenging mandate: "Have this mind among yourselves, which you have in Christ Jesus . . ." (Phil 2:5). It is likewise the truth proclaimed in John: "No longer do I call you servants . . . I have called you friends" (Jn 15:15). This too has its mandate: "Love one another as I have loved you."

The mystery of Christ is a mystery of love, a mystery of relationship. It is the love between Abba and Christ who is Son. It is the love between the First-born and all whom he calls and gathers into himself. This profound relational mystery finds expression in our ritual acts in word, where the assembly opens itself and gives itself over to God's ways revealed in Christ, in consecration, where the God who raised Jesus from the dead once again makes firm commitment to and covenant with those who are gathered with Christ and claims and consecrates them as God's own people, and finally in communion, where relationship with Christ and with the Abba of Christ sets all who enact the mystery into relationship with each other. These four—word, offertory, consecration, and communion—find expression not only in the eucharist but in all the sacraments of the church.

Because the mystery of Christ is a personal mystery, the symbols that bring it to expression must include persons.

Things alone cannot express a mystery of love. Thus it is that the people of the church are said to make Christ present in their very gathering, that the presiding minister of liturgical prayer is said to act *in persona Christi*, that the minister of the word gives human voice to the Christ who speaks in word, and that the consecrated food, that so tangibly makes Christ present in the eucharist, remains, as the Council of Trent proclaimed, *ad manducandum*, that is, food shared by people through the ministry of people. Full and active participation of the people, and the ministries of liturgical ministers in the assembly, are required so that the personal mystery of Christ may be personally brought to expression.

THE SACRAMENTAL LIFE OF THE CHRISTIAN

A clear thread running through the Constitution on the Sacred Liturgy is that sacraments aim at human transformation, a transformation that can be humanly described and humanly recognized. This transformation is not, and cannot be, understood as something taking place all at once. It is a human process, and therefore a slow process, one indeed which unfolds throughout one's life. Sacramental actions are not independent of life's journey. It is this very journey which they encapsulate, express, shape, and deepen.

It is at this point that Vatican II stretches our imagination even further. The scholastic theology of sacraments simply did not have a mechanism, nor even the language, to relate participation in sacraments to the ongoing transformation into Christ. It did, of course, name "sanctifying grace" as an increased share in the life of Christ, but, beyond affirming it, there was little in scholastic theology to describe just what that meant or how it took effect. It did speak as well of "actual grace," which is the help sacraments give for living one's life, but even here there was little intrinsic connection drawn between the actual enactment of the sacrament and the grace that ensued. Sacraments were envisioned episodically, that is, as individual experiences with their own specific value and effect, and not within the process view that ongoing transformation into Christ calls for.

Fortunately, one of the most remarkable achievements of

the postconciliar liturgical reform, namely the Rite of Christian Initiation of Adults (RCIA), brought forward such a mechanism and such a language. The RCIA identifies the intimate relationship that exists between baptism, confirmation, and eucharist, and calls for their celebration together in a single ritual enactment. Much more, however, it locates these three sacraments within a life process which is Christian initiation. Initiation unfolds in stages, though the sacraments themselves do not constitute the stages. Instead, they emerge from the process already underway for those being initiated, raise that process to a new level, and lead back into the process which must continue throughout one's life.

The RCIA recaptures Augustine's insight into the eucharist that the eucharist itself is the repeatable sacrament of initiation. If one holds the RCIA together with the restored rites of Christian burial, the full scope of initiation is made clear. The funeral rite calls on the baptism of Christians to proclaim that what was enacted throughout one's life in sacrament has finally been realized in Christian death. In death one passes through in fact what one has passed through ritually in baptism, in the eucharist, and indeed in all the sacraments enacted throughout one's life.

With the concept of initiation offered by the RCIA, it is possible to view each sacrament, and every enactment of the sacraments, as part of the initiation process, and as part of the sacramental life of each Christian. It is a process that has a structure, a shape, and a goal, captured and enacted in the sacraments that are *of* initiation. All who are placed with Christ (the primary symbolism of baptism) are anointed and consecrated by the Father (the primary symbolism of the anointing of confirmation) and set in union with Christ and with each other by God's own Spirit placed within us (the primary symbolism of the eucharist). The sacramental life of each Christian is lived toward the achievement of this reality, and every enactment of the sacraments enacts this reality into our life and our history. This is the hope in which Christians live, and the destiny planned by God from the beginning to be realized by all at death. It is this goal toward which the church's sacraments invite and lead us.

What both the Constitution on the Sacred Liturgy and the

reformed liturgical rituals call for is nothing less than a sacramental spirituality. The language of journey, the language of process, a language which will relate sacramental enactments not only to each other but even more to the gradual transformation of human life into the truth which sacraments express, will be essential to such a spirituality and to a theology of sacraments which must underlie it. Sacraments truly deserve to be treated under the heading: "The Office of Sanctifying in the Church."

THE SACRAMENTAL LIFE OF THE CHURCH

The final expansion of the term sacrament envisioned by Vatican II is in many ways a return full-circle to the point at which these reflections began. There the church itself was named to be sacrament, and this naming was said to be foundational to both the theology and the praxis that has come from the conciliar reform. The liturgical acts that are named sacrament express this sacramentality of the church. Moreover, these acts cannot be seen in isolation from life, but need to be seen as part of the transformative process of Christian initiation into which each Christian is invited by the Lord. This needs now to be taken one step further, beyond the individual Christian to the church as a whole.

It is necessary to remember that what is proclaimed in the sacraments involves Christians in a tension that is fundamental to the church itself. What is proclaimed has both the finality of an accomplished fact, namely, the once-for-all redemptive act of Jesus Christ, and the unfinished-ness that attends the unfolding of that fact in human history. On God's part, what is proclaimed in sacraments is complete; in human life, however, and indeed in the life of the church, it is yet to be fully realized. For any Christian, this process of realization is the life-long venture that is Christian initiation. For the church it is the same process writ large, the history of the church as it moves toward the *eschaton*.

The church is called the sacrament of Christ and, as noted above, this is a statement of both its identity and its mission. This sacramentality of the church is, on the one hand, an accomplished fact brought about in the death and resurrection of Christ and in the coming of the Spirit which that death and resurrection unleashed. The identity and the mission of the church share in the once-for-all redemptive act of Christ. On the other hand, however, the truth that the church is the sacrament of Christ is only partially realized by the church at any point in its passage through human history. The church too is on a journey of initiation and transformation which will not be complete until "he comes again."

The statement that the church is the sacrament of Christ is, therefore, in addition to being a statement of identity and mission, a self-summoning statement. The very proclamation of it summons the church more deeply into its own truth. Whenever it is proclaimed, as it is each time the church enacts its sacraments, it calls the church to be and become more deeply that which is proclaimed. It is not only the individual Christian, but the church itself, which must undergo a continual process of transformation into Christ.

The RCIA envisions the sacramentality of the church to be most vividly displayed in the life of a local church, and not exclusively in liturgical ritual moments. It envisions a people who pray, believe, relate to one another, and serve one another in the manner displayed in Jesus' own life. It envisions a people who do what Christ did, namely, speak of God, heal and forgive, call to reconciliation, and live the new life that belongs to the children of God. "By this all will know you are my disciples, if you have love for one another" (Jn 13:35). Echoing an insight from the sixteenth-century Protestant reformation, Vatican II acknowledged that the church must always undergo reformation. Transformation into the ways of Christ is the stuff of this reformation. As with the individual Christian, so too with the church as a whole, sacramental life is larger than ritual moments. What goes on in assembly serves to foster what must go on in the church as a whole if the church will be faithful to the mission and ministry given it by Christ.

* * * * * *

Vatican II was indeed a major moment in the history of the church, and specifically in the history of liturgical worship and sacramental understanding. The six points outlined above

capture at least in skeletal form the extent to which postconciliar Catholic Christians, and any others who choose to be guided by Vatican II, are challenged to expand and deepen their
understanding: how they understand themselves in relation to
Christ, how they understand what they do when they enact
that relationship in liturgical, sacramental act, and how they
understand what they are summoned to become whenever
they gather in assembly to "express in their lives and manifest
to others the mystery of Christ and the real nature of the true
Church" (SC 2). The sacraments of the church are not only vehicles of grace. Together they constitute the life of the church
and allow that life to grow and deepen.

2

Sacraments in
a Human Church

ANYONE WHO IS COMMITTED TO THE TASK OF LITURGICAL REFORM and renewal must inevitably stop from time to time to ask how well the project is proceeding. At that point of question, a certain irony presents itself. To the extent that one continues to be enthusiastic about reform and renewal, there will always be a sense of beginning. The nature of the task is such that the work undone will always far exceed that which has already been accomplished, and new possibilities for the future will continue to present themselves for study, exploration, and implementation. The ongoing question for renewal and reform remains: "What next?"

At the same time, one cannot help but notice that the enthusiasm of the liturgical reformer is not shared equally by all members of the church. Many bishops, priests, and lay members of the church seem to think and act as though the liturgical reform called for by Vatican II has already come to pass. Either they have become quite bored with the whole thing or else are content that the church has accomplished everything it set out to accomplish. Nothing remains but some very practical issues: the training of liturgical ministers, programs for Christian initiation, time for first confession, employment of inclusive language, and so forth.

In the meantime, what might be called a liturgical "dark side" has begun to appear to challenge, if not shatter, the optimism that once more generally attended liturgical renewal and reform. The growing shortage of ordained priests, for example, has shifted the liturgical conversation in the direction of liturgical restriction rather than possibility, with curious phrases such as "priest-less parishes" and "Mass-less Sundays" gaining unfortunate currency. The continuing disparity between men and women with regard to placement in liturgical ministries, as another example, has shifted the conversation to that disparity and away from the creative possibilities both for those ministries and for the liturgical assembly as a whole.

Both the irony and the dark side signal an inevitable frustration for anyone who would seek to serve liturgical reform and renewal. As in the days of the great liturgical pioneers, those who would serve the church at prayer find themselves talking to a church that grows more and more reluctant to listen. They continue to suggest change and movement to a church which seems more eager to cling to some measure of liturgical stability, and in some instances even to retreat to an earlier day when liturgical forms and patterns of prayer were familiar and secure.

From the perspective of a committed liturgical reformer, the years since Vatican II have seen the fulfillment of many dreams. They have also seen the end of an unforeseen illusion—namely, that change in liturgical form and language would solve all the church's problems with worship, In fact, the church now finds itself with far more questions than answers, questions which reach into every area of Christian theology and every facet of Christian life. An ongoing task of liturgical reform is to take note of these questions as they arise, and explore them thoughtfully as essential to the ongoing "new beginning" which liturgical reform and renewal involve.

Liturgical renewal has given rise to liturgical theology, a systematic attempt to understand and serve the ways of the church at prayer. As a branch of theology it is itself young and in the process of taking its proper shape. It is more than a theology of the liturgy because it is more than reflection on the liturgy itself. It takes place at the intersection of theology, liturgy, and life, and involves the conditioning interaction of these three: the theological models or patterns which sacramentalists have structured to interpret the church's prayer, the pastoral and practical insights which have come to liturgical ministers in their attempt to work creatively with the church's prayer, and the limitations imposed on both by the praying church which is, and must always remain, finite and human.

The theological reflection that follows here is an essay in liturgical theology. The issue addressed is an issue of the human church at prayer, namely, the all too observable discrepancy between actual liturgical celebrations in the church and the claims which faith makes for those celebrations. Catholic theology asserts, for example, that the eucharist is the sacrifice of Christ renewed, a memorial of the Christ event, and a pledge of eschatological fulfillment. The liturgical calendar maps out a rich fare of festivity and celebration to mark the various moods and movements of the church's prayer. In actual liturgies, however, it is frequently difficult to locate more than suggestions of this rich theological promise and festive affection in either the awareness of the praying Christian or the actions which the community performs. It anything has become clearer in the years since Vatican II, it is that neither touch-and-go experiment nor carefully controlled liturgical rites have been able to overcome this discrepancy. The issue involved lies somewhere else.

DEFINING THE ISSUE

Where does the issue lie? The suggestion I would like to explore here is that the issue lies not so much in the arena of doctrinal truth or liturgical correctness, but rather in the arena of credibility and honesty. Under what conditions is the church's prayer an honest enactment of the claims which the church makes for it? Under what conditions are the church's claims for its prayer to be rendered credible? This involves a shift from a metaphysical mode of reflection to one which is more phenomenological in tone. It implies a pursuit of criteria for success or failure in which the question of truth, is it true that Christ is present or is it true that the Mass is the sacrifice of Christ, will not be the primary concern. The concern will be rather the extent to which the liturgical enactment of the church's sacraments honestly and credibly presents the truth of the church's faith.

The question of truth arises when the validity of an interpretation of the church's prayer is no longer convincing. A failure of this kind calls for theological argument to re-present and re-convince one of the truths of the church's faith. On the other hand, the question that arises when the ritual enactment itself no longer presents the church's faith honestly, or when the people of the church no longer receive it credibly, will not be adequately met with argument alone. A different response is required.

Part of the response must address the quality of faith which a community brings to its worship. The quality of faith is a serious controlling factor for the success or failure of the church's prayer. Sacraments presuppose faith (SC 59). Faith that is brought to worship is deepened in worship. In addition, "the very act of celebrating them most effectively disposes the faithful to receive this grace to their profit, to worship God duly, and to practice charity" (ibid.).

It should not be automatically supposed that this is simply a question of catechesis. Nor should it be automatically assumed that because Christians have been baptized they possess the faith required to participate in sacraments fruitfully. Whatever theological validity there may be to the concept of faith as an infused habit of the soul, this does not seem to be a particularly helpful concept when seeking the quality of faith which must be a minimum prerequisite for a particular liturgical celebration. We must be ready to acknowledge and seek the theological implications of what has already begun to emerge on the intuitive-pastoral level, that in some situations the quality of faith is not adequate to the intended celebration. The reluctance of some priests to baptize a child whose parents show no serious participation in the Christian community is but one case in point.

A second part of the response to the question of credibility and honesty can be guided by the striking insistence in the Constitution on the Sacred Liturgy: the liturgy "involves the presentation of man's sanctification under the guise of signs perceptible to the senses and its accomplishment in ways appropriate to each of these signs" (SC 7). *Sanctification* is a symbolic word which gathers together all the models which theologians have constructed to interpret and understand the

Christ-event-for-us. All these models together constitute what the church has come to understand about its worship. They also constitute what the church promises to those whom it invites into its worship. Liturgists cannot proceed independently of these theological models. More than anything else it is their task to structure a worship service that will render what the church promises perceptible to the senses. At the same time it is important for theologians to remember that the ultimate test of their theological model is not its theological correctness, but the ability of the praying church to recognize in its prayer the richness which the model promises.

The praying church, we are reminded over and over again, is not some abstract ideal existing everywhere but nowhere. It is, in the concrete moment of its worship, a group of human beings. There is an incompleteness to their gathering which cannot be ignored. They are not-quite-yet a community; their faith is not-quite-yet fully formed. They are sinners not-quite-yet under the full power of redemption. They are, in short, the church, not-quite-yet the kingdom of God.

To affirm this not-quite-yet-ness of the church is to affirm some serious limitations on the possibilities for its prayer. All too often these limitations take the form of practical and political obstacles: obstinancy on the part of a bishop, inability on the part of a celebrant, unresponsiveness on the part of the community. My suspicion is that such limitations are more than practical and political; they have theological significance as well. A theology of the church is greatly chastened by the recognition that it is not yet the kingdom of God. A liturgical theology must likewise be chastened by the recognition that liturgy is always the prayer of the church.

The criteria of credibility and honesty arise quite naturally out of the liturgical understanding that has grown in the church since Vatican II. The worshiping community in its moment of worship is involved in a dual act of proclamation. On the one hand, it is the whole church, with all its history and the richness of its heritage, proclaiming to this here-and-now community something about itself in the hope of leading this community more deeply into the mystery of who it is. "They [the sacraments] not only presuppose faith, but by words and objects they also nourish, strengthen, and express it" (SC 59).

On the other hand, it is this human community proclaiming its union with the whole church and proclaiming itself as a saving reality to the world. Worship is thus a language, and the church must always question itself if it is using that language honestly. To the extent that the living members of the praying church back by their lives what they say in ritual, to that extent their ritual will be honest and credible.

THE METHOD

This essay in liturgical theology is gradually taking shape. We have explored the problematic which must be addressed, the major ingredients, and the central question which must be attended to. It remains now to consider the question of method. If the reflections of theologians, the discoveries of liturgists, and the limitations of the praying church are to interact, how is that interaction to take place? An obvious first response would be a linear movement from the theological models through liturgical form to the praying church, with the theologians offering promise and expectation, the liturgists structuring areas of recognition, and the praying church serving as ultimate test of success or failure. Let us explore this a bit to see if it is adequate.

With his encounter model for sacrament and worship, Schillebeeckx managed to breathe life into the four hundred-year-old Tridentine heritage and make that heritage accessible to the contemporary church.[1] His work stands as a perfect transition, maintaining continuity with the theological past, yet opening the doors for new forms of creative reflection. Since his work first appeared in English in 1963, several other models have developed in dialogue with contemporary theological currents. To recall just a few, we can name a biblical model, with its accent on *anamnesis*; a secular model, like the one proposed by George McCauley;[2] and a humanizing model, outlined in Joseph Powers' *Spirit and Sacrament*.[3] The plurality of models suggests a first question—namely, how these can and should relate to each other.

There will always be, I suppose, the tendency to consider the latest model the most relevant (that awful word), to view the models as somehow in competition, and to search for a compromise model or even a super-model which will embrace them all. We are all Cartesians at heart, endlessly looking for a clear and distinct point from which to begin. Behind this tendency, of course, is the search for clarity which the human mind must have if it is to understand.

In a liturgical theology, however, we are concerned with more than the understanding. The moment of worship is a moment of invitation as well. It is a moment when all that the church understands about itself is celebrated in order to invite people more deeply into the mystery. Clearly no model adequately embraces the mystery. Even the totality of all models, which together express the church's understanding of itself and its worship to date, cannot be said to embrace the mystery of who the church is. Every worship event involves a living people interacting with the mystery and contains at least the possibility of adding new data for theological reflection and of inviting the church to a new level of self-understanding. The question, then, is: Under what conditions do theological models become invitational?

My point can be made somewhat clearer by introducing a distinction between two kinds of language, declarative and evocative. Often enough the same words can serve as both. I call language "declarative" which is informational. It aims at clarity and, when used well, has the power to satisfy the human mind. "Evocative" language, on the other hand, serves more to transform than to inform. It suggests, it invites, it excites. Its aim is not clarity all all, but rather the as yet unprobed richness and depth which language can convey. Declarative language is the language of control. It manipulates one through the logic of argument and hopefully terminates in some form of agreement. Evocative language surrenders control and all forms of predetermined manipulation. It is the kind of language which stimulates the freedom of the listener and activates that freedom to creative response.

A theological model in its reflective phase of development is indeed declarative language. It seeks to understand. When the same model, however, again enters the living world of the church's prayer, it must shift its mode and be seen as evocative. If this does not take place, the theological model can become destructive of the worship event which it is meant to serve. Consider, by way of example, the reading of a poem, an analysis of the poem, and the subsequent return to the poem itself. It is possible that the second reading of the poem will be confined, predetermined, by the analysis that just took place. In that case the reader, while going through the motions of a second reading, will in fact be merely rehearsing in the mind the clear understanding he or she has just obtained. The second time around the person is not reading the poem at all. Analysis will only serve a second reading if it frees the reader to look for new levels of experience in the reading, either new meaning as yet undiscovered or a deeper appreciation of meaning already found. In terms of the distinction offered here, the analysis cannot remain declarative language during the second reading. It must translate itself into evocative language instead.

If the language of theological models remains declarative in the celebration, the worship may be clear and understandable, but it will be without depth or mystery. If, however, the models are offered evocatively, they can give the worshiper something to look for and awaken the dynamic of expectation, giving free reign to what theologians speak of as *grace* and the power of the word. I take this to be the intention of the Second Vatican Council's statement: "But in order that the liturgy may be able to produce its full effects, it is necessary that the faithful come to it with proper dispositions . . ." (SC 11). Without this sense of expectation freed from the control of any predefining model, the worshiper will merely go through the motions of liturgy; he or she will not be worshiping at all.

In suggesting that theological models be finally viewed evocatively, I am imposing a demand that theologians surrender control and submit their reflections to a test of credibility outside their own reflective domain. They cannot declare in advance what the worship event should be. At the same time, in imposing the criterion of credibility, namely, the ability of the praying church to recognize in its worship the richness of the theological models, I am also denying to the liturgist any form of manipulative control. Whatever creative input either theologian or liturgist makes to the worship of the praying church must finally be vulnerable to the freedom of a worshiping people and the action of God within them.

There is an element of *kenosis* emerging from these reflections. I am inclined to think that a kenotic movement must be essential to any liturgical reform and renewal. It is the enduring scandal of Christianity that all the richness of theological reflection about the mystery of God takes visible, tangible, historical shape and form in a human person. "Isn't he the son of the carpenter?" It must continue to be the enduring scandal of Christian worship that all the theological richness which has gathered through the centuries about the worship event must also always take visible, tangible, historical shape and form in men and women and in the very ordinary human actions they do together as part of Christian worship.

There is a real danger in not taking this kenotic element with sufficient seriousness, a danger which echoes the ancient theological distortion known as Docetism. If theologians forget that their interpretive models must ultimately become perceptible to the senses, their model may well become so overpowering in what they claim that no human ritual and no human church could ever render them credible. When that happens, the question must turn from credibility to truth, and the locus of criteria for evaluation must shift from the praying church to the world of theological thought. Since ritual can no longer express the richness which the church promises, it must be seen as pointing to it. Crassly put, while people do this, God does that, and God's activity in fact takes place somewhere else. This kind of separation gives rise to the very dualism that has afflicted the church's worship for too long. If we are to proceed in the ongoing task of reform and renewal, this dualism must be laid to rest wherever it appears.

The suggested movement from theological model to praying church is, of course, necessary. It should be clear at this point, however, that it is not sufficient to specify the mode of interaction among the three elements. Some form of reverse movement is equally necessary. The liturgist must evaluate the realistic possibilities for liturgical prayer and ask how the demand for sensual perceptibility conditions both the language and structure of theological models. There is also need to reflect on the limiting conditions within which the church must pray, limitations of finitude, incompleteness, and sinfulness, and ask how these limitations condition both the theological model and the liturgical form.

A final point suggests itself in a section of the constitution already cited: human sanctification is accomplished in ways appropriate to signs perceptible by the senses (SC 7). The demand here is for a careful analysis of the very human actions which constitute Christian worship, to determine the extent and possibility of their redeeming power. The richness of the theological model must not only become manifest in a way that is perceptible to the senses. The actual unfolding of what it claims must be understood to take place within the human actions and in a manner that is proper to these actions. Whatever sanctification is effected in the eucharist, for example, must be understood and recognized as effected not merely in the sharing of bread and wine but in the very human dynamic that is proper to the sharing of bread and wine.

Once again we are confronted with a dualism, this time a language dualism, that must be destroyed. Theological models tend to use symbols whose meaning is explicated in terms of other symbols within the same model. There is need to break this theological enclosure and carefully locate the meaning of theological symbols in the world of normal language and everyday experience. There is no reason why words such as life, love, forgiveness, and the like should behave any differently when the discourse shifts from everyday experience to theology and worship. Granted the theologian hopes to enrich these ordinary symbols with an intentional fullness they do not ordinarily have. Nonetheless, the continuity between ordinary and theological language is shattered at our peril. Only if this continuity is maintained will it be possible to recognize that theologians do in fact speak about this human life and not some ideal life form abstracted from the world of the familiar. Only then will we begin to understand that the promise of our theological models is in fact actualized in the human activity and human interaction that constitute our Christian worship.

I have spoken of limiting conditions arising out of the humanity and finitude of the praying church. Many suggest themselves. Let me here briefly mention three: security, obstinancy, variety.

Theologians of late have called on the church to view itself in images of journey. They speak again of faith as response to the revealing mystery of God and urge the death of all false securities that hinder this response. True faith rests secure only in the mystery of God. Nonetheless, the church continually exhibits a resistance to journey and spends much time and energy building new golden calves even as old ones die. Given the persistence of idolatry in the church, it is a valid question to ask just how much insecurity a human church can live with. Liturgical reform and renewal must take seriously the possibility, perhaps even the inevitability, that the church must always dance with idolatry even as it celebrates to deepen its faith.

A second limiting factor is obstinacy. I have often wondered why it is so difficult to preach the word, whether in the pulpit or on the city street. The word always calls for repentance and conversion, and a human church must inevitably offer resistance when that call to conversion is spoken. We are not, a theological tradition reminds us, naturally drawn to the invitations of the Gospel. Particularly when liturgical theology must address itself to the question of proclamation, this resistance to conversion must seriously be taken into account.

A final haunting question emerges from the fact of variety within the praying church. All disclaimers to the contrary, we still encounter over and over again the confusion of community with conformity. Not everyone comes to worship with the same level of faith, of understanding, of expectation. Perhaps we never will. Liturgical renewal must realistically determine possibilities for community which not only tolerates such variety but is positively nourished by it.

These are three very concrete limitations that must be taken into account both by liturgical theology and by efforts at liturgical renewal. Just how these limitations will condition liturgical models and liturgical forms is a question yet to be explored. But a theology which would make light of them, or even ignore them, buys cheap freedom indeed. It gains the freedom to theologize without being hindered by the tensions these limitations produce, at the cost of no longer theologizing about or for a human church. And a liturgical renewal that would make light of them, or even ignore them, will not fare much better. The worship events it will bring forth will be many things; credibility and honesty, however, will probably not be among them.

Notes

1. E. Schillebeeckx, *Christ the Sacrament of Encounter with God* (New York: Sheed & Ward, 1963).

2. G. McCauley, *Sacraments for Secular Man* (New York: Herder & Herder, 1969).

3. J. Powers, *Spirit and Sacrament: The Humanizing Experience* (New York: Seabury, 1973).

3

Three Languages
of Christian Sacraments

ONE OF THE MORE VALUABLE INSIGHTS TO HAVE ENTERED SACRA-
mental theology with and since Vatican II is the realization
that the liturgy of Christian sacraments is itself a language
which speaks and conveys meaning. The linguistic nature of
sacramental worship is attested to both in official church documents and in the recent work of several liturgical theologians. The Constitution on the Liturgy, for example, recalls
that sacraments, because they are signs, *instruct*; and that, as
signs of faith, they not only nourish and strengthen faith, they
also *express* it (SC 59). The constitution also notes that in the
liturgy human sanctification is *presented* by "signs perceptible
by the senses" (SC 7), and one of the guiding principles it sets
forth for liturgical reform is that "texts and rites should be
drawn up so as to *express* more clearly the holy things which
they signify" (SC 21).

This sense of liturgy as conveyor of meaning is echoed in the
General Instruction of the Roman Missal (GIRM), particularly
in its careful presentation of the structure, elements, and parts
of the Mass. The hope is that each part of the liturgy might be
properly understood and enacted, and so *instruct* the faithful
who worship. Liturgy speaks, and it is important both reflec-
tively and pastorally to attend to the ways of its speaking.

29

This chapter is an attempt to explore the language structure of Christian sacraments. It is based on the conviction that there are three different languages or language matrices operative in sacramental worship, and that these must learn to work together for successful and faithful liturgy. It is likewise based on the converse conviction that many of the pastoral miseries which still afflict the liturgical life of the church stem from the fact that these languages are not always properly understood. They often speak different, even conflicting messages to those who worship. There is thus an intensely pastoral concern to this chapter. If some clarity can be achieved concerning the way in which these languages behave, some helpful guidelines for liturgical prayer might emerge.

The three languages which I have in mind can be given an initial introduction before the sources which unveil and illuminate them are examined. The first is the reflective language of theology which attempts in a variety of ways to explain the event of Christian worship. It is also the language of the catechism, and of that not always happy intrusion on worship, the liturgical commentary. This language is declarative in tone, and directly instructional in that its primary intentionality is to impart information. The second is the language of song, prayer, and proclamation, by which the faith meaning of the event is announced upon it. This language behaves quite differently from the language of theology. It is evocative and inviting, and only indirectly instructional. Its primary intentionality is to announce the word of God, which is always more inclusive than simply revealed information. It speaks, not *about* God, but in direct address *to* God. The first language seeks the response: "I understand"; the second seeks rather the response of surrender: "Amen, so be it." The third language, perhaps the most neglected of all, is the language of the event prior to and independent of the word which is proclaimed upon it. It is the language of space, of movement, of interaction. It speaks, expresses, and instructs as surely as do the other two, and, precisely because it is the least attended to of the three, it is most frequently the source of conflict and confusion.

These three languages need to be examined, both in themselves, and more importantly in their interrelationship, if the proper behavior of each is to be observed. To do this I propose to draw on two sources. The first is a remarkably pregnant affirmation about liturgy already cited in part from the Constitution on the Liturgy. The second is the structure and behavior of symbols set forth in the writings of Paul Ricoeur. Together they can help us better understand the threefold linguistic structure of sacraments and provide some helpful pastoral insights for liturgical *praxis*.

The Constitution on the Liturgy

The statement from the Constitution on the Liturgy reads as follows: "It [the liturgy] involves the presentation of man's sanctification under the guise of signs perceptible by the senses and its accomplishment in ways appropriate to each of these signs" (SC 7). This statement repeats the classic distinction in sacraments between sign and that which is signified. However, it goes far beyond mere repetition.

This affirmation represents an expansion of the word "sacrament" by indicating that it is much more than simply a name attached to the seven saving actions of Christ in the church. It is a description as well as a name. To call an event "sacrament" is to make two claims about an observable phenomenon which is constituted by song, prayer, action, touch, word, interaction. The first claim is that this complex perceptible reality is the language God uses to speak the meaning of Jesus Christ and his saving action to the believer. It is proclamation. Reflective theology may explain the event and illuminate it, but the event itself is the primary mode of communication to the person who worships. The second claim is even more far-reaching. It concerns the way in which the saving action of Jesus Christ unfolds concretely in human life. The Vatican II document declares that all the human dynamics involved in the sacramental ritual are integral to its effectiveness. They are not incidental to the process of sanctification; nor are they merely the occasion on which God, in some mysterious and undefined way, brings this sanctification about. The human dynamics of the sacrament constitute the very way in which this sanctification happens.

The full import of this affirmation will be missed if one gives only a minimalist reading to "signs perceptible to the senses," and focuses too narrowly on the essential matter and form of the sacraments. Simply to focus, for example, on bread, wine, and words of "consecration" at the eucharist, or on water poured with the trinitarian formula at baptism, does not serve well the truth about Christian sacraments which the Vatican document is bold to affirm. It may have been more than adequate when the church's concern was to preserve another truth, namely, that sacraments effect what they signify. When the concern is reversed, however, to ask if the sacraments signify all we believe they effect, the entire liturgical event, which is filled with signs perceptible to the senses, becomes equally as important as that which an earlier tradition called essential (GIRM 5). One may have a valid eucharist which is clearly inadequate as sacrament because too little attention is given to the complex set of messages sent to the whole person, which speak and effect human sanctification. In other words, the essentials of our sacraments may indeed be necessary, but not always sufficient for an action to be adequate as sacrament.

The dual claim made by calling an event "sacrament" makes it all the more urgent that proper attention be given to the linguistic structure of Christian worship. All the theological orthodoxy in the world will not save it if the ritual speaks a distortion of God's saving word and work. Neither will theological correctness suffice to open the believer to God's word and work. In fact, refined theological acumen is in some ways a luxury. The sacrament will speak its meaning and accomplish its purpose provided that the complex language of the ritual addresses the believer properly, and provided that the believer is properly prepared for and open to what the ritual speaks and accomplishes.

This is little more than to say in a new key what the classic *ex opere operato* tradition tried valiantly to maintain. It is true that, at its worst, this classic tradition made sacraments sound much like magic. At its best, however, it set down two crucial conditions for sacramental efficacy, without perhaps fully understanding the reasons behind them. On the one hand, the celebrant had to intend what the church intends, which, to avoid any artificial dichotomy between intention and action, is the same as doing what the church does. On the other hand, the believer had only to put no obstacles in the way. In other words, openness to the power of the ritual is openness to the power of God who accomplishes his saving work in Christ according to the dynamics of the ritual itself.

The statement of Vatican II goes far, on an explicit level, to establish and illuminate the linguistic nature of liturgy as distinct from, and in some ways more important than, the language of reflective theology. It does not, however, except in an implicit way, distinguish languages within the liturgical event itself or relate each of the languages to the others. For this I have found Paul Ricoeur's reflections on symbolism extremely helpful. The structure of a symbol as Ricoeur identifies it so closely parallels and complements what Vatican II affirms about sacraments that his thought can be tapped generously for an understanding of Christian worship.[1]

Paul Ricoeur on Symbolism

For Ricoeur, the symbol arises in language in the class of multimeaning expressions. This is its first characteristic. Within the class of multimeaning expressions, however, there is a further characteristic which distinguishes the symbol from all other such expressions. In a symbol there are two levels of meaning intended, a first or literal level, and a second, bound intimately to the first, which in religious symbolism expresses the human relationship to the Sacred. Thus a spot, stain, or a mark mean something in themselves. They are such, however, that people have used them as linguistic vehicles to express and communicate the experience of brokenness, not-quite-rightness, of sin. Likewise, a water bath is a washing which has meaning in itself arising in ordinary life. It too, however, is such that it can speak a deeper meaning of healing and cleansing from sin. What is crucial to the symbol is that the deeper meaning is bound to the first level meaning which is its vehicle of expression.

This bound relationship, deeper meaning to literal meaning, suggests other characteristics of symbols which must be respected if symbols are to preserve their symbolic identity. In the first place, the deeper meaning of symbols cannot be objectified in such a way that it achieves a life of its own. It remains bound to the first, accessible to consciousness only in and through that first level meaning. As Ricoeur has it, one must "walk in the aura" of the symbol, that is, meditate on its first level meaning, if one would properly come to know the symbol's deeper meaning. In the second place, there is an ambiguity to symbols or, as Ricoeur calls it, a "mixed texture." Symbols both reveal and conceal. Symbolic expressions never completely capture the reality which they bring into speech. There is always something left unsaid. This mixed texture allows symbols to serve as the proper language for what Christian theology calls "mystery," and demands that symbols be engaged in such a way that they can always speak something new.

Ricoeur will not allow a symbol to be replaced by an explanation which pretends to express the symbol's meaning without remainder. He recognizes that "a symbol gives rise to thought," but he also recognizes that thought and its yield are not the end, but only a step in the process of engaging symbols. One must always return from thought to the symbol in what Ricoeur calls a "second naivete." This return is characterized by an openness to and respect for the symbol as a giver of meaning which is aided and even urged by the intervening reflective process. One does not return to the symbol knowing already what it means. This alone would rob the symbol of depth. The return demands a wager that, if one engages the symbol again, that person will find in a deeper way the meaning which thought has evolved and more. The meaning, however, must be sought in the symbol itself, and specifically in a meditation on the symbol's first level intentionality.

One can, for example, achieve a good deal of reflective yield toward an understanding of eucharist. Certainly the dual tradition of real presence and sacrifice constitutes a large part of this reflective yield. Ricoeur would caution, however, that neither tradition can be be properly understood unless the imagination is trained upon *all* that the church does when it celebrates the eucharist. The actions and interactions of the eucharist speak the meaning of real presence and sacrifice into our consciousness. Any attempt to understand these rich traditions apart from the action and interaction of the eucharist will only result in their distortion.

If the deeper levels of meaning drawn from symbols cannot be objectified, there is nevertheless a way in which that meaning can be articulated. An examination of this way will establish the language matrix of proclamation as distinct from either the language of human dynamics (first level literal meaning) or the language of reflective theology (symbol brought to thought). Ricoeur observed in his study of evil that symbols of evil evolved into myth, for example, the story of Adam and Eve, before they evolved into the doctrine of original sin. He recognized further that myth, which he is careful to distinguish from its popular associations with fantasy and falsehood, is a definite way of telling symbolic truth. Myth tells in a fuller way the same truth as the more primitive symbols from which the myth is evolved. Moreover, in order to give the myth a proper hearing it must be traced back to those more primitive symbols, for it is there that its truth has its experiential base. In other words, the truth of any given myth is dependent on the symbols from which it evolved, and can only enter human consciousness by a passage which engages those primitive symbols. For the truth of a myth to be arrived at, the first level literal meaning of its original symbols must be the center of focus.

Myth does not intend to be a literal statement of fact, and should never be read as such. Nor can the narration of a myth make any sense if the link to the basic human experience which it intends to portray is severed. Unlike a scientific treatise, myth only indirectly intends to communicate information. Its primary intentionality is to speak of fundamental human experience in such a way as to lure the hearer back to that experience to affirm it and embrace it. Whether Adam and Eve are indeed historical figures is quite beside the point. The truth of the story is not to be found in either a literal acceptance of it or in a historical-critical demolition of it. The truth can only be found at the intersection of the experience of brokenness and not-quite-rightness and the original expressions of that experience as they enter speech.

This brief look at the Constitution on the Liturgy in light of the structure of symbols given by Ricoeur allows us to be more specific concerning the linguistic texture of Christian sacraments. The three languages can be identified and related with Ricoeur's aid. The first language speaks a literal meaning, namely, what the action and interaction mean as a human phenomenon. The second language speaks in the form of myth the deeper meaning of the first. This second language can only be heard properly if the imagination is trained on the first. The third language aims to explain and illuminate the event which is constituted by the first two languages. It speaks, however, not simply to satisfy the mind. It speaks to send the believer back to worship in search of its truth there. At the same time, it exercises an influence on the shape of worship when its truth is translated into the first two languages and gets spoken into the event itself. The insight of Vatican II allows a concise summary statement: theology *explains*, the myth *proclaims*, and the human dynamics *accomplish*.

The First Language

It is now possible to examine each of these languages in the specific context of Christian sacraments. Viewed in its integrity as a symbolic event, each of the sacraments reveals this typical linguistic structure. There is action, there is word, there is theological reflection. The first language, namely, that of the human dynamics, should be obvious. Yet, as I noted earlier, it is the language which is most neglected in actual worship. Tokenism has no place here if this language matrix is to be respected. Each sacrament is a genuine human event constituted by action and interaction which have meaning in themselves. The eucharist remains a shared meal before it is anything else that faith claims for it. What is important in this language matrix is that the eucharist must look like and behave like a shared meal if it is to be anything else that faith claims for it. Likewise, initiation is a process of welcoming into the community which is constituted by this shared meal, and should look like and behave like a genuine welcome. Its various steps, which include the water bath, the medicinal anointing, the dual claim of anointing and the laying on of hands, and a welcome at the eucharistic table for the first time, should be fully enacted so that they signify as completely as possible the deeper truth which we believe them to accomplish. Penance is an apology and a word of forgiveness, and marriage is nothing if it is not the public expression of love between two people. Though some of these actions and interactions may be more culturally familiar than others, each has its own literal meaning which should be unashamedly spoken. I contend that this language matrix is the most important in sacramental worship. What this does or does not speak, what it speaks well or poorly, will determine the success or failure of the other languages involved, as well as of the sacrament itself.

The Second Language

The second language along with the first constitutes an action as sacrament. This communion of languages is a tradition at least as old as Augustine who required that a word be proclaimed upon the human reality (*materia*) to open it up as a visible sign of the invisible gracious activity of God. The word articulates that invisible gracious activity of God and so identifies the deeper level meaning of the action itself. Many forms of proclamation announce that word throughout the total sacramental ritual, namely, song, Scripture, a variety of prayers. There is, however, a privileged way of announcing the word upon the action, and this should be examined and understood for its inner behavior. All other forms of attending proclamation should take their clue for proper behavior from this privileged form which they aim to amplify and serve. This privileged form, clear in the case of eucharist and ordination, less clear, perhaps, in some of the other sacraments, is variously called the blessing prayer, the *berakah*, the euchology, or eucharistic prayer. There is a definite inner dynamic to the blessing prayer which specifies both its own proper behavior and the proper behavior of those who would pray it.

The blessing prayer is essentially a narration of the Christian myth, the *magnalia Dei* accomplished for us in Christ. It intends, however, far more than simple narration. It is indeed a prayer of thanksgiving, though it also intends far more than thanksgiving. The ecology of the prayer is such that it summons people and their God to a meeting in the here-and-now event of Christian worship. It is a reminder to us that God has acted in our past; it is also a reminder to God that God has acted in our past. But with the reminder it is a request that God will act again in and through what we do together as sacramental worship. The request, which is spelled out explicit in a good blessing prayer, calls our attention to the action/ interaction of the sacrament itself as the way in which God will fulfill the request. Thus, in the ordination of deacons we pray: "Almighty God, we ask you to be with us in this rite . . ."

and further specify this request in the invocation of the Spirit: "Lord, we pray, send forth upon them the Holy Spirit so that by the grace of your seven gifts they may be strengthened by him to carry out faithfully the work of the ministry."[2] Likewise, in the eucharist we specify the request in the dual invocation of the Spirit (1) to consecrate the bread and the wine, and (2) to fashion those who share it into the unity of Christ.

In both cases it is God the Holy Spirit who is invoked upon the human action. Theologically, this is fitting since the Spirit, in Christian theology, signals God's wedded presence to and within human life and activity. In both cases, moreover, the prayer so directs the attention of the believer that a response to the prayer must necessarily and at the same time be a response to the action which is prayed upon. "So be it, Amen, let it happen!"

The evolution of Christian sacraments exhibits clearly Ricoeur's observation that symbols evolve into myth before they evolve into dogmatic assertions. Primitive sacraments were the action of the church in which people recognized the saving action of God in Christ. As the church did in its sacraments, it gradually evolved in the form of blessing prayers the meaning of what it did. Only later did the church move its action and prayer to the level of theological reflection. The action itself remains the concrete moment in which the truth of the myth-prayer as well as the later reflection can enter human consciousness. The blessing prayer itself recognizes this as it lures the believer back to the concrete action in which and by which the truth of the prayer unfolds.

Our understanding of the behavior of this language matrix can be deepened by further tapping Ricoeur's thought. He speaks of the process of "creative interpretation" as the proper way to engage symbols.[3] This process involves three intertwined stages which the person passes through in a meditation "in the aura" of a symbol. The first seeks to understand a symbol in terms of other symbols. It is an expansive stage aiming to draw on all available resources to open up and illuminate the given symbol. Culture, nature, heritage, all come together to enrich the symbol at hand and allow it to speak. This is the stage where the myth is born and where the myth proclaims. The second stage brings persons into the process where they can no longer be outside observers. It seeks to understand the symbol in terms of oneself and one's life. "What does it all mean for me?" It is only in the third stage that the symbol moves to thought, and, since this third stage follows on the second, it reminds us how personally invested theological reflection is, or should be. This third stage has two interrelated moments. Thought asks, "what does it mean?" and seeks to understand. Thought also asks, "what might it mean?" and seeks to explore it for new possibility. All three stages are carried out with the imagination trained on the first level literal meaning of the symbol. The result of this threefold meditative process is to create an "imaginative lure" which does not coerce, but which invites. It invites one to entrust oneself to the truth which the process unveils. It invites not merely assent to the content of truth, but consent to the truth itself. It asks the person to choose to live according to the truth which is revealed.

Consent is a category which has special meaning in Ricoeur.[4] It completes the imaginative or meditative process by internalizing the truth and incarnating it in life. It is commitment, vulnerability, and a willingness to let something happen in life. In the case of Christian sacraments, consent is the proper meaning of Amen. It is a surrender to the truth proclaimed in the myth. It is also, and in the same act, a surrender to the ways or human dynamics of the event which reveal and accomplish the truth proclaimed.

The act of consent is crucial. Short of consent, the truth of sacraments will remain external to the faith life of the Christian as information about realities of faith. Of all the words which attend the proclamation, the Amen is in some ways the most important. It constitutes the very openness to God's gracious presence and activity which Trent called "putting no obstacles in the way." It is important to recognize, moreover, that, since the act of surrender is to the truth of the sacrament, that is, to the truth spoken by both languages together, the two languages cannot speak conflicting messages without harm to the integrity of worship and to the possibility of a proper faith response on the part of the believer. The two languages must speak in harmony if they will evoke an unambiguous Amen.

The Third Language

But what of the third language matrix, that of reflective theology? If Ricoeur's caution is to hold, as I think it should, this language too cannot be employed properly unless the imagination is trained on the first level of meaning of the sacramental action. Nor can it be properly employed without an attentive listening to the proclamation which is made upon the event. Theology aims to explain and understand in its own way the very same truth which the other two languages speak in the worship event. It cannot forget, however, that what it is talking about continues to happen in the church, and that its own truth is vulnerable to the test of experience in actual worship.

Unfortunately, theological reflection on sacraments has for too long been conducted at too great a distance from the worship event, and has attempted to speak its truth by its own inner logic. The result is that many believers, who have learned their catechism well, can recite truths about the sacraments, but seldom if ever recognize the claim of those truths on their lives in actual worship. The truths about sacraments get varying degrees of assent; the truth seldom evokes consent. The full task of theological reflection on sacraments is not completed until its truth is spoken back into the worship event itself.

In order to do this, theology must be translated into the language of movement and the language of proclamation. It can only speak its truth into worship by way of the other two. A purely instructional homily or a liturgical comment designed to "explain" will not do the trick. Some instances of translation are already in evidence, and serve to exemplify the task that must be done on a much wider scale. Theological reflection on the eucharist as meal translated into turning the altar around. Theological reflection on the role of the Spirit translated into the restoration of the epiclesis, the invocation of the Spirit, into the proclaiming prayer. It would have done no good simply to announce either insight in the form of an instructional comment if no change had taken place in either the language matrix of movement or the language matrix of proclamation. With the changes, moreover, such an instructional comment is unnecessary. Turning the altar around and restoring the epiclesis are the proper ways in which those specific theological insights are spoken into worship.

The Misuse of These Languages

It might be helpful at this point, before concluding with some pastoral suggestions, to give a few examples of the misuse of these languages which shows itself in conflicting messages to the believer. On the humorous side, I think of a cartoon which once appeared in *Critic* which depicted priest, deacon, and sub-deacon garbed in classic black funeral garb. Smoke arose in abundance over the coffin upon which they looked with somber scowls. The caption spoke the word proclaimed on this event. It read: "I am the resurrection and the life."

A second, more serious example involves the current practice of offertory procession coupled with the usual mode of receiving communion. People bring the bread and wine to the altar; they later return individually to the altar to receive what was consecrated. This movement amply speaks the very same theology of eucharist which was proclaimed for centuries in the Roman Canon: "Almighty God, we pray that your angel may take this sacrifice to your altar in heaven. Then, as we receive from this altar the sacred body and blood of your Son, let us be filled with every grace and blessing."

I am not interested at this point in debating the merits or non-merits of this theology. I only wish to suggest that the message spoken by this kind of movement is in sharp conflict with the message spoken by the language of proclamation when the newer eucharistic prayers are prayed. These new prayers invoke the Spirit to change the bread and wine *so that* we who share it may be fashioned into a unity. These prayers proclaim the theological insight that Christian communion is the union of people through the action of Jesus shared. Yet the language of motion continues to speak communion as "Jesus coming to me alone." One can go to communion and remain a stranger to those who likewise go to communion. The prayer calls attention to the sharing of the meal while the action says little or nothing about the sharing.

A final example concerns the ritual of marriage. However much a couple realizes that they are coming before the Christian community to proclaim their love and to hear the church's proclamation that in their love they will find the saving love of God, just try to get them to enter the church and walk down the aisle together. True, it is beginning to happen in some places, but the time-honored practice of "giving the bride away" still holds a strong footing. It is a wonder that more feminists have not moved in on that one, since the movement language speaks all too clearly that the bride's father is "delivering the goods."

Other examples could be cited, but perhaps these are sufficient to identify the problem of conflicting languages, and to urge both a respect for the proper behavior of each language, and the importance of having all three languages speak in their own way the same message. Each must be adequate to its own function, yet congruent with the others in the whole nexus of word and action. What remains, by way of conclusion, is to set forth some pastoral suggestions which emerge from this analysis of the language structure of sacraments.

Pastoral Suggestions

The first set of suggestions concerns the language matrix of human dynamics. It is important that celebrants, liturgical planners, and indeed the people who worship begin to examine the actions and interactions which constitute our sacraments in view of the way in which sacraments achieve their effect. Whatever we believe to be the effect of the eucharist on us happens to us because it is a shared meal. The eucharist should then be experienced as a shared meal, and care should be taken that the nonverbal language in the liturgy of the eucharist foster the interaction of a shared meal. Perhaps the table should be set from the very beginning, with some other gesture devised to signify our part in Christ's offering. Certainly the kiss of peace should not be an isolated intrusion on an otherwise private encounter with God. Whatever before, during, and after the liturgical service will foster true communion among the people is proper to the behavior of the eucharist. Whatever creates in the people a sense that they are simply alone before their God speaks a message that is in conflict with true Christian eucharist.

Similarly, rituals of welcome should be just that, and people should be invited to extend a genuine welcome to the new member. This is not the same thing as having a baptism at a Sunday eucharist where the people sit back and watch. All the attending actions which constitute the ritual of initiation should be so carried out that they speak a washing, a healing, and a claim to the initiate. As obvious as it may sound, the forgiveness of penance should be real forgiveness, and not simply the announcement of forgiveness. In short, the sacraments are very human activities, and they should unfold fully in all their humanity in order that (1) they may achieve their effect, and (2) there be a human reality upon which the word might be proclaimed.

The second set of suggestions looks to the language matrix of proclamation. I would urge again that the blessing prayer is the privileged way of proclaiming the word upon the event. The blessing prayer is the proper way of "explaining" the action, rather than the liturgical comment or didactic homily. If the prayer is attentively and well-prayed, liturgical commentary will prove to be unnecessary. Furthermore, if the prayer is understood as the truly representative prayer of the church, all other forms of proclamation, Scripture, homily, song, auxiliary prayers, will have found their proper behavior and culmination. The church's eucharistic prayer proclaims in order to invite Amen to the word and to the action it identifies.

To do this, it is important that celebrants, liturgical planners, and indeed the people who worship understand the inner movement of the blessing prayer and the full significance of the Amen it invites. Sound catechesis will be helpful, but the best instruction is the proper use of the blessing prayer itself. I strongly urge that the blessing prayers given in the rituals for each of the sacraments be given their proper place in the celebration, even where the prayer is not canonically essential for a valid sacrament. The blessing prayer over the water at baptism, for example, and the nuptial blessing at a wedding are integral, if not canonically essential, to the sacramental action, for they proclaim the word, identify the action, and invite the Amen no less than does the eucharistic prayer or the consecration prayer at ordinations.

The third set of suggestions concerns the language matrix of theological reflection. Needless to say, those who have responsibility for worship should be theologically formed in how the contemporary church understands its sacraments and intends them to be enacted. It is still a good maxim to intend and do what the church intends and does. The rituals themselves, and their attending introductions, are the best source for such understanding, and should be studied carefully. My principal suggestion, however, concerns the way in which theological knowledge enters into the arena of worship. Here I can only repeat what I have said above. Theological insight influences worship by effecting change in the other two languages. The language of movement and the language of proclamation are the proper way in which theological truth is spoken into worship.

Notes

1. The reader interested in a more detailed study of Ricoeur on symbolism might consult the following: "The Hermeneutics of Symbol and Philosophical Reflection," *International Philosophical Quarterly* 2:2 (May 1962) 191-218; and *Freud and Philosophy: An Essay on Interpretation*, trans., Dennis Savage (New Haven: Yale University Press, 1970) 3-56, 344-551.

2. Similarly, for the ordination of presbyters: "We ask you, all-powerful Father, give these servants of yours the dignity of the presbyterate." Attention is focused on the laying on of hands which this prayer interprets.

3. The process of creative interpretation is outlined in Ricoeur's article already cited, "The Hermeneutics of Symbol."

4. For a fuller treatment of the concept of consent, see Ricoeur, *Freedom and Nature: The Voluntary and the Involuntary*, trans., Erazim Kohak (Evanston: Northwestern University Press, 1966) 341-486.

4

Understanding Sacraments: Vatican II and Beyond

AS HAS BEEN NOTED EARLIER, THE LITURGICAL REFORM SET IN MOtion by Vatican Council II has had two significant components: a new way of celebrating the sacraments and a new way of speaking about them. The first is embodied in the revised liturgical texts for the eucharist and the other sacraments. It involves in some cases a modest and in other cases a radical restructuring of the way in which the church conducts its sacramental-liturgical prayer. The second is presented both in the Constitution on the Sacred Liturgy and in the various *praenotanda* or instructions that accompany the revised liturgical texts. This second involves in all cases a radical restructuring of the rhetoric employed to name and to explore the meaning of the church's sacramental prayer. In this chapter I propose to examine the second. By tracing the recent history of sacramental theology and the various stages along which this restructuring of language has taken place, I hope to identify what might be called "current directions" in sacramental understanding, and to propose some possibilities for future development.

By way of initial contrast, a sharp distinction can be drawn between preconciliar sacramental theology and its postconciliar shape and garb. Preconciliar reflection on sacraments in the

West developed according to the dyptich "sacraments in general" and "sacraments in particular," where the former identified what the seven sacraments held in common, and the latter then applied these common notes to each individual sacrament. The language was structural, objective, quasi-scientific. Postconciliar theology departs from this tradition in several significant ways. The language now employed to explore what is common to the church's sacraments is liturgical rather than structural. Emphasis is on their relationship to the mystery of Christ and to the church as a whole, both of which are expressed in each liturgical act. The concept of *sacramenta in genere* has receded somewhat, and, if it were to gain renewed attention again, it would do so only after due consideration of individual sacraments in their uniqueness; it would not be the point of departure. In postconciliar reflection on sacraments, priority focus is given to the richness of each sacrament as a unique liturgical act, and to the relationship that exists among them in the sacramental life of the church.

Symptomatic of this radical shift in rhetoric is the contrast between the way sacraments are identified in the 1917 Code of Canon Law and in the revised code of 1983. In the former they are listed under the heading *de rebus* (on things); in the latter, under the title "The Office of Sanctifying in the Church."

The plan of this chapter is to present a brief survey of the evolution in sacramental theology from its preconciliar scholastic garb to its contemporary theological "shape," where its language is liturgical, its methodologies are garnered as much from the human sciences as from philosophy, and where it has taken its place firmly in the arena of Christian spirituality. I will consider (1) the gains and limitations of scholastic sacramental theology, (2) the first level move from the scholastic mode to a more personal and phenomenological mode of discourse, and (3) a second level move into a more properly liturgical mode of discourse. Finally (4), I will suggest some tentative directions for the future.

SCHOLASTIC THEOLOGY

The scholastic methodology which dominated Catholic theology in the West from the thirteenth to the twentieth century can rightly boast of a number of achievements in regard to the understanding of the sacraments. It advanced the distinction between sacraments and sacramentals, thus securing special significance for the (then) seven distinct liturgical actions that displayed and continued the saving mission of Christ. It struggled to preserve the effectiveness of these actions, and rooted this effectiveness firmly in the action of Christ. In an articulation that was not always correctly understood, it identified Christ's gracious presence and action as the "within" (*gratia continetur*) of the sacraments, and insisted that only two things were required for Christ to touch people effectively through them. Those responsible for enacting the sacraments had to do so according to the mind and intent of the church (*ex opere operato*), while those who participated in the sacraments as "recipients" (people ministered to) needed to do so with no obstacle placed in the way (*ex opere operantis*). In other words, fidelity to the church's action and an openness to the ways of these actions allowing the saving grace of Christ to be appropriated by believers through the medium of Christian sacraments.

Scholastic theology employed a specific model in its reflection on and examination of the sacraments. It looked on them as "objective realities," quasi-scientific objects, which could be observed and analyzed from without. Appropriately, it asked questions of sacraments that were fitting to scientific objects: who made it? where did it come from? what constitutes it to be what it is? when does it cease to be itself? who may use it? when? and for what purpose? This question set allowed theologians to weave together a well wrought network of understanding which rooted the institution of sacraments directly, or at least indirectly, in the life of Christ, which insisted that these actions were indeed the actions of Christ, and which examined the conditions under which sacraments are properly celebrated and made effective for the people who receive them. The heart of scholastic reflection was to see the church's sacraments as sacred objects (holy signs) given by Christ to be received by all through the ministry of some, usually ordained priests.

In spite of its achievements, however, scholastic theology labored under some severe limitations. It lacked a sound ecclesiological base, for it had replaced the Augustinian image of the *totus Christus* (Christ in the midst of the church, together with the church which is gathered into union with him) by an image of *Christus solus* (Christ alone, present in the ministry of the priest, and acting on behalf of the people). The sacramental theology of the Scholastics also lacked a proper sense of the relation between word and sacrament, a deficiency that became particularly poignant during the sixteenth-century Reformation. A third burden was the conflation of the trinitarian structure of sacramental worship into a purely Christological framework, with serious neglect of the role of the Holy Spirit as the agent of transformation of all that is united with Christ. Western theology paid a heavy price for having replaced the *epiclesis* of Eastern prayer with the *verba Jesu* of Ambrose. Finally, and with added force at the time of the post-Tridentine liturgical reform, scholastic theology lacked the sense of the liturgy itself as a theological locus. Liturgical forms were frozen to protect doctrine; they were neither seen as, nor given free reign to be, living expressions of the church's living faith.

It is this set of limitations, and the growing awareness by the mid-twentieth century that they were in fact limitations, that gradually exposed the scholastic mode of reflection as no longer adequate to the task of understanding the church's sacramental life. This awakening came about because of a number of converging factors: the liturgical movement of the nineteenth and twentieth centuries, the advance in biblical scholarship in both Protestant and Catholic circles, the non-scholastic theological ventures of Maurice de la Taille and Odo Casel, and such official pronouncements from Rome as *Mystici Corporis* (1943), which recaptured the church as Christ's Body, and *Mediator Dei* (1947) which brought new focus to Christ himself as sole mediator between God and humankind.

BEYOND SCHOLASTIC THEOLOGY

While the "mystery theology" of de la Taille and Casel had already suggested to the theological imagination other ways of pursuing an understanding of the church's prayer, it was not until the now classic work of Edward Schillebeeckx, *Christ, the Sacrament of the Encounter with God* (English translation, 1963), that the break with scholastic theology began in earnest. Drawing on patristic and biblical richness, Schillebeeckx reestablished the proper sacramental relationship between Christ and the church, and identified this relationship as foundational to any theology of sacraments. Christ was present *as one to be encountered* in his primary sacramental manifestation, the church, and specifically in the church as it gathers for prayer and its sacramental acts. Schillebeeckx introduced a paradigm shift, a new hermeneutical lens through which to view sacramental faith and the sacramental tradition of the church. Moreover, in replacing the "object model" of scholastic reflection with the more phenomenological and experiential model of "human encounter," he turned sacramental theology away from the extrinsic *quid pro quo* language of economic exchange (to do this and receive grace) to the interpersonal language of relational human experience. As a result, theology could no longer be content simply to be explanation of the church's faith (the *fides quaerens intellectum* of Anselm); it had to be seen in addition as "promise" (*intellectus quaerens fidem*), pointing to and unveiling a meeting with Christ that continues to unfold in the church.

Schillebeeckx set several things in motion which continue to influence theological reflection on sacraments. He broadened the resource base of sacramental theology by rediscovering, as it were, the biblical and patristic roots of the sacramental tradition. He introduced a distinction that had been seriously neglected in earlier sacramental reflection between the unique manner of existence that is peculiar to human persons and the objective mode of "being there" that is proper to things of nature. He insisted that religion is a saving dialogue between human persons and the living God, and that, according to the Christian confession of the incarnation, the God who addresses us does so *as human among humans*. By employing a personalist model for his theology, in contrast to the objective model of the Scholastics, he unveiled the fact that all sacramental theology in fact employs models in its investigation of Christian worship. He thus opened the door for the employment of other models as well.

The rhetorical shift which Schillebeeckx effected in sacramental theology found a complement in the language employed at Vatican II, especially in the Constitution on the Church (*Lumen Gentium*) and the Constitution on the Sacred

Liturgy (*Sacrosanctum Concilium*). Both documents reflect the fruit of the liturgical and biblical scholarship that had been underway since before the turn of the century. Both secure the language of sacrament for the church in its relation to Christ, and both name the mystery of Christ as a mystery of personal presence in and to the church.

The Constitution on the Sacred Liturgy did not offer a new definition of sacraments. Rather, it began to speak of sacraments in a radically new way. It reinstated the primitive concept of liturgy as *the work of the people*, and it unequivocally included all the sacraments firmly within its scope. The image of sacrament as "vehicle of grace administered by some to others" was quietly replaced by one which was more active and inclusive. Sacraments are not things at all, but lively expressions by the whole assembled church of its faith and its mission to embody and make accessible the saving work of Christ. "For it is the liturgy through which, especially in the divine sacrifice of the Eucharist, 'the work of our redemption is accomplished', and it is through the liturgy especially, that the faithful are enabled to express in their lives and manifest to others the mystery of Christ and the real nature of the true Church" (SC 2). In addition, the constitution stated in a way that is both appropriate to and directed to human experience the time-honored tradition of sacramental effectiveness: "It [the liturgy] involves the presentation of man's sanctification under the guise of signs perceptible by the senses and its accomplishment in ways appropriate to each of these signs" (SC 7). If scholastic theology had labored to root sacramental effectiveness in the action of Christ, to the neglect of the way in which this effectiveness was achieved (i.e., *significando*, by signifying), Vatican II brought forward with remarkable force this complementary truth. The scholastic tradition insisted that sacraments effect what they signify; Vatican II demanded that sacraments signify all that they effect, because it is by signifying that sacraments are effective for those who enact them.

The initial impact of *Sacrosanctum Concilium* on the church was to guide and direct the liturgical reform and revision which it called for. Its primary first contribution to sacramental theology was to bolster the major insights advanced by Schillebeeckx and others (e.g., K. Rahner): the centrality of Christ and the church in sacramental reflection; the dynamic notion of sacrament as action; and the call for experiential language both to name the reality of sacraments and to describe the effects which sacraments have on people. Only later, when its initial pragmatic task was accomplished in the issuance of reformed liturgical rites, would the Constitution on the Sacred Liturgy have an even more radical effect on the procedures of sacramental theology.

The decade or so that followed Schillebeeckx's introduction of a new model for sacraments can well be called the decade of models in sacramental theology. Bernard Cooke (*Christian Sacraments and Christian Personality*, 1968) and Joseph Powers (*Spirit and Sacrament: The Humanizing Experience*, 1973) drew insights from psychology and personality development to explore the question of meaning in sacraments and to name the process through which the sacramental experience might lead one. Cooke aimed to "explore the function of sacraments in the actual living of Christianity and in the development of the Christian person" (p. 10). The goal of all sacramental activity is the development of a mature Christian person; sacraments are *formative*. Powers, on the other hand, focused on the human experience that lies behind all sacraments. It is, in the first instance, the experience of "no-thingness" in the face of the Transcendent, and in the second instance, the experience of being drawn along the path of self-transcendence. The purpose of sacraments is to provide a new quality of consciousness and a new quality of living marked by an ever increasing freedom, hope, and possibility for love. If Cooke sees sacraments as formative of the mature Christian person, Powers sees them as *transformative* of human consciousness. For both, sacraments advance the quality of human life.

George McCauley (*Sacraments for Secular Man*, 1969) employed a sociological model to unearth the human meaning which sacraments hold. Sacraments are "secular gestures; they deal with secular reality; they promote a greater secularity than we are accustomed to associate with human existence; in themselves they embody secular experience" (p. 15). An enriched human life on the secular level is the fruit of sacramental worship. McCauley's model drew sharp attention to the human reality which underlies the church's sacraments.

A further insight of Schillebeeckx (*God, the Future of Man,*

1968) that the church is to be sacrament of dialogue with the world, coupled with his and Rahner's earlier perception of the church as sacramental embodiment of Christ present and active in the world, gained new force in the political model employed in the liberation theology of Juan Luis Segundo (*The Sacraments Today*, English translation, 1974) and others in Latin America. If the mission of Christ in the church is to thwart and overcome all forms of oppression among people, the church as sacrament of Christ must be about that saving business. In function of that mission, Segundo sees sacraments primarily as signs to the church of what it must be about, and they will be effective "to the extent that they are a consciousness-raising and motivating celebration of man's liberative action in history" (p. 55). If there is no raising of consciousness toward the liberative force of human action in the world, then however perfect the ritual enactment of sacraments might be, there is no Christian sacrament to speak of. Liberation theology calls forth the ethical dimension of Christian sacraments.

Still other models were employed. The categories of process thought, for example, shaped Bernard Lee's investigation of church, sacrament, and the structure of Christian experience (*The Becoming of the Church*, 1974) and raised to sacramental theology the need to speak of God, the church, and Christian sacraments in the language of *becoming* rather than the language of *being*. In Great Britain structural analysis, as well as considerations of the symbolic imagination, guided Bruno Brinkman (in *The Heythrop Journal*, 1972-1973) through his exploration of "sacramental man," and called attention to the experience of intimacy, interiorization, and social relationship as integral to sacramental prayer. Later, George Worgul (*From Magic to Metaphor*, 1980) examined the ritual experience through the combined eyes of sociology and anthropology to draw out the relationship between sacraments, human life, and social interaction.

In some ways the "model" approach continues to be employed in more recent theological works: for example, David Power (*Unsearchable Riches*, 1984) draws heavily on the "symbol" structure of Paul Ricoeur, and Michael Lawler (*Symbol and Sacrament*, 1987) develops an understanding of sacrament as "prophetic symbol," but these show as well the influence of the second shift in sacramental theology since Vatican II, the movement from sacrament as theological concept to sacrament as liturgical act. They can therefore be considered both continuous and discontinuous with the first level shift which Schillebeeckx set in motion.

BEYOND SACRAMENTAL THEOLOGY

The first movement away from sacramental theology raised the issue of meaning in experiential categories. It sought to relate Christian life and Christian worship within sacramental theology itself. This second movement continues that project, yet adds an additional dimension. The focus of attention is on the liturgical enactment of the sacraments, rather than on sacrament as an abstract theological concept. At this second stage, the term "sacramento-liturgical theology," or simply "liturgical theology" arises to name the theological venture. Its guiding motto is the age-old adage of Prosper of Aquitaine, *ut lex orandi statuit lex credendi* ("it is the law of prayer that establishes the law of belief").

One of the primary gains in this move from sacramental to liturgical theology is the recovery of the liturgical act itself as a *theological locus*. It has been classically known and accepted that faith gives rise to theology. In the first move from scholastic modes of reflection, it became equally known and accepted that theology must feed back into, and in some sense be verified in, the experience of faith. In this second move from sacramental to liturgical theology, the liturgical act arises as the necessary intermediary between faith and theology. Paul Ricoeur's noted phrase, "the symbol gives rise to thought," is very much to the point. Faith gives rise to theology only after it finds its first articulation in the form of myth and symbol, that is, the stuff of liturgical ritual. Conversely, theology does indeed return to faith by way of promise, but it is in the engagement with symbol and in the enactment of liturgical ritual that promise is made, received, and actualized. Liturgy expresses and manifests the mystery of Christ (SC 2); it is itself a primary statement of both theology and faith.

Liturgical theology is still very much in the process of being formed. It moves in a variety of directions and weaves together in its own project a variety of ingredients: the doctrinal, the biblical, the historical, the liturgical, the aesthetic, and the pastoral. Liturgical theology studies liturgical texts as privileged expressions of the church's faith. It examines as well the inner movements of faith which ritual action calls forth. It examines the correspondence between what is portrayed in ritual and what is lived by individuals and the community. It calls on the arts, the human sciences, and pastoral experience as well as the more traditional sources of doctrine, philosophy, and liturgical history. The liturgy of the church cannot be studied in isolation from the life realities and the faith realities which it both brings to expression and fosters. It is open to any source and any method which serves to link worship, faith, and human life.

By holding the liturgy itself as a central theological locus, a new understanding of sacraments emerges based on what the church in fact does. There is an understanding of sacrament embedded within the ritual actions themselves. This realization led David Power to advance fresh insight first into the theology of orders (*Ministers of Christ and His Church*, 1969) and, later, into the wider spread of ministers and ministries that are evolving in the contemporary church (*Gifts That Differ*, 1980). It guided John Barry Ryan to explore the eucharist from the texts of the eucharistic prayers (*The Eucharistic Prayer*, 1974), a venture which was taken further for the ecumenical church by Frank Senn (*New Eucharistic Prayers*, 1987). And it has guided a number of theologians to examine the various sacraments from the revised liturgical texts which present them to the church: for example, Aidan Kavanagh (*The Shape of Baptism*, 1978) on the initiation rites; Gerard Austin (*Anointing with the Spirit*, 1985) on confirmation; James Dallen (*The Reconciling Community*, 1986) on penance; Charles Gusmer (*And You Visited Me*, rev. 1989) on pastoral care of the sick; and Richard Rutherford (*The Death of a Christian*, 1980) on rites of Christian burial.

Liturgical theology is concerned, however, not only with ritual text, but also with the dynamics of ritual action which constitute the inner workings of the text. Exploring this terrain, Edward Kilmartin (in *The Sacraments: God's Love and Mercy Actualized*, ed., Eigo, 1979) examined the word dimension of

Christian sacraments and its intrinsic relation to the action that is both called forth from and empowered by its proclamation. Regis Duffy (*Real Presence*, 1982) has studied the sacramental fare in terms of the human commitment which sacraments call forth and engender. Similar studies appear in the volumes of *Alternative Futures for Worship* (1987), especially by Jennifer Glen on the experience embedded in sickness and healing and my own reflections on the process of conversion in reconciliation. Concern for dynamics also gave rise to new studies on the rhythms of liturgical time, for example, Marion Hatchett (*Sanctifying Life, Time and Space*, 1976) and Thomas Talley (*The Origins of the Liturgical Year*, 1986), and essays in liturgical spirituality, for example, Kevin Irwin (*Liturgy, Prayer and Spirituality*, 1984).

Liturgical theology also seeks to intersect with issues and concerns in the broader field of systematic theology. Three works in particular deserve note. Geoffrey Wainwright (*Doxology*, 1980) offered a full systematic theology with specific and illustrative links drawn to corresponding liturgical texts. Aidan Kavanagh (*On Liturgical Theology*, 1984) presents a more finely focused systematic slice where the liturgical enactment of Christian faith is considered, not simply one theological locus among many, but the premier expression of Christian faith. Finally, Edward Kilmartin (*Christian Liturgy*, 1988) delivers what may be seen as either a foundational theology for Christian worship or a liturgically based fundamental theology. His work stands in the tradition of *sacramenta in genere*, but unfolds on a much more profound level.

The allied issue of church order and its relationship to the sacramental life of the church gains particular urgency in a time when the possibilities for prayer in local church communities are increasingly restricted by the availability or non-availability of ministers ordained to the task. Edward Schillebeeckx (*Ministry*, 1981) stirred up some measure of conflict and controversy by urging a reversal of the traditional Roman Catholic view that the possibilities for liturgical prayer are determined by available ministers. He has suggested that the church has a right to its sacramental-liturgical prayer, and that this right is to be served even if the local church must call forth extra-ordinary ministers to serve them. In his suggested reversal, the right to prayer determines the ministry; it is not the other way around.

In addition, there are voices from outside the traditional arena of systematics or liturgics who contribute to the task. Social moralist David Hollenbach (in *The Faith That Does Justice*, ed., Haughey, 1977), to cite but one example, has urged liturgical theology to recover its ethical dimension, and to include within its scope questions of faith, justice, and the community's social responsibilities. This intersection between sacramental liturgy and ethics continues to be raised at the annual meeting of the North American Academy of Liturgy, and lingers as the as yet barely-recaptured heritage of Dom Virgil Michel and other liturgical leaders of the 1940s.

There is a multi-faceted ferment within contemporary liturgical theology that can only be suggested in this essay. As the living church continues to experience its renewed liturgical forms, new issues and new areas of investigation will continue to shape its ongoing task. The impact, for example, of liberation movements, of feminist theology, of liturgical evolution in non-Western, non-European parts of the globe is only beginning to make itself felt. These must be addressed by liturgical theology as well.

A FORWARD LOOK

Efforts to understand the sacramental life of the church continue as they must. Liturgical theology, as all theology, explores the realm of mystery, of God's gracious freedom in engaging men and women in their lives. Mystery continues to unveil its secrets. It will never be completely grasped; it must always be explored anew. What then might lie ahead in this ongoing task of exploring the church's sacraments? At least some tentative suggestions might be allowed.

It is probably safe to say that the future of liturgical theology will be both continuous and discontinuous with its present contours. Lines of continuity can more easily be drawn. Certainly liturgical theology will continue to be "liturgical," namely, it will continue to learn from the liturgy as it is enacted by the living church. It will continue to explore the interface between sacramental rituals and human life realities which those rituals presuppose and embody. It will continue to engage fundamental theological realities such as the trinitarian God, church, salvation, and grace, and locate itself more firmly at the center of those investigations. It will continue to be enlightened by new modes of discourse, new paradigms, and new methodologies. Points of discontinuity are harder to name.

One point of potential discontinuity lies in the introduction of local languages and customs into the liturgy and the encouragement given in the Constitution on the Sacred Liturgy (37-40) that the tradition be adapted to the various peoples of the world. It remains to be seen just how radical that adaptation will be, and what impact such adaptations will have. It could be that the process will simply issue forth in rituals that differ one from another only in nuance. It is equally possible, however, that adaptation will lead to ritual forms as different from the current praxis in the church as Gentile ritual differed from Jewish-Christian ritual, or as Byzantine ritual differs from Coptic, and both from the liturgies of the West. Karl Rahner once named the contemporary moment in the church as the "emergence of the world church." If such be the case, it is reasonable to expect that emerging ritual forms at least could be unlike anything the church to date has known. If this were to happen, liturgical ritual *as theological locus* would present a radically new face to the church's faith and therefore present a radically new challenge to the liturgical theologian who seeks to understand that faith.

A second point of potential discontinuity depends on how seriously the church takes the symbolic nature of its liturgy, and how deeply theology takes Aidan Kavanagh's assertion that liturgy is the "premier" statement of the church's faith. The place where this will impact the most is on the ecumenical reality of the church, and ultimately on the issue of church unity. To date, the ecumenical task seems to be the pursuit of church unity by reaching some level of agreement forged in bilateral and multi-lateral discussions. Agreement is sought on the level of doctrine, which is essentially the level of interpretation, and the task rests on the assumption that agreement can be reached. Yet, what if it were the case that agreement can and should never be reached; that unity should be sought on a level different from that of doctrinal agreement? If it is true that the nature of symbol demands a plurality of interpretations, it might well be discovered that the disunity which the churches are trying to overcome does not in itself really exist, and, on the deepest level of the church's life and prayer, never did. It may well be that we people of the church have allowed division where division was in fact not called for. Deep appreciation of the symbolic nature of ritual may force the church to confront the fact that, while different communities of Christians disagree as to what they *think* they are doing sacramentally, nonetheless, within a reasonable range of deviation based on culture, language, and perception, all Christian communities continue to *do* the same thing. The impact of such a realization on the theology of Christian worship, and indeed on Christian life and theology in general, would be enormous.

The future of liturgical theology remains essentially a task to be pursued: to explore the human events that are Christian sacraments both as human and as liturgical (i.e., as works of the entire assembled church); to penetrate ever more deeply the truth which faith names as the "within" of those events; and to draw lines of connection between sacraments and those realities of everyday life which sacraments both draw on and point to. It must be done in many directions and on many levels at once. Christian worship proclaims and enacts the transformation by God of human life, of human history, and of creation itself. The ways of liturgical theology can be no less than the ways in which humans seek to understand their life, their history, and their world.

Selective Bibliography on Sacraments

Bouyer, Louis. *Eucharist.* Notre Dame: University of Notre Dame Press, 1968 (French orig. 1966).

Fink, Peter, ed. *The New Dictionary of Sacramental Worship.* Collegeville: The Liturgical Press, 1990.

Hollenbach, David. "A Prophetic Church and the Sacramental Imagination." In J. Haughey, ed., *The Faith That Does Justice.* New York: Paulist Press, 1977 (pp. 234-263).

Kavanagh, Aidan. *On Liturgical Theology.* New York: Pueblo Publishing Co., 1984. Also, *The Shape of Baptism: The Rite of Christian Initiation.* New York: Pueblo Publishing Co., 1978.

Kilmartin, Edward. *Christian Liturgy.* Kansas City: Sheed and Ward,

1988. Also, "A Modern Approach to the Word of God and Sacraments of Christ." In F. Eigo, ed., *The Sacraments: God's Love and Mercy Actualized*. Villanova: Villanova University Press, 1979 (pp. 59-110).

Schillebeeckx, Edward. *Christ the Sacrament of the Encounter with God*. New York: Sheed and Ward, 1963 (orig. 1960).

Vaillancourt, R. *Toward a Renewal of Sacramental Theology*, trans., M. O'Connell. Collegeville: The Liturgical Press, 1979 (French orig. 1977).

Sacraments:
Particular Questions

5

The Significance of the Meal in Christianity*

FROM THE BEGINNING OF CHRISTIANITY, AND EVEN BEFORE THE DISCI-
ples of Jesus were themselves known as Christians, table fellowship with Jesus and with each other stood at the center of
the Christian experience of God. It began in Jesus' own life-
time; it continued as a matter of course after the experience of
Jesus' death and resurrection. Throughout the history of the
Christian Church the table has been the privileged place
where Christians meet the Risen One. It has likewise been the
privileged place where they meet the God who raised Jesus
from the dead.

I would like here to offer some reflections on the significance of the meal in Christianity. To be more specific, I would
like to speak of the eucharistic meal and of its significance
within the Christian experience of God. The eucharist continues to be the central worship event for Christians, and, in spite
of the many disguises it has worn over the centuries, the eucharist remains most fundamentally a meal that is shared
among people. It is shared in the context of faith; it is shared
in the context of relationship established by faith. The eucharist is the Christian meal *par excellence*.

---

*This chapter was originally delivered as an oral presentation at a
Jewish-Christian dialogue.

I would like to begin with two preliminary remarks. The first is to identify an important recovery in current liturgical scholarship among Christians, which is the vantage point from which I speak. The second is to make my topic a bit more modest by noting a diversity even among Christians as to the significance of this central worship event. I must acknowledge from the outset that I write as a Roman Catholic theologian, and hence from but one perspective within Christianity itself.

Current liturgical scholarship among Christians enjoys a recent recovery which fulfills the wonderful description by T.S. Eliot: we have returned to the place from which we have started, and have seen it as though for the first time. After a very long period of amnesia, Christians have recovered the Jewish roots of Christian worship. A brief sketch of that amnesia might be instructive.

We can safely say that, in its origins, Christianity was a Jewish experience. Jesus himself was a Jew, and the earliest Christians were likewise Jews who did not imagine themselves as anything other than a movement within Judaism. When these early Christians experienced the death and resurrection of Christ, they began to interpret this Jesus and their own experience of him by calling on resources from their Jewish religious heritage, such as Son of Man, Suffering Servant, Messiah, and the new age of God's Spirit prophesied by Jeremiah and Ezekiel.

We can also safely say that very early in its history Christianity, thinking itself to be universal, became dominantly, almost exclusively, a Gentile experience. This demanded a translation of Jewish religious symbols for a people who were not steeped in that religious tradition. As is true with all translation, some symbols made it intact, some did not make it at all, while most were changed to some extent in the process.

The unfortunate and embarrassing part of that history is that the Christian imagination, for reasons on both sides too numerous to list, began to develop in opposition to its Jewish roots, with greater emphasis put on discontinuity than on continuity. Thus, for example, the New Covenant was imagined as abrogation of the Old, and the Christian experience itself was thought to render the Jewish experience outmoded, passé, without meaning except as a preliminary stage of God's plan now brought to its fullness.

Insofar as liturgy is concerned, the people pray as they understand themselves. If the Christian religious experience is seen to be a new thing, over against the old, then Christian liturgy must likewise be seen as a new thing over against the old. It might take the Jewish Scriptures to itself, and incorporate the psalms as a mainstay of its prayer. Its real genesis, however, must be located just about anywhere except within the Jewish worship of God.

It is the particular grace of our own day that the amnesia and the antagonism that urged it are being gradually laid to rest. In the field of Christian worship it has been both exciting and enriching for us finally to recover our Jewish roots. Scholarly works such as Louis Bouyer's *Eucharist*,[1] which successfully traced the eucharistic prayer to the Jewish *berakoth* (blessing prayers) have helped us recover a continuity which goes far deeper than form or structure to the very style of faith and prayer that is intrinsic to both Jewish worship and Christian worship alike.

A second preliminary remark. Let me say a brief word about another dimension of Christian liturgical history, and about another form of embarrassment that is a peculiar in-house problem for Christians today. This, as I mentioned above, is to make the topic of this presentation a bit more modest.

The various traditions within Christianity have developed different styles and different understandings of Christian eucharist. In both East and West elaborate rituals have evolved with at times so much ritual overlay that it is difficult to recognize in these liturgies the contours of a simple meal shared in faith. In the medieval West the meal became a divine drama attended by so much distortion and even superstition that it became a major factor in triggering the sixteenth-century Reformation.

Nor did that Reformation do much to cure the ills. The Reformers so shifted the focus of Christian worship to the word of God that the centrality of the eucharist was severely damaged. Moreover, they removed the words of institution from any eucharistic prayer context, and hence from the already meager context of thanksgiving accorded them by the Roman Canon. Meanwhile, the Roman reaction to the Reformers served only to fix even more firmly the objectified *sacrificium* which bore only token resemblance to a meal shared in faith.

In our own day, while most Christian traditions are once again recovering the eucharist as central and the eucharist as shared meal, many disagreements still exist. No single articulation of the significance of the eucharist will gain universal acceptance among Christians, a fact that still leads us to remember our common Lord at separate tables.

I can speak, therefore, as but a single voice within the diverse Christian community. My own tradition embraces a strong sacramental principle not shared by all Christians. Thus my remarks must be more properly named, "Some Significance of the Meal in Christianity," offered to enhance not only the dialogue between Christians and Jews, but also among Christians still divided.

What I would like to do in unfolding this one perception of the role or significance of the meal in Christianity can be done in four stages. Since I speak from a strong sacramental principle, it will be helpful first to explain what that is, and what it is not. Secondly, I will look at some of the Christian biblical material where meal-stories are recounted, to get some sense of the meaning perceived in meals by the foundational Christian Church. Thirdly, I will examine with you some liturgical testimony to the Christian meal *par excellence*, specifically the prayer prayed over the eucharistic food. Finally, in what may be the most difficult part of this presentation, I will attempt a brief phenomenological analysis of the meal in the light of a specifically Catholic tradition, namely, the eucharist as sacrifice.

A STRONG SACRAMENTAL PRINCIPLE

I use the term *a strong sacramental principle* to denote a particular approach to those activities of faith which Christians call sacraments. I realize that this term needs carefully to be understood to avoid turning Christian sacraments into a form of magic. It does not mean the possibility of putting controls on God. God's gracious activity must always remain gracious. Nor does it mean the possibility of gaining salvation automatically, with no conditions on the faith of those who are saved. Salvation always demands vulnerability before God's gracious action, and an open responsiveness which alone is worthy of the names obedience and faith.

What a strong sacramental principle does involve is a willingness to take the concrete here and now with radical seriousness, convinced in faith that God's gracious activity is actualized in concrete human actions. With regard to the eucharist it means that the meal as meal, and as *this* meal, is the concrete locus of God's saving action. The meal is not an empty reminder of something from the past, nor an empty projection of something yet to be realized. Images of God's activity, be they past or future, enter the present *as present*, that is, as the depth dimension of what is visibly and tangibly taking place here and now.

Vatican II's Constitution on the Sacred Liturgy (*Sacrosanctum Concilium*) gives a concise statement of this sacramental principle. "It [the liturgy] involves the presentation of man's sanctification under the guise of signs perceptible by the senses and its accomplishment in ways appropriate to each of these signs" (SC 7). This sanctification embraces everything which Christians believe God has done for us in raising Jesus from the dead, and everything God continues to do in God's own gracious love. This includes freedom from sin, inner transformation by God's own Spirit, formation into a people of covenant, and a share in the promise of God's kingdom. Of this sanctification Vatican II asserts two things. There is a way we can come to know this sanctification: it is spoken in the signs and symbols of our worship. Moreover, there is a way that this process of God's action takes concrete human shape: the ways of these signs and symbols. With regard to the Christian meal of eucharist, it is the meal itself, including the blessing prayer prayed over it, which must reveal the meaning of sanctification, and it is the very dynamics of a meal so blessed and shared that constitute the ways of this sanctification.

A strong sacramental principle says simply that God's activity takes concrete human shape, and that all one must do is to allow that human activity faithfully to unfold. This principle explains why, in an earlier and often misunderstood articulation of the same truth, the minister had only to intend and do what the church intends and does, and the people had only to put no obstacle in the way. It is at least as old as the decision not to re-baptize Christians who were baptized in "heretic" communities, as urged in the second and third centuries. If its history is properly traced to its Jewish roots, this principle stands as a Christian articulation of 1^e *zikkaron, anamnesis, memorial*, where human actions done in faith are the concrete locus of God's active remembering.

BIBLICAL WITNESS

Since a strong sacramental principle demands that we focus careful attention on the eucharistic meal as a meal, it will be helpful, as a second movement of this essay, to examine some meal stories of the Christian Scriptures to find in that biblical witness some of the things that the early Christians saw as the ways of the meal.

A first text that suggests itself is taken from the ninth chapter of Matthew.

> As he sat at table in the house, behold, many tax collectors and sinners came and sat down with Jesus and his disciples. And when the Pharisees saw this, they said to his disciples, "Why does your teacher eat with tax collectors and sinners?" But when he heard it, he said, "Those who are well have no need of a physician, but those who are sick. Go and learn what this means: I desire mercy, and not sacrifice. For I came not to call the righteous, but sinners (9:10-13).

In this first selection we see that the meal is the place where sinners are welcome. It is the place where mercy is given and reconciliation is found. In the early Christian Church the eucharist was recognized as the prime place of forgiveness. Baptism, and later penance, were likewise named "for the forgiveness of sins," but these activities or sacraments never stood alone, isolated from the eucharist. In fact, they were ordered to eucharist which was in turn their intrinsic completion. Baptism initiated one into eucharistic communion; penance reunited those who had lost communion by their sins.

The story of the multiplication of the loaves and fish brings out further dimensions of meal richness. Matthew's version is as follows.

> And as he went ashore he saw a great throng; and he had compassion on them, and healed their sick. When it was evening, the disciples came to him and said, "This is a lonely place, and the day is now over; send the crowds away to go into the vil-

lages and buy food for themselves." Jesus said, "They need not go away; you give them something to eat" (14:14-16).

And when Jesus had prayed upon the five loaves and two fish that were brought to him,

> the disciples gave them to the crowds. And they all ate and were satisfied (14:19-20).

Most charming is the note of compassion that introduces this story. And most startling is the Lord's command to his weary disciples, "You give them something to eat." It is the responsibility of those who gather with Jesus to offer food and welcome to all who come. None shall be turned away.

If we turn now to the Gospel of John, we find a developed theological meditation on the early Christian experience of eucharist in chapter six. A brief section brings forth the thrust of John's proclamation.

> Jesus said to them, "Truly, truly, I say to you unless you eat the flesh of the Son of Man and drink his blood, you have no life in you; he who eats my flesh and drinks my blood has eternal life, and I will raise him up on the last day. For my flesh is food indeed, and my blood is drink indeed. He who eats my flesh and drinks my blood abides in me and I in him. As the living Father sent me, and I live because of the Father, so he who eats me will live because of me" (6:53-57).

One of John's theological tactics is identification, so that one may appropriate for oneself that with which one is identified. For example, in his account of Jesus' last days, John has Jesus die at the same time the lambs are being slaughtered in the temple, thus identifying Jesus with the Passover lamb. In so doing he appropriates even more richly for the Christian experience of God the full heritage of Passover. In the passage given above, John identifies the bread and wine of the eucharist with the living reality of Jesus so that the one who eats and drinks is proclaimed as gaining intimate union with Jesus. This is union, moreover, with the Risen One who will never die again, and therefore gains for the Christian the promise of everlasting life.

A final selection of the Christian biblical material on the meal is taken from Paul's First Letter to the Corinthians. In Paul we expect to find the accent on the unity of the church which is a central theme of his whole theology. Paul views the church as the *soma Christou*, the Body of Christ, the ongoing enfleshed presence of Christ until he shall come again. The body is established by unity, fractured by disunity, healed by reunion. And the Body is made visible in all its fullness at the meals which Christians share.

Paul's concern for unity comes forth in chapter eight when he is speaking of food that is sacrificed to idols. Since idols do not exist, a knowledgeable person might very well eat such food with a clear conscience. It is, he maintains, an indifferent matter because of the knowledge we have received. But Paul issues a strong caution nonetheless, since not all have received this knowledge.

> Take care lest this liberty of yours become somehow a stumbling block to the weak . . . [lest] by your knowledge this weak man is destroyed, the brother for whom Christ died. Thus, sinning against your brethren and wounding their conscience when it is weak, you sin against Christ (8:9-12).

Concern for unity comes forth again in a specifically eucharistic section of chapter ten:

> The cup of blessing which we bless, is it not a participation in the blood of Christ? The bread which we break, is it not a participation in the body of Christ? Because there is one bread, we who are many are one body, for we all partake of the one bread (10:16-17).

It comes forth finally when he admonishes the community at Corinth because divisions exist among them, divisions illustrated when they come together to eat. It is unworthy for some to humiliate others at the table, and Paul's judgment on this is severe:

> Whoever eats the bread and drinks of the cup of the Lord in an unworthy manner will be guilty of profaning the body and blood of the Lord . . . So then, my brethren, when you come together to eat, wait for one another, lest you come together to be condemned (11:27,33).

Paul's word on the meal is clear. It is the place of reconciliation and welcome, the place of union with the Lord, and the place of unity with those whose faith fashions them into the one Body, the *soma Christou*.

This brief look at some of the biblical testimony concerning the meal in Christian experience is not intended to give an exhaustive picture or a well-honed argument. It is given simply to suggest some of the dimensions of the meal that were alive in the consciousness of the early church. Of course, the picture would be seriously defective without some look at the accounts of Jesus' Last Supper, but these actually take us into the third stage of this essay, namely, the liturgical testimony and the eucharistic prayer.

LITURGICAL WITNESS

The texts of the Last Supper in Matthew, Mark, and Luke present the meal as a Passover supper eaten by Jesus with his disciples. Christian tradition, particularly in the West, has taken this event to be the originating moment of Christian eucharist. For a long time these texts were taken as the literal moment of institution, when Jesus himself reworked the Passover ritual and gave it new meaning. This particular reading of the texts is difficult to sustain in light of contemporary biblical scholarship, which informs sacramental theologians like myself that an actual reconstruction of that supper, if indeed there was one, is difficult if not impossible.

At least it can be said that it was the intention of the foundational church to make it perlucidly and inescapably clear that Christian eucharist originates in the Passover faith, and can only be understood in light of that faith. Alas for Christian history, we did manage to escape it, and the eucharistic piety that has dominated Christian experience since at least the fourth century is quite seriously adrift of that Passover faith.

It is certainly not possible within the space of this presentation to trace in any detail the movement away from the faith of Passover over Christianity's two-thousand year history. However, a brief look at some segments of two major eucharistic prayers within the Christian Church can at least suggest the magnitude of the shift, from which we are only beginning to recover in our own day.

The dominant piety and theology of the eucharist which has prevailed in the Christian West from at least the sixth century until very recently is enshrined in the Roman Canon, now called Eucharistic Prayer I. Thanksgiving, always a cornerstone of the Jewish *berakah*, can scarcely be called a central motif of this prayer, which is much more petitionary in tone. Nor is the focus primarily on the wonderful deeds of God, but rather almost exclusively upon the eucharistic gifts: gifts offered, gifts consecrated, gifts received. Two brief sections from the Roman Canon illustrate the movement of faith shaped by this prayer:

> Father, accept this offering from your whole family . . . Bless and approve our offering; make it acceptable to you . . . Let it become the body and blood of Jesus Christ . . .

and a bit later in the prayer,

> We pray that your angel may take this sacrifice to your altar in heaven, that, as we receive from this altar the sacred body and blood of your Son, we may be filled with every grace and blessing . . .

The prayer envisions individuals before God seeking the gifts of God for their own spiritual nourishment and enrichment.

The dominant Eastern tradition, captured in the Byzantine prayer of John Chrysostom, represents a somewhat different shape of eucharistic faith, but one still removed from the Jewish Passover faith. While preserving the thanksgiving context and narrative context for the words of institution, it too gives strong emphasis on the gifts to be consecrated, and on the individual sanctification of those who partake:

> Send down thy Holy Spirit upon us and upon these gifts lying before us . . . and make this bread the precious body of thy Christ and that which is in this chalice the precious blood of thy Christ, having changed them by the Holy Spirit . . . so that for those who receive them in communion, they may serve as a cleansing for the soul, for the forgiveness of their sins, as a communion of the Holy Spirit, and a full participation in the kingdom of heaven.

In both the Roman and Byzantine traditions eucharistic piety very early moved away from the sense of eucharistic food that forms us into a people toward the eucharistic food which forms holy individuals before God.

How different these are from an earlier third century prayer, the anaphora of Hippolytus, which gives the more primitive sense of communion:

And we beg thee to send thy Holy Spirit upon the offering of
thy holy Church, to gather and unite all those who receive it.[2]

This prayer reveals the clean lines of what we can now see a
Jewish *berakah* would look like when translated into a language apt for the Gentile converts. Its principal shape is that
of a thanksgiving narrative which outlines the *mirabilia Dei*,
the wonderful deeds of God. The words of institution form an
integral part of the narrative to interpret the meal precisely as
a meal of Passover faith. There follows a twofold prayer, classically called *anamnesis*, we remember, and *epiclesis*, God sends
his Spirit in his active response of remembering. In other
words, there follows in the Christian eucharistic prayer the
full sense of *l^e zikkaron* of Jewish faith: we remember in order
that God will remember and act once again.

A most important link of Christian eucharist with its Jewish
roots is a prayer from the *Didache*, dated about 110 A.D. It is
not a single eucharistic prayer, but rather three distinct blessings, which can be interpreted as a pre-Gentile, pre-
translation, Jewish-Christian prayer. There is a blessing over a
cup, a blessing over bread, and a second blessing over a cup.
The context is clearly a meal. I interpret the three as all that a
Jewish-Christian would have to do with the familiar meal
blessing prayers in order to "Christianize" them, that is, bring
them to focus on God's new deed, Jesus Christ. For example,
the blessing over the bread:

> We give you thanks, our Father, for the life and the knowledge
> you have revealed to us through Jesus, your Child. Glory to
> you forever.

> Just as this bread which we break, once scattered over the hills,
> has been gathered and made one, so may your Church too be
> gathered from the ends of the earth into your kingdom.

It is this final link between Christian and Jewish meal-worship
that awakens the possibility of reading again the experience of
Christian eucharist in the light of its Jewish roots.

Because space does not allow further elaboration, let me
simply draw a parallel between Jewish Passover and Christian
eucharist that urges recognition of the same style of faith and
prayer for each.

In the Passover faith, the lamb was slaughtered in order to

acknowledge God as God. The slaughter was thus true sacrifice. The blood was poured out, not as a movement toward God, but to acknowledge a movement of God toward Israel, that is, the promise and seal of the covenant. Finally, the lamb was eaten in order to unite the people under the covenant and to bring the people into access to that covenant. It was done as a memorial, that the God who made covenant long ago will remember and give now to this people the same faithful love and deliverance.

In the Christian Passover faith, Jesus, the Lamb, was slaughtered once for all. His blood was poured out, again as a sign of movement from God to God's people. It is the "blood of the covenant." In fact, the more primitive articulation of the words of institution in the Christian Scriptures does not say, "This is the blood of the covenant" (Mark, Matthew), but rather, "This is the new covenant in my blood" (Luke, Paul). The blood of Jesus is the sign of the covenant sealed. Finally, the meal is shared in order to form and unite the people under the covenant, and to gain for them true access to God's love and deliverance. It is done as memorial, that the God of covenant whose faithfulness was shown in raising Jesus from the dead, will remember and give now to this people, united with Jesus, that same faithful love.

For the Christian faith, this recovery of our Jewish roots allows us to understand why the eucharist is a meal, and why it must do for us the things a meal does. It must make us a people under covenant; it must establish relationship before God in whom we believe, for that relationship is the very shape of the sanctification God gives us in the eucharist. To look for it elsewhere is, in another fine phrase of T.S. Eliot, to look "in the wrong place." In short, the contemporary liturgical renewal among Christians, still in its early phases, might well be called the rediscovery of the role of the meal in Christianity, and indeed the recovery of the eucharist as a meal.

There is a fact that we, Jew and Christian alike, must acknowledge, jolting perhaps at first though ultimately quite obvious, and an interesting speculation which might possibly open up new vistas of common research for us both. The fact is a simple observation in regard to two people who both proclaim with integrity, "Hear, o Israel, the Lord your God is one

God." Eucharist and Passover are done as *memorial*, that is, a people remember in order that the God of covenant might remember us.[3] Is it not proper to say at least that *the same God of covenant* might remember? How foolish and blind we would be to imagine that we do not worship the same God. Our common proclamation of this Deuteronomy text binds us, I think, to the fact that it is to one and the same God that we pray. The speculation is a bit more risky, though it is not without some solid ground. Is it not possible that it is not only the same God, but the *same covenant*? The term "new covenant" which the Christians clearly employed does not in itself imply, as a later Christian theology came to interpret it, a rejection of the Jewish covenant. "New Covenant" is itself a concept within Jewish faith and prayer, rooted especially in the prophecies of Ezekiel and Jeremiah. Raymond Brown, in commenting on the Christian understanding of Jesus in light of Jeremiah 31:31-34, notes: "For Jeremiah this was more a renewed covenant than a totally new covenant, and this was probably the earliest Christian interpretation as well . . ."[4] Surely this is a suggestion rich with possibility in an age when Christians are discovering again their Jewish roots, and when some Jews, such as Samuel Sandmel, are beginning to suggest that Christianity is a form of Judaism.[5]

As a beginning step toward this, I can offer a possible reconstruction of the origins of Christian eucharist. It is just that: a beginning, and possible. I would imagine it in this way. Jesus went to his death because, in his life, he was obedient to God. He went to his death in the faith of Passover, the only faith the Jewish Jesus had at his disposal. He trusted that the God who promised deliverance would remember and would deliver him, even though the deliverance might have to take a shape not originally imagined within the traditional Passover symbols. In the proclamation of Jesus' resurrection, the Jewish disciples spoke forth their conviction that God did indeed remember and deliver Jews from the exile of death. It was principally a proclamation of the fidelity of God to God's promise. It was a proclamation that the covenant was not abrogated, but rather was given one more sign that it still held, and that God was still the faithful one to be trusted. Why would they not continue, as is noted in the Acts of the Apostles, in the breaking of the bread, proclaiming now this new wonder of their faithful God?

Time would force upon Christians the language of discontinuity, and this fact of history cannot be swept away. But even if, in honesty, we must attend to that development, and explore it for what truth it may contain, we must likewise attend to the strong possiblity and even probability that discontinuity is not the original experience of Christianity. It remains to be explored whether the subsequent discontinuity rests on a necessity of faith, Jewish and Christian, or only on the accidental contours of history.

SACRIFICE MEAL

At any rate, let me move to the fourth stage of this presentation. This last part I must do sketchily, but even so, I hope to bring out from the tradition of eucharistic sacrifice one final dimension of what I see as the role of meal in Christianity.

Ironically, the tradition of eucharist as sacrifice has often stood in apparent opposition to the meal, so much so that emphasis on the meal seems to detract from or threaten the tradition of eucharistic sacrifice. I have been forced by my own convictions to explore the meal *as sacrifice* and the sacrifice *as meal*, beyond any apparent opposition they might have. Let me share with you briefly some of that exploration.

The Roman Catholic tradition has insisted that in the eucharist a true and proper sacrifice is offered, yet one which is different from Christ's sacrifice *only* in the manner of offering. It *is* Christ's sacrifice. Words such as bloody-unbloody, or original-sacramental, attempt to maintain a unity in distinction and distinction in unity which sounds almost contradictory. We affirm that Christ's sacrifice was offered once-for-all, and yet the eucharist repeated in the church is nonetheless this once-for-all sacrifice. The Reformation position, particularly in Luther, saw only the contradiction, and therefore needed to downplay, even deny, the true sacrificial nature of eucharist. But the strong sacramental principle of Roman Catholic tradition could not allow it to empty the eucharist of its true sacrificial character.

In an effort, then, to be faithful to my own tradition, and to the strong sacramental principle I enunciated earlier, I find it necessary to ask two related questions. What is there in a meal that would allow it to be the actualization of Christ's sacrifice, and what is there in Christ's sacrifice that allows it to be actualized as a meal?

The method of pursuing these questions begins with the sacrifice of Christ, which is all too often looked at narrowly in terms of the crucifixion, read in the light of Isaiah's fourth servant song. It is necessary to push back to a more general understanding of sacrifice in order to arrive at an understanding of Christ's sacrifice which includes, but goes much deeper than, the crucifixion.

The term "sacrifice," as it is used among religious peoples, and particularly among Jewish and Judaeo-Christian peoples, is a complex category referring to a variety of religious activities. Frances Young, in her *Sacrifice and the Death of Christ*,[6] rightly cautions against the reduction of the category to any one simple meaning. Nonetheless, across the spectrum of "sacrificial" activities, there are two common notes: sacrifice as worship and sacrifice as seeking favor. The act of worship acknowledges God to be God, and in a variety of ways commits the worshiper to an openness and an obedience to God. It is the dual intention of acknowledgment and obedience that makes the act a religious sacrifice.

The basic Christian proclamation about Jesus' life is that it was a life of total obedience ("obedient unto death"—Phil 2:8), guided completely by the *malkuth schamaim*, the kingdom of God (Mk 1:15). This kingdom shaped his life, and unfolded in his life. Because of this, every event of Jesus' life, and not merely his death, can and ought to be regarded under the heading "sacrifice." Jesus' death was the final act of obedience in that he chose to die rather than deny the inner summons of God, which from the beginning shaped his life. Thus his crucifixion is sacrifice in that, one with the rest of his life, it expressed and was embraced in obedience to the *malkuth schamaim*. His death, freely embraced in obedient love, was the definitive seal on his whole life ordered to the worship of God.

Johannes Metz, in *Poverty of Spirit*,[7] draws together Jesus' obedience to God and his act of becoming human under the rubric "poverty," which at its "dregs" is worship. This will be developed more fully in a later chapter. Suffice it to say here that the Christian imagination affirms the uniqueness of Jesus' sacrifice, and does so by specifying the journey of Jesus' obedient life as the *incarnation* of the Son of God, that is, the journey of God becoming the completely human one. In turn, it identifies the process of becoming fully human as obedience to the God who is within. One can say, then, that the unique sacrifice of Jesus, the Obedient One, was his journey of becoming human "even to death" in spite of the outside voices that would have shaped his life otherwise. He was obedient to God, and he trusted that God would deliver him.

With this brief reflection on the sacrifice of Jesus before us, we can turn to the phenomenon of a shared meal in the hope of understanding how it can actualize that sacrifice. The case rests on a perception of the shared meal as an invitation to true humanity. Let us consider this briefly.

A meal shared among friends is an expression of friendship, a moment together where people need not be anyone other than who they are. Friends at table can simply entrust themselves to each other. At a meal one cannot be angry, or else one must leave the table. At a meal one cannot be phoney or artificial, or else the meal becomes a bore and people get restless. When people do not behave as the meal asks them to behave, some signal of this manifests itself, and the meal collapses. At its best, however, when people can simply be with each other, the meal can go on and on, with very little attention paid to the time it takes. Such a meal is, and has the power to be, a most gracious moment among friends, and worthy of the name *communion*. Such a meal needs no motive; its gift is motive enough.

In the Christian meal of eucharist, something which is spontaneous among friends becomes universalized in faith. We place ourselves in a position where the power of this most intimate of human actions can work upon us, not with existential friends, but frequently enough with people we hardly know. In faith we call them sister and brother, but in fact we may not treat them as such, or even want to. Yet, if we are vulnerable to the power of the meal shared, and generously allow that power to unfold upon us, something must happen, gradually, eventually.

For this we must have a motive. The Christian experience presents that motive by identifying the meal with the life-journey *sacrificium* of Christ. Thus it appropriates as motive the faithfulness of God who once-for-all has declared himself faithful to the Jesus journey. The humanizing that is actualized at the table is risky business for those who allow the meal to work itself out upon them. It is risky to do in a strange place what ordinarily we would dare do only with friends. Yet the risk is warranted, for it is the summons of God, and we who take our place at the table of the eucharist and express our baptismal unity with Christ acknowledge God as God, and commit ourselves in obedience with Christ to the humanizing journey that is made manifest and accomplished by the meal. Christ's sacrifice is actualized as our own, and our sacrifice is both embraced by and articulated as his.

* * * * * *

As a final summary statement I can say that, in the Christian experience of God, or at least in this one perception of the Christian experience of God, the meal is nothing less than a powerful force that can make human beings out of us, and that can form us into an open, trusting, and loving people. At least that is what we are invited to surrender to when we speak our Amen to the prayer and to the meal. That force, moreover, is not impersonal or abstract or distant. It is rather an incarnation, in the here-and-now meal that is shared, of the power and the grace of a remembering God.

Notes

1. L. Bouyer, *Eucharist: Theology and Spirituality of the Eucharistic Prayer*, trans., C. Underhill Quinn (Notre Dame: University of Notre Dame Press, 1968). The major insight of this classic work is now taken for granted; in its initial publication, however, it was considered quite revolutionary. For a more recent presentation of the relationship between Jewish and Christian worship, see Peter Fink, ed., *The New Dictionary of Sacramental Worship* (Collegeville: The Liturgical Press, 1990): (a) "Jewish Roots of Christian Worship" by A. Kavanagh, pp. 617-623; and (b) "Jewish Worship" by L. Hoffman, pp. 623-633.

2. This anaphora, contained in the *Apostolic Tradition* of Hippolytus, ca. 215 A.D., has formed the basis of Eucharistic Prayer II in the Roman Missal of Paul VI.

3. Though there are many interpretations of the word *zikkaron*, memorial, I am relying here specifically on that proposed by Brevard Childs in *Memory and Tradition in Israel* (London: SCM Press, 1962) and by Joachim Jeremias in *The Eucharistic Words of Jesus* (Oxford: Blackwell, 1955). A full discussion of the various interpretations can be found in Fritz Chenderlin, *"Do This as My Memorial"* (Rome: Biblical Institute Press, 1982).

4. Raymond Brown, *The Gospel According to John XIII-XXI* (Garden City: Doubleday, 1970) 614.

5. See S. Sandmel, *Judaism and Christian Beginnings* (New York: Oxford University Press, 1978).

6. F. Young, *Sacrifice and the Death of Christ* (Philadelphia: Westminster, 1975). See also R. Daly, *The Origins of the Christian Doctrine of Sacrifice* (Philadelphia: Fortress, 1978).

7. Johannes Metz, *Poverty of Spirit*, trans., J. Drury (New York: Paulist Press, 1968).

6

Perceiving the Presence
of Christ

IT HAS BEEN MORE THAN TWENTY YEARS NOW SINCE EDWARD SCHIL-
lebeeckx introduced the now familiar notion of personal encounter into the language of sacramental theology. To enact
the sacramental actions of the church is personally to encounter, to meet, to engage the mystery and the person of Jesus
Christ. It is likewise more than twenty years since the Constitution on the Sacred Liturgy of Vatican II broadened the categories in which the church speaks of the presence of Christ in
the eucharist. Christ is present in the word, in the assembly, in
the presiding minister, and in the eucharistic food. This fourfold presence stands in marked contrast to the long theological
tradition which limited discussion of the presence of Christ to
the bread and wine alone. Christ is present in the eucharist,
and the modes of his presence are several. Christ is to be encountered in the eucharist, and the modes of his presence govern how this encounter is to take place.

The aim of this essay is to reflect on the presence of Christ
in the eucharist, and in particular to explore and guide the
process of encounter. The biblical warrant for such an exploration is the Lucan *Emmaus account* where the disciples were
said to have "recognized" Christ in the breaking of the bread.
The fact of his presence was known because the person was

somehow met in the doing. The conciliar warrant is the call for full and active participation of all the people in the eucharistic action, a goal which the council insists is "to be considered before all else" (SC 14). The participation envisioned by the constitution is not simply participation on the level of external, physical activity. It is much more on the level of awareness of both the human reality and the faith reality which the eucharist is. Participation at its deepest level *is* the meeting in faith with the living Christ. Finally, the theological warrant for such an exploration is the doctrinal tradition that has proclaimed and defended the real presence of Christ *within* (*continetur gratia*) the eucharistic action. It is a metaphysical presence, and therefore can never be scientifically proven. It must be recognized or perceived through the eyes of faith, and the full truth of the church's proclamation will lie hidden until such recognition takes place.

This exploration into the presence of Christ in the eucharist unfolds in three stages. The first is to examine the faith of the church and to get the largest possible purchase on what it is that the church affirms about the presence of Christ. At this stage the task will be to form proper images of the Christ who is present, and proper images of the ways of his presence. The second stage is to ask how that presence might be known and engaged. This will entail an understanding of myth and symbol, and the process of being drawn into comprehension of the truth which myth and symbol convey. It will also involve some remarks on the importance of ritual care when the church's eucharist is enacted. The final stage will be a brief assessment of the ontological conditions that must hold for the presence of Christ to be perceived and recognized.

THE FAITH OF THE CHURCH

In the revised liturgy of the eucharist in the Roman Sacramentary, the minister proclaims to those who approach the table, *Corpus Christi*, "The body of Christ." This is a deliberately multivalent statement meaning at one and the same time the bread, the eating of the bread, and what we, the church, become in the eating. This simple acclamation capsulizes the process which the full epiclesis of the eucharistic prayer calls forth, namely, that the food become the body and blood of

Christ, and that we who eat and drink become one body and one spirit in Christ. Because it is a process that is announced, and not simply a statement of fact, the proper response to the acclamation is *Amen*, "so be it, let it happen." It is not agreement but surrender. An unfortunate reductionism occurs when the eucharistic minister alters the acclamation and announces instead, *"This is* the body of Christ." It becomes less an invitation to transformation, and more a declaration that seeks assent and nothing else. Still more unfortunate is the occasional announcement, "This is Jesus." Not only is the symbolic richness of the invitation lost, the acclamation itself is theologically inaccurate.

The church proclaims the presence of Christ, and as obvious as it may seem, it is the presence of Christ, not the historical Jesus. The theological position that tried to identify the consecrated bread and wine with the Jesus of history was happily laid to rest at the subtle hands of the Scholastics who named it a metaphysical, not a physical, presence. Unfortunately, the images of popular piety, such as "Jesus descending upon the altar," or "Jesus lonely in the tabernacle," have not always preserved and respected this subtle distinction.

To speak of the presence of Christ in the eucharist is to name the presence of one who has passed over into the heavenly realm, who therefore transcends the limits of space and time, and who, though his presence may be made manifest through the medium of historical realities, can never be equated with those historical realities.[1] Images that do suggest the equation are not helpful, for they inevitably posture us face to face with, and therefore over against, the historical Jesus rather than drawing us into the one who has become the Christ. To serve the faith of the church, especially as it is proclaimed in the baptismal "incorporation *into*," images of Christ's presence need to be more fluid and more subtle.

A first step in restoring proper images of Christ's presence is to recapture the Augustinian sense of the *totus Christus*, that is, the person of Christ gathered with and gathering all those who by baptism are united to him. The organic metaphor of the body which Paul so skillfully used remains a privileged image of the Christ. Thus it is that the Constitution on the Sacred Liturgy maintains that all the liturgical actions of the gathered church manifest and express "the mystery of Christ and the real nature of the true church" (SC 2). With the image of the *totus Christus* it is more proper to speak of Christ's presence made manifest by the church doing the eucharist than of Christ present "in" the eucharist. This second is really derived from the first.

A second step is to call upon the Jewish experience of the presence of God, and the complex symbol set they used to name this experience, and to keep in mind that it was this same complex image set that Christians used for Christ once they named him to be "what God is."[2] The Jews knew a fourfold experience of the presence of God, and drew up a set of stories and symbols to identify each shade of that fourfold experience. God was the God who *comes*, on his own initiative and at his own time. God was likewise the God who *leads*, who goes before, who prepares the way. God was also the God who *abides*, dwelling freely among his people. And God was the God who *hides*, with the primary mask of the hidden God being the people themselves. In the experience of the Risen One the early Christians named Jesus Christ in exactly the same way. He is the Christ who *comes* ("Maranatha"), the Christ who *leads* ("I go before you"), the Christ who *abides* ("I am with you all days"), and the Christ who *hides* ("You are the body of Christ").

Two of the image sets, namely, he *comes* and he *hides*, capture the presence of Christ as transcendent, elusive, never under human control. The other two, in different ways, speak of the immanent Christ, tangibly accessible to human experience. All four must be held together in order to preserve the true reality and experience of Christ. The transcendent images alone threaten to lose Christ in otherness; the immanent images alone threaten to bring Christ under human control.

The irony of Christian theology is that it has indeed preserved all four image sets, but has parceled them out in different theological directions. Images of the Christ who *comes* have shaped both the theology of the word and Christian eschatology. Images of the Christ who *leads* have given rise to the theology of eucharistic sacrifice which, in the scholastic tradition at least, was held distinct from the theology of real presence. Images of the Christ who *hides* formed the theology of the church, while only the images of Christ *abiding* found their way into reflections on Christ's presence. Once the irony is recognized, however, it is possible to draw all four strands together and see them as varied statements about the presence of Christ, which presence is enacted into history when the church gathers to do its eucharist.[3] It is also possible to see how the apparently new proclamation of the fourfold presence of Christ, in word, in ministers, in eucharistic food, and in assembly, is but a naming of these four kinds of experience which together constitute the experience of Christ present. In word Christ comes; in presider Christ leads; in food Christ abides; in assembly Christ lives hidden.

There are other dimensions of the church's faith in the eucharistic presence of Christ that need to be recalled if the images we form of that presence are to serve and not hinder the encounter. It is a *personal* presence, and not an impersonal one. On the negative side this urges us to avoid any imagery which would make of Christ a sacred object, or even a sacred *persona*, with which we interact in less than human ways. Positively, it points to the primacy of an interpersonal paradigm to guide both reflection and interaction. Moreover, the Christ who is present is *active*, and not simply "there." Christ is eternally *coram Patre*, and therefore eternally giving forth of himself to Abba. He is likewise *pro nobis*, a relationship which combines generous giving of himself to us and an active gathering of us to the Father. Nor is the Father absent from the Christ who is present. He is eternally present to the Son with the same dynamic force that drew from Jesus his "obedience unto death," that raised Jesus from the dead, and that continues to draw all things together under the Lordship of Christ. In other words, the eucharistic presence of Christ is not well served by Christological imagery alone. Christ's presence is a *trinitarian* presence, Father and Son present to each other and to us in the loving interchange that is the Holy Spirit.

It is very important to grasp the proper images of the presence of Christ because that presence is never immediately accessible to us. It is a *signified* presence. It is always mediated to us through symbols that signify. It is always a sacramental presence. The Constitution on the Sacred Liturgy named four modes of Christ's presence, and pointed to four liturgical signifiers that mediate his presence to us. Word, minister, euchar-

istic food, and assembly are themselves the proper images of
the presence of Christ, and will serve to lead us into that presence provided that their own special dynamic as signifiers is
observed. These images, moreover, need to be seen in the fullness that is theirs within the living liturgy of the church. None
of them is a sacred object, and none can stand apart from the
ritual network which brings them to life and holds them in relation. The word is the word proclaimed, the minister is the
leader of the assembly's prayer, the food is always for the eating (*ad manducandum*), and the assembly is gathered, nourished, set in action, and sent forth. The word signifies by being
proclaimed, the presider by leading in prayer, the food by being shared and eaten, and the assembly by enacting the full
ritual in all of its complex movements. These liturgical signifiers are the primary images of the presence of Christ in the eucharist. No other images properly illuminate or serve the
church's faith in that presence.

Yet for all that, this personal, active, trinitarian presence of
Christ is signified, and can only be made known through the
mediation of symbols, the presence of Christ within the eucharist remains actual and *real*. Signification is not a projection
of an "elsewhere" upon the event. Nor is it an imaginative
lure that takes us to an "elsewhere." The Christ who is accessible to us through the mediation of symbol comes to us from
the depth of the symbol itself. There is no "elsewhere." The
Christ who is present in the symbol will be met, encountered,
and engaged the more deeply we are drawn into the symbol
toward the one whom the symbol signifies.

THE PROCESS OF ENCOUNTER

This reflection on what it is that the church proclaims about
the presence of Christ in the eucharist, and the realization that
the four modes of Christ's presence affirmed by Vatican II,
provide the question of how it is one may come to encounter
the Christ who is present. It should be clear that the place to
start theologically is not with any one particular manifestation
of Christ's presence, be it the food, the word, the minister, or
the assembly, but the total eucharistic action *as* an expression
of the Christ who is present.[4] Recall again the declaration of
Vatican II: ". . . it is through the liturgy, especially, that the

faithful are enabled to express in their lives and manifest to others the mystery of Christ and the real nature of the true Church" (SC 2). Because the eucharist is action, it can be an expression of the active Christ, and the very dynamics of the ritual itself exhibit the dynamics of Christ's action among us. Because it is prayer, our prayer guided and shaped by the prayer of Christ, our prayer made in union with Christ, it captures and portrays the trinitarian dimension of the presence of Christ. Because it is a meal, it can speak the presence of Christ as one who both nourishes and unites us, and allows the food to be a tangible and focused sign of the Christ who so nourishes and unites. And because it is an action of all the people, who by that very action are set in relation to each other, it embodies the interpersonal or relational mode of Christ's presence to and for us. Within the action that is the eucharist, the signifiers of Christ's presence are *enacted signifiers* with the persons who enact them being integral to the signification itself.

Once it is realized that the total action of the eucharist is the primary manifestation of Christ's presence, it becomes possible to correlate the modes of Christ's presence with the various signifiers, and to focus on these various signifiers for what they are; not the presence of Christ, nor even a sign of Christ's presence *simpliciter*, but a sign which carries within it the *way* in which Christ is actively present. As I mentioned above, Christ is not simply "there." The various dynamics of Christ's presence require a variety of signifiers which together exhibit the *active* fullness of that presence. In addition, because the ritual arranges these signifiers in a patterned relationship that spells out a process, it is possible, and indeed necessary, to understand the relation between the various modes of presence and the process they represent. Finally, it is possible to discover in the modes of Christ's presence, their relationship to each other, and the process which that relationship reveals, the path to perception of the Christ who is present.[5]

At the beginning of the eucharistic action there are two interrelated signifiers, each of which speaks the presence of Christ to the other. The presider who calls the assembly to worship signifies to the assembly the Christ who calls them together. This fact, that it is Christ who calls them together, is a fundamental truth of the eucharistic assembly, and critically important for what is to follow. The assembly is gathered by invitation only. Likewise the assembly constitutes in its gathering a manifest presence of Christ. "Where two or three are gathered in my name . . ." There is a sacredness to the assembly in its gathering because in the gathering the *corpus Christi* becomes a corpus, visible, tangible, enfleshed. This sacredness of the assembly as *assembly* calls the presider before the One whom the presider is asked to serve. Together they signify the *totus Christus*, the Christ who gathers and the Christ who is gathered. Together, as a manifestation of the presence of Christ, they are foundational to any liturgical act.

The readers proclaiming the word embody the next movement in signification. Through them the Christ who has gathered now speaks and reveals to the assembly the ways of God. It is only in response to the approach of God that Christ sets in motion his saving mission and thus gives obedient worship to the Father. It is likewise only after hearing the word proclaimed that the *corpus Christi* can enact Christ's prayer and actions. This prayer and action require a complex set of signifiers. Those who present the gifts to the presider, and finally the presider himself in the act of presenting, manifest once again the once for all offering of Christ, and serve further to gather the assembly, now into Christ's own offering. The presider proclaiming the words of institution and invoking the Holy Spirit signs Christ giving of himself for his friends *and* asking the Father to send the Spirit upon them. Finally, the ministers of the table who take the eucharistic food to the assembly sign in the distribution Christ nourishing and uniting. That which is heard and taken as food lives on as the within of the people assembled, and they are sent forth more the Body of Christ than they were when they gathered. This transformation into the "more" names the goal of the eucharistic process.

Christ is not present in the eucharist simply to be; he is present to do. He is present to lead people into his own prayer relationship to Abba, and he is present to form people into a true *koinonia* of love and service. The four signifiers of his presence enacted according to the ritual form allow Christ to awaken people to his own prayer and to form people into his own desired relationship. True encounter with Christ allows both the awakening and the forming to take place.

At the outset of this essay I said it was all important to form proper images of the Christ who is present, and gradually led to the point of seeing the liturgical signifiers as the proper images. At this point it should be said with equal force that it is important to form proper images of the encounter itself. Encounter does not mean, as is sometimes conveyed in descriptions of personal contemplation, holding before oneself an image of Christ and talking to that Christ so imaged. The presider is not that kind of an image of Christ. Nor is the word, nor even the eucharistic food. The presider is asked to lead the prayer of the church and to shape that prayer into the prayer of Christ. The word is proclaimed in order that Christ speak God's ways to people. The proper response is to listen, and to allow Christ to awaken something within us. The movements of the presider, first presenting our food offerings and then imploring God's consecrating Spirit upon those offerings, are to call forth generous giving on our part and then humble, even awe-filled reception of God's transformation of what we bring. Generous giving and humble reception are the proper response to Christ at that point. And the food passed among us remains food to nourish and unite. Christ is among us to nourish us and unite us. The proper engagement of that Christ is to allow oneself to be nourished and united. If Christ is present to do something with and for us, true encounter with Christ allows him to act and surrenders to his actions. Amen is the word of encounter. No other words can take its place.

At the same time, encounter with Christ, in keeping with the human dynamics of the human paradigm, allows for and in fact demands varying degrees of depth and awareness. It is important to remember this, lest we place too heavy an existential burden on the process. Christ is the within of the eucharistic action, and it takes time to penetrate the signifiers and to name the Christ who is their depth. Too quick a naming holds the risk of transposing the signifiers into sacred objects, and so thwarting the true dynamics of the encounter. Christ comes through the signifiers from their depth as one who appeals to the freedom of people and urges them to choice. The responses of listening, giving, receiving, and being set in relationship to others are choices made in the face of other possible choices. Christ comes to us as motive for the choice, and it is precisely by being drawn to address Christ in the vocative "you," and by knowing oneself addressed by Christ in the same way, that one is drawn deeper into the encounter and to deeper levels of awareness. Initially, however, one may only see the signifiers, with the presence of Christ as their depth more a word of hope and promise than a reality consciously experienced.

The language of Paul Ricoeur remains a helpful guide in the process that leads to this deeper level of awareness. Second levels of meaning for symbols reside within first levels, and are accessible only by way of the first. One must "walk in the aura of the symbol," that is, attend to the first, and allow oneself to be drawn by the first into the second. At first one may only submit to the ministry of the signifiers on the first level, be guided to prayer by a presider who prays, be inspired to listen by a reader who reads with clarity and conviction, or be moved to relationship by a greeting of peace or by the sheer geography of the space. The human dynamics may be all that are attended to. Nonetheless, even there, where Christ may not yet be named with any explicit force, a first level of encounter with Christ is taking place. Friendships begin long before the friendship is noticed and named. Attention to the liturgical signifiers on their human level is that kind of beginning. Without those first unnoticed steps true friendship might never develop. Without attention to the first level of signification in the liturgy, awareness of Christ as the one who is in fact engaging and being engaged might never take place. Or an imaginatively imposed relationship with Christ may replace the true encounter that Christ yearns for.

The path to deeper levels of encounter demands attention to the ritual signifiers as human interactions. There is no other path to the Christ who is their within. From the viewpoint of liturgical ministry, this realization heightens the importance of exercising care that the signifiers really signify, and that the liturgical ministers exercise that ministry well. Only a reader can bring human depth to the reading; only a presider can invest the role of presider with those human affections of care, reverence, generosity, and awe that complete that particular mode of Christ's presence. Only a eucharistic minister serving at the Lord's table can bring to the food being given the human presence of him who calls us "not servants but friends." And only an assembly which truly cares for one another can bring the "body of Christ" to incarnation. Liturgical care is the personal side of *ex opere operato*. It is simply doing what a human church intends.

THE ONTOLOGICAL CONDITIONS
THAT THIS MAY BE SO

Much of what has been said above remains on the descriptive, phenomenological level. Yet, if this is so, the question remains, how is it so? Paul Ricoeur, whose own phenomenology of symbol is heavily relied upon here, never really brings the discussion to the ontological level, though he does imply that such is the nature of symbol, and not simply what people make of symbols. Nevertheless, the question of ontological reality is very much at the heart of the church's faith in the eucharistic presence of Christ. The teaching on transubstantiation names an ontological change in the eucharistic food. The sacramental characters of initiation and ordination identify an ontological change in the assembly of Christians and its ordained presider. And the theology of inspiration struggles to say that scriptural proclamation is human proclamation somehow invested with God's own word. To speak of Christ as the within of the eucharist, and to name Christ as the one who reaches out from the depth of the human signifiers of his presence does name something about the reality of those signifiers and not simply something which the church imposes on them.

One difficulty with the language of ontological transformation is that it all too often sounds like an alchemist's feat, which separates some bits of church from the whole church, and some bits of creation from the rest. The language of process does help mitigate this somewhat. Together with this, however, lines of continuity rather than discontinuity must be drawn. Sacraments are not only sacraments *for*, they are sacraments *of*. The church, which in its eucharist and other sacraments, enacts the mystery of Christ into history is itself a piece of that history and a signifier to human history of its own God-given destiny. The signifiers of Christ's presence are not bits of creation separated from the rest. They remain bits of creation whose mission it is to name and identify something that is true of all. The mystery of God in Christ is the depth of all creation, and the emergence of that mystery from within is the ongoing process of creation. It is also the Christian name for the process of all human history. Conversely, the path to the Christ within requires that we take creation and history seriously, and immerse ourselves within it. To name the Christ as the within of the eucharistic action, and to see the transformation into Christ as the dynamic process of that action, does not separate the eucharist from all else. It allows the eucharist to be *sacramentum* of all else, both of creation and of history. This it can be because it is a human act that is both creative and historical.

The language of ontological changes does not well serve to name the church's faith in Christ's presence if it is spoken and heard in the image of the alchemist, namely, something becoming something else which is totally different from what it was. It needs to be both spoken and heard in the more subtle tones of the Scholastics who named the change *esse melius*, that is, it becomes something more truly itself. The biblical source for such an ontological "becoming" is the splendid vision of Romans 8, all creation yearning for its transformation into Christ. Against this horizon of cosmic transformation proclaimed as the full fruit of God's action in Christ, it becomes less extraordinary to name the action of the eucharistic assembly as an advance action of God which signals God's plan for it all. It becomes equally less extraordinary to speak of that same transforming action of God *per modum sacramenti* in reference to the various signifiers of that action, and to see the Christ as the within of what they are and do. In the Christian proclamation of creation and redemption, ontologically it is but the nature of things. And within the Christian mission to advance the saving work of Christ, cognitively it is the horizon of choice to help us enter both creation and history and to guide them to realize their own inner truth.

The perception of Christ in the eucharist is of a piece with the perception of Christ in creation and in history. As with the relationship between assembly and presider described above, these two stand in relation to nourish and guide each other.

Perception itself remains a journey to be made, impelled by the promise of those who have gone before, urged on by the presence of him who waits to be met.

Notes

1. See E. Schillebeeckx, *Christ the Sacrament of the Encounter with God* (New York: Sheed and Ward, 1963) 25-45.

2. See W. Brueggemann, "The Presence of God," in *The Interpreter's Dictionary of the Bible*, Supplementary Volume (Nashville: Abingdon, 1976) 680-683.

3. See, for example, W. Hill, "The Eucharist as Eschatological Presence," *Communio* (Winter 1977) 306-320.

4. See E. Kilmartin, "A Modern Approach to the Word of God and the Sacraments of Christ: Perspectives and Principles," in *The Sacraments: God's Love and Mercy Actualized*, ed., F. Eigo (Villanova: Villanova University Press, 1979) 68-71.

5. For a careful mystagogy of this process, see E. Diederich, "The Unfolding Presence of Christ in the Celebration of Mass," *Communio* (Winter 1978) 336-343.

7

Investigating the
Sacrament of Penance

A CONSTANT THEME THROUGHOUT THIS VOLUME IS THAT THE SACRA-
ments of the church, in both theology and praxis, are in a state
of transition. The static model of scholastic theology has yielded to a more dynamic model embraced by the Constitution on
the Sacred Liturgy which chose to view sacraments as communal acts of the church in assembly, and to stress much more
forcefully than before the relationship between what is effected and what is signified. Similarly, the rigid juridical control
over the execution of the sacraments, familiar since the Council of Trent, has yielded to a set of guidelines aimed at adaptation and evolution rather than uniformity and ritual stability.
Moreover, the revised rites themselves, with varying degrees
of clarity and success, present the *ecclesia orans* with a signifi-
cantly altered image of itself and of its different sacramental
actions. It is inevitable that what has been set in motion by
Vatican II will gradually give rise to new perceptions of faith,
new theological understanding of that faith, and even further
altered sacramental rituals to express, nourish, and deepen
that faith. In the meantime, the church finds itself caught in
tension between an old sacramental consciousness that has not
yet disappeared and a new sacramental consciousness that is
only in early stages of gestation.[1]

This investigation of the sacrament of penance, as any investigation of the sacraments today, must insert itself in the midst of this tension. The task is to draw out as well as possible the main lines of this new sacramental consciousness and to seek understanding of the sacrament in its light. The hope is to gain insight into the direction of the reform and its projected future in such a way that it might serve as a pastoral guide in the process of evolution that has only begun.

THE PROBLEM

Of all the sacraments, the sacrament of penance has fared least well in the transition thus far. The new rite is incredibly schizophrenic, with more than one foot still dragging in the preconciliar *Zeitgeist*, and only a toe or two pointing toward the world envisioned by the liturgical reform. For example, in spite of the conciliar charge that communal celebrations involving the presence and active participation of the faithful are to be preferred to celebrations that are individual and quasi-private (SC 27), the introduction to the rite insists that the only ordinary way for reconciliation remains individual, integral confession and absolution.[2] Moreover, though the same introduction speaks of the whole church acting in different ways in the work of reconciliation, and of the sacraments as an act in which the church proclaims its faith, gives thanks to God, and offers its life as a spiritual sacrifice of praise,[3] it nonetheless speaks much more abundantly in the familiar juridical concepts of priest as judge, penance as satisfaction for sin, and absolution as decision of forgiveness in accord with the power of the keys. Finally, without subtle analysis of the ritual as a whole, the individual form of the sacrament looks like and acts deceptively like the preconciliar private confession. The prayers and readings that surround the confession and absolution are more likely to seem an awkward intrusion on the intimacy of the event than a radical alteration of its basic dynamic. In short, one suspects from occasional hints that a new thing is aborning, but this is easily drowned out by an abundance of language which allows one to see the same old thing in new ritual dress.

This ambiguity creates a host of pastoral and theological

questions. Some of these can be brought forward by two situations and two observations.

The first situation involves a parish anointing of the sick where those who felt spiritually, mentally, or physically troubled were invited forward to seek the Lord's healing in the sacrament. Everyone came forward. Afterwards one priest wondered: "Since Catholic tradition maintains that the sacrament of the sick also forgives sins, were all these people forgiven?" Since the answer is indeed yes, one is forced to question the exact role of the classic formula of absolution in the sacramental act of forgiveness of sins.[4]

The second situation grows more familiar and problematic as nonordained men and women serve as spiritual directors or retreat guides. Frequently dialogue with the directee enters the arena where sin is explored and named, and a deep sense of peace is given to the "penitent." Two questions surface: since I can't give absolution, does the person have to go through it all again? And, what is the point of going to a priest when the sacrament seems to have taken place?

The first observation recalls that this sacrament exists as a gospel and ecclesial response to the experience of sin, and takes its proper shape in accordance with the way sin is experienced. Recall that in the first five centuries of the church serious sin was experienced as excommunication, that is, real separation from the eucharistic communion of the church. The proper sacramental response was re-communion or reconciliation with the church. Other sins did not fall under the domain of this sacrament, but found their healing within the eucharistic assembly itself. In the second phase of the sacrament, which spans the tariff penance of the Irish monasteries *and* the law-court model of the post-Tridentine church, sin was experienced in some form or other as code violation. The sacramental form took new shape and responded accordingly. In our own day, when the experience of sin seems to be shifting away from code violation to a less neatly defined sense of sinfulness, one must ask what form or forms will properly address this experience with the healing power of Christ in the church. One must also wonder what will happen in the transit to the familiar categories of integrity, satisfaction, and judgment.

The second observation notices that the sacrament of penance has over the centuries taken on two other functions in addition to the original reconciliation of serious sinners: the process of spiritual purification and growth once accomplished through intercession and other acts of the eucharistic assembly, and, in the case of children prior to their first eucharist, characteristics more akin to initiation than reconciliation. In light of the restoration of confirmation to its proper place between baptism and first eucharist accomplished in the Rite of Christian Initiation of Adults, and of the prominence gained by spiritual direction, communal anointing of the sick, and other services of healing particularly among charismatic groups, the question arises whether the sacrament of penance ought not be honed down in its usage, and other sacraments or actions of the community brought forward to fulfill what penance has absorbed. At any rate, with the ritual of penance now addressing three different kinds of experience without distinction, it is difficult to see how the nature and purpose of the sacrament has been rendered any more intelligible than before.

Questions such as these may not lend themselves to ready solutions, but they do urge a fresh investigation of the sacrament of penance which will ask what the church is doing in its variety of ministers and ministries when it assembles to enact this sacramental action. It is toward this goal that I propose the following experiment. I mean to establish a controlled environment shaped by the reforms of Vatican II and to investigate the behavior of the sacrament of penance in that environment. I wish to seek in both human terms and in faith terms a description of the sinner's approach to God in the church and of God's response in Christ enacted in the sacrament of the church.

The cue for this experiment is drawn from the Constitution on the Sacred Liturgy (no. 2), which says that the liturgy is the outstanding means by which the faithful express and manifest the mystery of Christ and the nature of the church. The controls are thus drawn first of all from the paschal mystery of Christ, and then from the way this mystery is played out in the two principal manifestations of the church: eucharist and initiation. The presumption is that the patterns of this mystery so drawn will likewise be exhibited in the sacrament of penance, and will thereby help to illuminate its nature and behavior.

THE CONTROLS

The paschal mystery of Christ is a complex unity whose component parts must be drawn out and identified both for liturgical celebration and for human understanding.[5] These component parts are always ordered to each other, and if they seem to form a temporal sequence when drawn out liturgically or theologically, this must be recognized as a simplification, a needed concession to the human mind as it seeks to understand and celebrate in history what is not a completely historical reality.

With this caution, the paschal mystery of Christ can be set forth in four basic movements, the person of Christ himself embracing the first two. In Jesus we have both God's self-initiated approach to humanity and the perfect human response to that approach of God. This is the unity of revelation and faith, the unity of sacrifice, obedience, and incarnation. The faithful response of the human Jesus to the prior lead of Abba is the fundamental dynamic of his whole life culminating in and sealed by his death. The third movement is the Father's response to Jesus' obedient trust articulated and imaged variously as remembrance and deliverance, resurrection, anointing and consecration with the Spirit. The fourth movement is the historical realization of it all, the *Christos* made large by the gathering of all humanity into its Christic destiny, realized in sacrament, and anticipated as church, the gathered assembly, the people of God.

The direction of these movements, be it towards God, from God towards the human, or the horizontal movement towards unity among the people, is integral to each component part of the paschal mystery and must be carried by any ritual gesture which would seek to express it. Thus, whether one attempts to draw understanding from a ritual that already exists, or to construct a new ritual that will enact all or part of this mystery, care must be taken to observe the movement of the gesture as well as anything else the ritual or image might communicate.[6]

We would expect to discover the four movements of the mystery of Christ within the principal sacramental/liturgical exercise[7] of this mystery, which for the assembly is of course the eucharist. This becomes readily evident if we recall the classic division of eucharist into offertory, consecration, and communion, and take this as the combined second part enacted in response to the first, the word proclaimed. I am told that there was a very short-lived suggestion in the early days of liturgical reform to place the Scripture after the eucharistic meal where it could serve as a meditative response. This was rejected out of hand as a fundamental distortion of proper liturgical dynamic which demands that the community act only in response to the word. If liturgy is to express the mystery of Christ, proper liturgical dynamic must follow the dynamic of the Christ mystery itself.

Within the eucharistic assembly, the word is proclaimed as the initial approach of God-in-Christ to us, in light of which, and in response to which, the sacramental community enacts its vocation. In the eucharist, offertory is much less a "part of the Mass" than a dynamic of faith and prayer that seeks a variety of ritual expressions. The chaste Roman setting of the table, the elaborate medieval offertory rite, the Byzantine Great Entrance, all symbolize this fundamental dynamic of the *anaphora-oblatio*: Christ passing over in obedience to the Father and our union with Christ in that passing. It is the obediential act of Christ and the obediential act of the assembly made one. Similarly, consecration is much less a specific moment in the ritual than the eternal response of the Father towards Christ articulated upon those now joined to Christ in his offering. Transformation of the elements and transformation of the people are of a piece in this movement of consecration. Finally, communion, except for the fact that it has long been read solely in terms of a Jesus-and-me piety, is or ought to be obvious as the proper exercise of the fourth movement, the gathering of humanity into the unity that is Christ.

This same pattern can be observed within the eucharistic prayer itself. The prayer moves from a narrative proclamation of what God has done through a triptych of response. There is first *anamnesis* ("Mindful therefore, we offer . . ."), remembrance as an obediential act of offering. There is secondly invocation or *epiclesis*, which has a varied history of expression, but which aptly identifies the movement of consecration, God's response to the offering Christ. And finally, the conjoined invocation which calls to unity all who partake of the eucharistic food expressly completes the four-step exercise of the mystery of Christ.

It should be stressed that these four movements of the Christian mystery are inner movements of faith and prayer which seek a variety of modes of expression. The church can only be impoverished, and our liturgical possibilities severely limited, if we carelessly identify any or all of these movements with one or other mode of expression.

As is true with the principal exercise of the mystery of Christ which is eucharist, this pattern of four movements emerges again in another major enactment of the assembly, namely, initiation. This would not have been obvious before the conciliar reform because of the long separation in both praxis and theology of the three initiation sacraments. In the reformed ritual for adult initiation, however, baptism, confirmation, and eucharist are restored to their proper relationship within the initiation process, and are properly enacted only at the end of a long catechumenate which is explicitly focused on the proclamation of the word. In the new Rite of Christian Initiation of Adults it is not only possible to observe the same four movements of the paschal mystery which were perceived in eucharist, but to come to a richer understanding of both baptism and confirmation in the process.

The prior approach of God is clearly enunciated as the inner dynamic of the catechumenate, and indeed is the necessary condition for beginning the catechumenate at all. If this catechumenate is viewed, as it may properly be, in parallel with the liturgy of the word, then the single sacramental act by which the assembly baptizes, confirms, and welcomes into eucharistic communion reveals its close parallel with the tripartite offertory, consecration, and communion.

The total initiation action is to incorporate the person into the mystery of Christ, which is the mystery of the church in action. It is thus eminently proper ritual exercise to do something that will accomplish *significando* the fullness of this incorporation. The act of plunging into water aptly enacts the second movement of this mystery, for its speaks the inclusion of the person into Christ's dying and rising. God's response needs a different ritual statement, which the Christian community has brought forth using the laying on of hands, the anointing, or both. Having thus been brought from the water into the assembly and touched by the act of anointing and consecration, the new Christian is led to the final statement of incorporation, the act of eucharistic communion.

Much more can and ought to be said about the sacraments of initiation, but this much suffices for the purpose of this experiment which has been to establish controls for the investigation of yet another act of the church in assembly, the sacrament of penance. The effort has been to identify the essential dynamics of the paschal mystery of Christ and to note this dynamic within the two principal actions of the church which express and manifest this mystery. What we have seen can be summarized as follows:

Mystery of Christ	Eucharist (E.P.)	Initiation
↓ God's approach	↓ word (narrative)	↓ catechumenate
↑ Jesus' response	↑ offertory (anamnesis)	↑ baptism
↓ God's response	↓ consecration (epiclesis)	↓ confirmation

↔ Formation of the church↔communion (communion) ↔ eucharist

These controls provide the environment for the investigation of the sacrament of penance. Essentially, the question is: how are these same movements exhibited, and how do they illuminate what the church is doing in this further act of manifesting and expressing the mystery of Christ?

THE EXPERIMENT

The revised rite of penance offers three forms for the celebration of the sacrament: a one-on-one interaction, a one-on-one in the context of a communal word service, and a totally communal celebration. In spite of these differences, however, the three forms are structurally identical, and it is this common structure which reveals the patterns of the Christ mystery we are looking for.

Each form begins with a proclamation of the word. Even

though, in the first form, the word proclamation is given as optional, this should not lead to the immediate conclusion that it is irrelevant. The word here exerts the same influence on the subsequent actions as it does on any other sacrament. It is the necessary condition for the community to act at all, whether to confess, intercede, absolve, or give thanks.

It is not difficult to see in this initial proclamation of the word the first movement of the paschal mystery, the prior approach of God. What is perhaps less immediately evident is the impact of this word upon the actions that follow. In the law-court model of the preconciliar ritual the patterns of interaction between penitent and confessor were clearly defined by the model itself. The dominant motive for presenting oneself was guilt and sorrow arising from the knowledge of having offended God by the violation of a code. The presentation of oneself to God followed the pattern of self-accusation according to frequency and seriousness of those violations. Confessors prepared by carefully studying cases which would give the proper response, the necessary ingredients for their solution, and the conditions under which proper absolution could be given. As in a law court there was little room for surprise or deviation. The proclamation of the word as the immediate context for confession and absolution changes all that most radically.

Under the word of God the primary motive for turning to the Lord and seeking forgiveness can only be the love of God revealed in Jesus Christ. Whatever form it might take, the presentation of oneself to God is first and foremost a response to that word, and an effort to discern in oneself the demands here and now which God's love exerts. Similarly, the response of the confessor is predetermined by God's revealed love, and his principal concern ought to be to help the penitent hear that word of love effectively. As far as preparation is concerned, case studies may still have an important value, but I think the most important resource will be the word the confessor has heard in the face of his own sinfulness. At any rate, there can be no absolute certainty beforehand as to what he will say, for he must listen to the word speak in the immediacy of each penitential encounter.

The first movement of the paschal mystery in the sacrament

of penance is clear. The second can be observed with only a slight difficulty in the pentient's presentation of him/herself in acknowledging sinfulness. Under the controls set for this experiment, the act of naming one's sin appears to be one with the movement of offertory, sacrifice, incarnation. It likewise appears as a reaffirmation of the fundamental baptismal stance whereby the Christian is included in the Christ offering, and thus embraced by the same love with which the Father loves Christ Jesus.

In this environment the act of naming one's sin is much richer than self-accusation. It is first of all an act of claiming one's humanity and offering it with Christ as spiritual worship to the Father. More specifically, however, it is an act of claiming one's sin in the act of offering, and in that very act transforming what of itself separates us from God into a gift with which our God is pleased. To name sin in the context of our union with Jesus is already to be forgiven, and therefore already an act of forgiveness.[8] It ought not be surprising if the very act of naming our sin in some context that is church brings with it a measure of release and inner peace.

When the church enacts the sacrament of penance, the role of the assembly is to act in a variety of ways to help the penitent name his or her sin and so to make a full offering of self to the Father. The assembly itself presents to the penitent a living image of the *Christos* in loving stance toward the Father, and its act of intercession is nothing else but an activation of this movement toward God which the penitent is invited to join by naming his or her sin. Where there is need for one-on-one assistance, that interchange, be it with priest or other members of the assembly, is principally an act of preparation of gifts, that is, assistance toward naming one's sin completely in the presence of God with full acknowledgement of ownership and responsibility (integrity in a wider than juridical sense). This act of preparation is part of the ministry of reconciliation which the whole assembly shares and enacts in a variety of ways. It is the faith environment which makes the confession of sin possible and which keeps alive the expectation of forgiveness. In the ordinary run of affairs, it ought not be seen as the sole ministry of the confessor.

Forming an interface with the second movement, the third

movement of the paschal mystery is expressed, at least in the Roman West since the thirteenth century, by the declarative formula of absolution ("I absolve you"), now somewhat awkwardly conjoined with an invocation (*epiclesis*), and a laying on of hands. Recognition that this "absolution" is the same movement as what is elsewhere expressed as consecration and confirmation, namely, God's response to the offering Christ which now embraces the penitent's sins by his or her own act, highlights the fact that the absolution is a sacramental act whose purpose is to effect *significando*. It is not primarily a juridical decision within a juridical context. Nor is it necessarily the act which brings experiential release, which can take place in the naming of one's sins, or which may unfold more gradually through the aid of many ministers and ministries in the community. What it manifests and effects is God's response to Jesus Christ now articulated upon the sinner who has placed his or her sins before God in Christ. It transforms the reality of sin into non-sin, and though the historical realization of this transformation may need to unfold in a variety of ways, the transformation itself, effected in the public arena of the community's faith and prayer, is the causative act which justifies, motivates, and grounds all ministries that serve to enflesh it.[9]

As a sacramental act and a proclamation of faith, absolution is proclaimed as much for the assembly as for the individual penitent, and the penitent is revealed to exercise a ministry to the assembly even as the penitent enjoys the varied ministries of others. Just as the assembly in its obediential stance of love before the Father invites the sinner to name his or her sin as part of the movement of offertory, so the enactment of absolution consecrates the assembly and enlists it, as Paul says, as ministers of reconciliation. If the priest is seen solely as judge, with special powers given him from Christ, absolution will be seen as an act of the priest alone. However, when the proper role of the priest is recognized to be presider over the assembly, even if the assembly is not present, absolution is revealed to be an invocation upon penitent and assembly alike to activate and summon them all to the ministry of reconciliation. The sinner finds the forgiveness of God, not through the words of a priest proclaimed in a vacuum, but through words of a priest proclaimed in the church, in a community of men and women who reconcile and who enflesh by their very life together God's loving and forgiving stance toward the sinner.

This leads to the fourth movement of the paschal mystery which seems to be absent from the ritual of penance. It is possible to say at this point that the experiment breaks down. It is also possible, and perhaps more fruitful, to view penance in the same relation to the eucharist as the process of initiation views baptism and confirmation. What I prefer to see here is an ordering of penance to eucharist which once agains restores eucharist as the fullness of reconciliation. At present many Catholics view penance as required before the reception of eucharist. The relationship is extrinsic. My sense at this point of the experiment is that the intrinsic relation of eucharist to penance is once more unveiled. Eucharistic communion, with all the responsible and ministering relationships that eucharist expresses and summons us to, is the final movement of reconciliation even as it is likewise the final movement in the process of initiation. This would certainly allow us to understand why baptism, eucharist, and penance alike are named "for the forgiveness of sin," and why the sacrament of reconciliation in its fullness is indeed an act of the whole church in which it proclaims its faith, gives thanks to God, and offers its life as a spiritual sacrifice in praise of God's glory.

THE OUTCOME

A first result of this experiment is a confidence that the paschal mystery of Christ is indeed exercised in the sacrament of penance as the church acts to address and embrace the repentant sinner. A second is that it is possible to understand this sacrament as an act of the church in assembly, done by the whole church for the whole church. The sacrament of penance can never be simply an act between penitent and confessor alone. A third result is to recognize that the variety of ministries of reconciliation carried out by a variety of ministers is an integral part of the sacrament, and not simply helpful preparation or follow-up. Perhaps the most intriguing result of all is to acknowledge that the one most directly ministered to in the sacrament, namely, the sinner-penitent, exercises a ministry to the whole church as sinner-penitent.

If the experiment is successful in having exhibited the dynamics of the Christ mystery in the sacrament of penance, and if these begin to shed new light on what the church is doing when it enacts this sacrament, perhaps it can yield some light also on the questions raised at the beginning.

Confusion with regard to the "absolving" power of the sacrament of the sick can be alleviated somewhat by the recognition that the traditional formula of absolution is but one way of ritually articulating God's response to the naming and claiming of one's sin. Anointing, the laying on of hands, and invocation are equally successful symbols of the same movement, and, if properly intended in the ritual action itself, can serve to communicate God's forgiveness effectively. What is crucial to the question is to note that both sin and sickness represent strong resistance to one's ability to say *yes* to one's own human life, and the foundation of sacramental healing in either case lies in a transformation of sin and sickness that allows a person to make God's *yes* to this human life his or her own. Neither sin nor sickness as human phenomena are necessarily negated, and the existential enfleshment of that healing certainly requires many hands from among the community. The sacrament acts *significando*, and its power lies in its ability to give a new way of imaging the sin and the sickness that itself transforms sin and sickness alike.

If sin and sickness were held to be two non-overlapping realities, the enactment of the mystery of Christ upon them would unambiguously be named two different sacraments. Such it seems is the testimony of the early church where presbyters were called to anoint the sick and excommunicated sinners were reconciled to the church. One can question if such a neat separation can be made in all cases today. Just the fact that the assembly in question was made up of people who in some way considered themselves morally, physically, or mentally in need of healing indicates that those distinctions were not at the time held to be sacramentally important. Perhaps the best thing to say is that the same ritual act can address sin or sickness or both *depending on what is presented to God for response.*[10] Certainly if there is an experienced blur between sickness and sin, the sacramental ritual will necessarily reflect that same blur. At any rate, the phenomenon described, which I know has happened in many parishes, may in some way presage the emergence of a common sacramental form which will more adequately serve the whole assembly as the ordinary celebration of the sacrament of penance, with individual celebration of the sacrament reserved for those occasions which the penitent's own needs determine.

The questions posed by the nonordained can likewise gain at least the beginnings of an answer. The experience of forgiveness in the interaction means certainly that the sacrament has begun to be enacted, and the nonordained has ministered well in aiding the penitent to name his or her sin. We must not forget that the interaction with spiritual director or retreat guide is an assembly of the church, and constitutes one mode of the presence of Christ proclaimed in Scripture and recalled in the Constitution on the Sacred Liturgy.[11] Nor must we forget that without the ordained priest the fullness of the church in assembly is not made manifest,[12] and the action of the church in assembly *significando* must remain incomplete. This is not a question of power, but a question of sacrament, and it is the right of both the larger assembly and the penitent to seek this sacramental completion. In no way should the priest be seen as "doing again" what has already been done, and in no way should the penitent be required to "go through it all again" as if nothing had happened. Some recognition that the church in its variety of ministers has already begun the sacramental act of reconciliation is called for, with the priest bringing forth yet another ministry which complements what has begun and completes it.[13] The absolution of the presiding celebrant speaks the fullness of God's response to the penitent and summons the entire assembly into the ministry of reconciliation on the penitent's behalf.

A final question concerns what might be the most puzzling dimension of sacramental theology today, namely, the suspicion that the church may have been enacting one sacrament in fact all the while thinking it was enacting another. No matter how hard one tries, it is almost impossible to make reconciliation sense out of penance for children before their first communion. If, however, we realize that the children have, if not real sins, at least their baptismal selves to present to the Father in Christ, then the absolution spoken upon them might well be a badly used ritual to compensate for a misplaced sacrament. In other words, the terms of this experiment can support a case for identifying that use of the sacrament of penance as nothing more than a surrogate confirmation.[14]

But, as I say, the sacraments of the church, in both theology and praxis, are clearly in a state of transition. The church finds itself caught in tension between an old sacramental consciousness that is only in its early stages of gestation. Any investigation of the sacraments must insert itself in the midst of that tension . . . and for a long time yet to come remain there.

Notes

1. An excellent analysis of this transition is given in R. Vaillancourt, *Toward a Renewal of Sacramental Theology*, trans., M.J. O'Connell (Collegeville: The Liturgical Press, 1979). See also P. Fink, "Liturgy and Pluriformity," *The Way* (April 1980) and M. Hellwig, "New Understanding of the Sacraments," *Commonweal* (16 June 1978).

2. Introduction to the Rite of Reconciliation, no. 31.

3. Ibid. nos. 8, 7(b).

4. It is to be recalled in this regard that the churches of the East employ a form of absolution that is invocation rather than declaration. In the West too there is evidence of invocation and laying on of hands antedating the declarative absolution which is a late Latin development in the church.

5. Thus the church celebrates Incarnation, Christmas, Easter, and Pentecost, all elements in the single mystery of Christ. Thus too theology comes to focus on Christ, salvation, church, and sacrament, though these too find their unity in the one mystery of Christ.

6. Rising smoke, for example, can never speak of God's approach to us, but only our approach to God. Similarly, the imposition of hands does not express our approach to God but rather God's movement to us.

7. The Constitution on the Sacred Liturgy (no. 2) says that in the liturgy the work of our redemption is accomplished. The word "accomplished" translates *exercetur* which in an earlier edition (*The Documents of Vatican II*, ed., W. Abbott [New York: Guild, America, Association, 1966]) is translated as "exercised." More graphically than any other image, this metaphor "exercised" suggests that the doing of our liturgy is the doing of our redemption, and that we grow stronger, more redeemed, in the doing.

8. The context in which sin is named is all important, lest this seem to be self-forgiveness, and only a psychological victory. The baptismal imagery by which union with Jesus is the victory over sin is invoked here. It is important therefore that the place of naming in some way represent church and in some way evoke Jesus as the one in whom our sins are named.

9. Catholic tradition maintains that sacraments effect by signifying (*significando*). Much work remains to be done to understand this kind of effectiveness. I draw here on the power of imagination as set forth in the works of William Lynch, particularly in *Images of Hope* and *Christ and Prometheus*. Lynch maintains that reality is shaped by the images we form of it, and can be changed by changing the images we have. I maintain here that the Christian faith gives the wherewithal to alter images of sickness and sin, and so to change their very reality. In this lies the power of the sacraments to change reality and effect sanctification *significando*.

10. Recall that since the sacrament of the sick was reserved in praxis for the dying, the sacrament of penance in the area of private confession did absorb sickness as well as sin. Thus a blur has existed, though the mirror image of the blur is envisioned here.

11. "Lastly, he is present when the Church prays and sings, for he has promised: 'where two or three are gathered in my name, there am I in the midst of them' (Mt 18:20)" (SC 7).

12. The reality of the church is the union of Christ and his members, and one of the ministries of the ordained to the assembly is to *signify* the Christ who calls, who prays, who speaks, and who acts. The priest is both sacrament of Christ for the assembly and sacrament of the church when the assembly is not gathered. A local assembly is not yet the full manifestation of the church until the one it ordains for the ministry of signifying Christ in their midst calls them to assembly and stands in their midst.

13. I have presented a liturgical model for this in *Alternative Futures for Worship*, vol. 4, *Reconciliation*, ed., Peter Fink (Collegeville: The Liturgical Press, 1987) 109-126.

14. This confusion of penance with initiation is discussed in its immediate historical context by Aidan Kavanagh in *The Shape of Baptism: The Rite of Christian Initiation* (New York: Pueblo Publishing Co., 1978) 81-86.

8

The Sacrament of Orders: Some Liturgical Reflections

THE THEOLOGY OF ORDERS IS ONCE AGAIN IN FERMENT DUE TO A number of forces currently in convergence. There is, on the one hand, the classic *lex credendi*,[1] a noble tradition which has been passed on through scholastic theology and the decrees of the Council of Trent, which offers one set of images to understand those whom the church ordains. There is, on the other hand, a new *lex orandi*, embodied in the revised rituals of ordination and in the specific ministries assigned to the ordained. This latter offers its own set of images which are not completely consistent with the received *lex credendi*. To complicate matters, there is within this same *lex orandi* the emergence of new liturgical ministers who, together with the ordained, conduct an ordinary ministry to the assembled church.[2] Finally, there are reflections such as those of Bernard Cooke and Edward Schillebeeckx which call into question not only the current church order, but the underlying conception of church order which sees it to be determinative of the church's life and prayer rather than determined by it.[3] The challenge to a theology of orders is to bring together the *lex orandi* and the *lex credendi*, to understand these new liturgical ministers who hold a proper ministry of word and sacrament, and to clarify the relation between church order and church life and prayer.

In this chapter I hope to make a modest contribution to the task by offering some reflections on the *lex orandi*. They are in part systematic and in part pastoral, using as both starting point and control the liturgy of the church. This is a first level reflection in that I will bracket here distinctions between deacon, presbyter, and bishop, and use the term "ordained priesthood" for all who are recipients of the sacrament of orders.[4] What I am interested in is the place in the church's life and prayer of those who are ordained.

A SYSTEMATIC REFLECTION

The church ordains its ministers in liturgical assembly, and the rites of ordination are the public statements of the church's thought and intent when it ordains. These rites were revised in 1968 according to the general conciliar norm that the liturgy more clearly show the mystery of faith which the rituals express and enact. (SC 21, 34) This new liturgy of ordination, as indeed all the new liturgical rituals, has already begun to alter the images we form of ourselves as church, and in particular of those whom the church ordains for ministerial priesthood. As the images change, a new theological understanding is called forth.

Against the backdrop of this new *lex orandi*, I would like to ask three questions about the priesthood of the ordained. First, how shall we understand the place of the ordained within the liturgical assembly? Second, is the ordained priesthood one of power or of service? And finally, how shall we describe the relationship between this priesthood of the ordained and the priesthood of the faithful?

The Place of the Ordained in Liturgical Assembly

What is at stake here is the relationship between the ordained priesthood, the church as a whole, and Jesus Christ. The heart of the question is how we understand the church's profession of faith that the sacrament of orders, like the other sacraments, was instituted by Christ, and that Christ himself is its origin and source.

Prior to Vatican II the Roman Catholic tradition had advanced certain affirmations about the sacrament of orders which it saw primarily in terms of the presbyteral order.[5] It is indeed a true sacrament, establishing one in a priesthood which is different in kind, and not merely in degree, from the priesthood of the faithful. It was instituted by Christ at the Last Supper, even as he instituted the eucharist, for priesthood and eucharist were taken to belong to each other. In that received tradition, ordination involves an empowering by Christ to consecrate the eucharistic bread and wine, to offer sacrifice, and to absolve from sin, an empowering which was clearly set forth in the preconciliar ordination of priests: "Receive power to offer sacrifice to God and to celebrate Mass . . ." and "Receive the Holy Spirit; whose sins you shall forgive they are forgiven."[6]

The exact role of the church and of the Holy Spirit in this sacrament was obscured, such that theology imagined a simple passage: from Christ to bishop to priest to church. The ordained priest thus represents Christ to the church. Even in the postconciliar church this position can still be heard. In the Vatican Declaration on the Admission of Women to the Priesthood, for example, the argument was offered: "It is true that the priest represents the church, which is the Body of Christ. But if he does so, it is precisely because he first represents Christ himself, who is the Head and Shepherd of the church."[7] This is the key: the priest *first* represents Christ, and only then does he represent the church. Ordination is seen as an act of the ordaining bishop who, as representative of Christ and in his place, empowers one to act as Christ in specific sacramental situations.

In contrast, the *lex orandi* that has issued from Vatican II offers a different set of images to understand the agency of ordination. The Constitution on the Sacred Liturgy recognizes ordinations to be liturgical actions, that is, actions of the church in assembly (SC 27). As such, they are composed of different parts, with different parts pertaining to different people; they are not simply the action of the ordaining bishop (SC 26, 28). It is true that the bishop lays on hands and prays the prayer of consecration, the combination of gesture and prayer that lies at the heart of the ordination rite. That is his specific ministry in the ritual as leader of the community's prayer and as sign to the assembly of its continuity with the apostolic church. It is also true that the people assembled for the ordination must present the candidate, and must publicly approve the bishop's election. The assembly likewise prays for itself in the litany (". . . pray for us") because of what it, the assembled church, is about to do.

Within the ordination liturgy, whether of deacon, presbyter, or bishop, the consecrating words are words of prayer in which the Spirit of God is invoked upon the ordained that they be strong and faithful in the ministry assigned to them. They are words of prayer prayed by the ordaining bishop in the name of the entire church. The great Amen of the assembly which concludes this prayer of consecration is as important to its completion as is the great Amen of the eucharistic prayer. This liturgy of ordination is a complex act of the entire church gathered in assembly.

To grasp the significance of this with regard to the source and origin of orders in the church and to the role of the ordained within the assembly, it must be stressed that nowhere in the revised rite of ordination is there hint of a direct intervention by Christ that by-passes the action of the church assembled for prayer. Neither visually, symbolically, nor verbally is there any intrusion on the action of anything that appears to originate apart from the assembled church. If we are to maintain, as we must, that this act of ordination is an act of Christ, it becomes necessary to image it as an act of the Christ who is present *in* and *as* the assembled church, and who acts *when* and *as* the church itself acts. (SC 7)

Seen as an act of the assembled church, the rituals of ordination belie the classic movement from Christ to bishop to priest to church. Rather, they illustrate an insight which Vatican II recaptured and advanced, namely, that the church assembled is the primary sacrament of Christ, and that all its liturgical actions are actions of the church expressing itself as the sacrament of Christ (SC 5-7).

Because of this sacramental identity between church and Christ, it cannot be accurately said that the priest represents Christ first, and only then the church. Rather, it must be urged that the Christ whom the priest represents is the Christ who is sacramentally present upon the earth *as church*. In other words, once the act of ordination is recognized to be a liturgical act of the church in assembly, it becomes necessary to hold fast to a new way of imaging the Christ who is source and origin of orders in the church. It is not a Christ who stands over against the assembly. It is a Christ whose full and proper expression is the liturgical assembly itself.

There is a profound implication to this image shift which has to do not only with the way we understand ourselves as the church and the ordained person in the midst of the church; it has to do with the way we image Christ in liturgical prayer. In other words, it has to do with the fundamental image structure of Christian piety and prayer.

Godfrey Diekmann and Joseph Jungmann both, many years ago, described what happened to Christian prayer in the Middle Ages as the divinity of Christ received excessive stress to the detriment of his humanness.[8] Christ became imaged, not among the people of the church, but with the Father, leaving the people with a need for someone, or a group of someones, to do for them what they could not do for themselves. Thus they called upon the saints in heaven to plead to Christ for them, and upon the earth they called upon their priests to be a sign of Christ and to do the things of Christ on their behalf.

Within that structure of Christian piety, the ordained priest was a stand-in for Christ. He offered Christ's own sacrifice, and spoke Christ's own words of forgiveness. In the popular imagination, moreover, he enjoyed a quasi-divinity that had no truck with his own humanness, a quasi-divinity that was patterned after the adopted images of Christ. Within this structure of Christian piety, moreover, the priest was imaged as a surrogate for the rest of the church. He did not call the church to offer sacrifice; he did not call the people to the ministry of reconciliation; he did not invite the assembly to initiate, to heal, or to bless. All these he did on behalf of the church. The work of Christ that properly belongs to the whole church became solely the work of the ordained, and must inevitably do so if ordination is seen to be an act of Christ that is independent of the assembled church.

A Priesthood of Power or of Service?

In some ways the question poses a false dichotomy, because ordained priesthood is about both power and service. An effective proclamation of the word is a service, yet it has the power to awaken hope in the desperate, peace in the troubled, courage in the frightened. An effective communication of God's forgiveness is likewise a service, and it has the power to strip away layers of human bondage and set people free. The power that is properly associated with the ordained priesthood is a power that is unleashed in the very ministry which the priest performs. To empty that ministry of its power is to take away the very purpose for which it is carried out.

It is true that the term "power" can be wrongly applied to ordained priesthood. One such misapplication was recognized in the older rites for ordination, and corrected in the liturgical revisions. Where once the bishop said to the new deacon, "Receive the power of reading the Gospel in the church of God . . .," he now says, "Receive the Gospel of Christ whose herald you are." Where once the bishop said to the new priest, "Receive power to offer sacrifice to God . . .," he now says, "Accept from the holy people of God the gifts to be offered to Him." Gone from the new ordination liturgy is any sense of a personal power being given to the ordained. In its place there is the assignment of specific ministries to the assembly which gather priest and people alike into the manifest power of God.

The true power that is associated with ordained ministry is nothing else but the fundamental empowering by God which is named the Holy Spirit. Theology in the West has tended to play this Spirit falsely by employing a "some Spirit for you, more Spirit for you" motif as it tried to distinguish baptism from confirmation, and both from ordination. But the Spirit of God is not a quantity; it is God's personal presence in the church. It is the active presence of God calling us, and empowering us, to be and become the church. It is the Spirit who enables us to pray, to proclaim, and to remember. It is the Spirit who gathers, unites, and transforms. It is the Spirit who causes us to be, as an assembled church, *sacramentum Christi*, doing the things of Christ in our sacraments, and becoming ourselves the presence of Christ into which our sacraments transform us.

We can see in the liturgical witness of the church's prayer that it has been a common and constant practice to invoke this Spirit of God when faith sought a transformation, or when faith saw a mission that could only be fulfilled with God's help. This invocation of God as Spirit is an essential part of the structure of Christian prayer. Thus, with some combination of prayer, anointing, and laying on of hands, God's Spirit is called upon the sick and the sinner for a healing, on the baptized for an inner transformation into Christ, and on the eucharistic meal, to change the food of eucharist and to transform the people who partake of that food. Thus also the prayer of the church invokes God's Spirit in blessing upon the married, and in consecration upon those who will hold the office of leadership and service in the assembly. It is not a question of "giving the Spirit," though that kind of imagery unfortunately finds its way into common usage. The Spirit of God was given to the church in its foundation, a gift that is one with the resurrection of Christ. To invoke the Spirit is to call upon a presence already within the church, and to place this action, this meal, this person at the disposal of God's abiding presence.

Listen to what the church prays when it invokes the Spirit upon the ordained. For the deacon: "Lord, send forth upon him the Holy Spirit that he may be strengthened by the gift of your sevenfold grace to carry out faithfully the work of the ministry." For the presbyter: "Renew within him the Spirit of holiness. As a co-worker with the order of bishops may he be faithful to the ministry that he receives from you." And for the bishop: "So now pour out upon this chosen one that power that is from you, the governing Spirit whom you gave to your beloved Son."[9] In each case the invocation of the Spirit is a function of the ministry that is being given: to proclaim the Gospel, to lead the community's prayer and worship, to govern the life and assembly of the church. It is an act of entrustment more than an act of empowerment. The church in its prayer entrusts the life and ministry of the ordained to the abiding presence and power of God.

There is no hint in the *lex orandi* that the Spirit is given to the ordained in order that they in turn may pass it on to others. That is an unfortunate image drawn once the church is funneled into priest and bishop, and once the personal presence of God becomes imaged as an entity to be doled out in different amounts. In that image set, one can only give what one has received. If the *lex orandi* is given a proper hearing, it becomes clear that the reason why the ordained person goes forth to invoke God's Spirit upon others is the very reason the Spirit was invoked upon him. It belongs to the structure of the church's prayer to invoke God's Spirit whenever a transformation is sought or when a mission is seen which can only be fulfilled by God's help. And within that structure it is the ministry of the ordained to lead, and thus pray, the prayer of the church. The Spirit of God resides in the church, manifests itself in the activities of the church, and is in fact constitutive of the church. Since the liturgy is the activity of the entire church, the power of God's Spirit in the church is the only power that can be invoked and made manifest.

The ordained are assigned ministries within the prayer and activity of the church, and as such their role is primarily one of service. It is a service, certainly, to the people of the church. Most profoundly, however, it is a service to the abiding presence of God-Spirit whose power is activated and made manifest when the ordained conduct their assigned ministries. The ordained are thus ministers of this power, not because they possess it any any special way, but because they are commissioned and authorized by the church to perform the very actions which manifest and contain that power. The heart of this image shift is the realization that the ordained in their ministry are placed at the disposal of God's Spirit. It is not the other way around.

The Relation between Priesthood of the Ordained and That of the Faithful

We begin this third question by recognizing that there is only one priesthood in the Christian experience, the priesthood of Jesus Christ. If we speak of the priesthood of the ordained and the priesthood of the faithful, we are in fact speaking of two manifestations of the one priesthood of Jesus Christ. The received *lex credendi* maintains that they are different in kind, and not merely in degree. That difference needs to be preserved, even if we are well advised not to pursue it in exclusive or oppositional terms. Nonetheless, however we do name the difference, we can never lose sight of the more fundamental fact that they both manifest the one priesthood of Christ, and therefore even though different, must be seen in relation to each other.

Earlier I offered the thesis that the ordained represent the church which is the primary sacrament of Christ. This thesis contains the relationship we seek. In order to get at this relationship, I'd like to use two terms: *embodiment* and *mutual iconography*.

First, *embodiment*. Church can be an abstract and amorphous reality until it becomes concretized somewhere. If the church is to be the sacrament of Christ, it must become manifest. In other words, it must be embodied.

The principal mode of embodiment is the liturgical assembly and its liturgical activity, as has already been noted above. This liturgical assembly does not, to be sure, exhaust the life and activity of the church, but it does concretize it, identify it, render it tangible and visible. What has not yet been noted about this church which is embodied in liturgical actions is that the church itself is ever becoming, called from its past and its present into a future that is proclaimed and actualized in the liturgical event (SC 59).

It is in function of the church's past, what we remember, and of the church's future, what we are summoned to become, that the ministry of the ordained has taken shape. The deacon is the herald of the Gospel; the bishop and presbyter proclaimers of the eucharistic prayer. In both, past is set before us as the very promised future that lures, invites, and shapes the entire assembly into it. Gospel and eucharistic prayer announce the largeness of Christ and the largeness of the church which remain only partially achieved in history. This largeness calls the church assembled into becoming. It is both a theological principle and an observable fact that without this dimension of largeness and its power to summon beyond what already is, a given assembly will close in on itself. Without the dimension of largeness, the very impulse for growth is taken away.

It is because of this largeness of both Gospel and eucharistic prayer that the ministers who proclaim them have come to be appointed by the college of bishops, and not simply through the local ministry of the local church. To serve the largeness of Christ and church, the ministers themselves must manifest and be rooted in that largeness. The ordained are asked by the church to embody and manifest this largeness of Christ *so that* the assembly may see in someone living among them what they themselves are summoned to become. No one takes on this ministry by virtue of baptism which, by incorporating one into Christ, entitles one to be a *member* of the assembled church. To carry out this ministry one must be appointed and constituted as an embodiment of Christ and the church by an additional decisive act of the assembled church. Because such an embodiment involves a transformation and a mission, this church once again in its prayer invokes the Spirit of God. The transformation is to be a sacrament of the ecclesial Christ; the mission is to exhibit in life, in action, and in the specific ministries which the church assigns, the identity and the destiny of the church itself.

This commissioning prayer of consecration, this act of embodiment which is ordination, establishes a mutual relationship between the ordained and the assembly which, by the very fact that it is a *sacrament*, is a signifying relationship (*sacramenta significando efficiunt*). This is what I mean by the second term, *mutual iconography*. The ordained person is commissioned to be an icon of the church in its identity as the sacrament of Christ. In the life and ministry of the ordained the church asks and expects to see a manifestation of its own identity and vocation. Conversely, the assembled church is itself the icon of the priest's identity and vocation. The one who will take on this ministry for the church can only discover what it is to be sacrament of the ecclesial Christ by observing that ecclesial Christ, that is, the assembled church, in action. In ordaining someone the church asks that person to *listen*: to listen to the word proclaimed in the church, to listen to the actions which the church carries out, to listen to the people who make up the church.[10] In submitting to ordination the ordained not only agree to do this, but in turn promise so to fulfill the task as to summon the church to be more itself. To forgive is at the same time a summons into the ministry of reconciliation (2 Cor 5:18-20); to offer sacrifice is at the same time a summons into the offering (Rom 12:1-2).

It is in this sense that the ordained priesthood is most properly seen to be ministerial, different in kind, from the priesthood of the faithful. Priesthood of the faithful is as *member* of the church; priesthood of the ordained as *sacrament* of the church. It is different in kind and degree, not in the sense of higher or more important. The ordained embody in sacrament the as yet unfulfilled destiny of the entire church.

The principal ministry of the ordained, by way of embodiment and mutual iconography, is to activate and thus call forth the priesthood of the church. This is in no way surrogate activity, the ordained acting *in place of* the church, for even in its most token expression all liturgy is the action of the entire church. It is not a kind of exclusive elitism, the ordained going where none can follow. It is in fact just the opposite, an inclusive elitism if you will, an advance journey *per modum sacramenti* into the future of the church in order to call and advance the church as a whole into that same future. I take this to be the proper sense of the ministry of leading the community in its prayer and proclaiming to the assembly the Gospel of Jesus Christ.

It is unfortunate that these two manifestations of the priesthood of Christ are frequently taken to be in opposition, as if to elevate one it were necessary to diminish the other. As a matter of fact, the two rise and fall together. The faithful will never know what their own priesthood is if they never see it embodied for them, nor will they be inclined to embrace and activate that priesthood if no one summons them to do so. Conversely, the ordained will never properly understand, much less fulfill their own ministerial priesthood unless they recognize it as ordered to and educated by that priesthood into which the assembled church is being formed. The control on both is the ongoing priesthood of Jesus Christ, a dimension of the Christ identity which is likewise a dimension of the church, begun but never completed until all are gathered into his worship of the Father and into his saving work for the world.

A PASTORAL REFLECTION

The first part of this chapter attempted to draw out some understanding of ordained ministry based on what the church *does* when it ordains someone. This second part seeks further understanding based on what the church *asks* of the ordained. Like the first, this too is a first level reading. It does not analyze liturgical ministry in all its detail. Instead, the ministry of the ordained is examined here under only two headings: presider at the community's prayer and the image *in persona Christi*.

As a context for this examination, two general reflections on liturgical action need to be recalled. The first has to do with perspective, that is, how we look at our liturgical activity, and the second, with effectiveness, namely, how liturgy is effective for those who enact it.

A Liturgical Context

First, perspective. The reform of Vatican II gave new emphasis both to the full and active participation of the people in the church's liturgy and to careful attention to the intrinsic purpose of each of the rites.[11] It reminded us that the actions, prayers, movements, and symbols of the liturgy each intend something, and called all who participate in the liturgy to penetrate and observe what the various parts of the liturgy intend. In contrast to the preconciliar perspective which placed the assembly by and large in the position of spectator, the outsider observing what is done by someone else, Vatican II has reinstated the entire assembly as insiders, where all we can see is each other, what we are doing together, and how we are doing it. Others may see the assembled church in action and be moved to find out what we are up to. This is, in fact, the first step envisioned by the initiation process of the Rite of Christian Initiation of Adults.[12] The people of the assembly, however, who are the within of liturgical action, must learn to see in a different way.

The members of the gathered assembly, people and ministers alike, are invited to look at each other, and what they do together, and attend to the startling, still scandalous confession of faith that this is what the *Christos* looks like, and this is how the *Christos* behaves. This is true of the breaking of the bread, and the proclamation in human voice of God's revelation in Christ. It is true of acts of sorrow and forgiveness, of healings and blessings, of welcome and invocation. It is thus that "through the liturgy, especially, the faithful are enabled to express in their lives and manifest to others the mystery of Christ and the real nature of the church" (SC 2). No one in the assembly is an outsider to liturgical action. Liturgy *is* only because people make it to be; liturgy is only *what* people make it to be. A shift in perspective from the outside to the inside, with all that that implies.

Second, effectiveness. This shift in perspective is essential if we are to understand the effectiveness of Christian sacraments, and learn to respect the ways of that effectiveness. In addition to its stress on full participation and the intrinsic purpose of the rites, Vatican II insisted that the rites clearly signify the reality of faith which they bring to expression (SC 21). If the church at the time of Trent was primarily concerned to insure that the sacraments effect what they signify, this concern has now been set in proper balance with another, equally important concern, namely, that sacraments signify all that the church believes they effect.

This stress on clear signification is not simply a matter of cosmetics. Scholastic theology had clearly stated, even if it did not give it proper attention, that sacraments achieve their effect by signifying.[13] *Causant significando.* This is a specific way of making something happen. If sacraments signify poorly, or worse, inaccurately, their effectivensss is put in jeopardy. *Significando.* That was the theological missing link that, if it had been properly attended to, might have saved the *ex opere opera-to* formulation from appearing like magic. The Constitution on the Sacred Liturgy not only brought this missing link into the spotlight; it expressed it with unprecedented force and clarity: "It [the liturgy] involves the presentation of man's sanctification under the guise of signs perceptible by the senses and its accomplishment in ways appropriate to each of these signs" (SC 7). Clear signification is not simply a matter of cosmetics. It is essential for the proper effectiveness of liturgical action.

If the way liturgy is effective is the way of signification, theology must be careful not to speak as if it achieved its effect in some other way. Negatively, this means two things: we must not neglect, or worse obscure, either the detail or the inner dynamic of ritual enactment, nor must we think of the effectiveness of sacraments as something automatic or instantaneous. The first is clear enough. The second calls forth a distinction between the *real* effect which is proclaimed by the church from the depth of its faith, and the *realized* effect that is actually experienced by people in their lives. Ritual action properly enacted signifies the real effect, but the path to realization of that effect is something else. It takes time for what is proclaimed to transform one's images, one's affections, and one's behavior. It takes time to penetrate and be penetrated by symbolic expressions of the mystery of Christ. It involves conversions on many levels, and a slow passage along the path of spiritual growth. It involves a host of ministers and ministries, and in fact a community life structure that nourishes and nurtures people toward the realization in life of that which the church proclaims. A proper understanding of the ways of signification will keep us from making excessive claims for sacramental effectiveness.

There is a positive side of this renewed stress on the ways of signification, and this gives shape to the first ministry of the ordained in the current church order, namely, to preside over the community's prayer and worship.

Ministry of Presider

With the liturgical reform of Vatican II, the ministry of presider has surfaced as a complex ministry which, even on the functional level, demands time, energy, and competence on the part of those who would fulfill it. Since I am trying to get a picture of the priest who is commissioned by the church to preside over its prayer, let me, as a first sketch, draw some lines of the functional side of this ministry.

First of all, it is a ministry that involves other ministers and ministries, people who need to work together for the success of the community's prayer. Gone are the days when the liturgy of the church was the sole preserve of the ordained. The principle set forth by Vatican II is now familiar: everyone should do that, and only that, which belongs to them (SC 28). Readers should read, deacons should proclaim the gospel and lead petitions. Musicians should enact and guide the musical dimension of prayer; table assistants should assist at the table. This means, certainly, that the presider should insure that there are other ministers, and not be ready to take on those ministries for the sake of convenience. It means too that the presider should work in harmony with the other ministers, realizing that their ministry is as integral to the liturgical action as his own.

Second, it is a ministry to ritual form. This is not the same as the slavish adherence to rubrics that characterized liturgical ministry prior to Vatican II. It recognizes that different parts of the ritual have different intrinsic purposes, and that it falls within the ministry of the presider to insure that each purpose is properly achieved.[14] Knowledge of the various rituals, and of the ways of ritual prayer, is essential to this ministry.

Third, it is a ministry to the people assembled. The liturgy of the church is no longer enacted toward the altar, or worse, toward the wall. It is enacted *coram populo*, where the Latin word *coram* means more than simply physical direction. The aim to be considered before all else, the documents say over and over, is the full and active participation of all the people. In this regard, perhaps *presider* is not a helpful term. It tends to convey the image of one simply "sitting there" coldly overseeing what is going on. Terms such as *enabler* or *facilitator* are closer to the mark, though they are probably more proper to a psychological group process than to the act of corporate worship. My own preference is to speak of *inviter* or even *awakener*, dreadful terms to be sure, but terms which do convey the full sense of the presider's ministry: to stir up and engage the people in an activity that is properly theirs.

Finally, still on the functional level, it is a ministry to a local community, as a reality in itself, and as a reality within the larger church. The presider has the principal responsibility for seeing that the liturgy is enacted according to the *full* norms of the church, and not according to any individual's liberal or conservative fancy. This includes making sure that the liturgy is appropriately the prayer of the local assembly. The stress given by Vatican II to adaptation makes it clear that no enactment of the liturgy can be universally successful (SC 37-40). At the same time, it is the liturgy of the church that is to be adapted. There is no call for a liturgical *creatio ex nihilo* each time the church assembles. This is a delicate balance which is not achieved by either the rigid or the careless.

More can be said of the ministry of presider even on the functional level. But the ministry of presider goes beyond the functional. Much more than being overseer, or adapter, or awakener, the presider is first and foremost the leader of the community's prayer. The presider's book is the sacramentary, and the sacramentary is preeminently a book of prayer.

This ministry of prayer calls on more than the skills that can be learned in a classroom, from a textbook, or before a videotape machine. It taps for public ministry something which must be deep in the heart of the presider. It probably should not need to be said, but it does, that no one can lead the prayer of others who does not pray publicly. There is no way around it. One cannot fake it, one cannot pretend, one cannot compensate with anything else. To lead in prayer is to pray publicly. It is as plain and as simple as that.

To lead in prayer involves creating an atmosphere of reverence where the presence of God can make its claim on the people assembled, and where the people can attend to and respond to God's approach to them. It is really an indirect ministry, one that, although it is center stage, does not call attention to itself. It is a ministry to silence, even when words are filling the air. It is a ministry, most profoundly, to the freedom of God and the freedom of the human person. It is not fulfilled simply by reading prayers, however splendidly the prayers may be written. There always remains the task of translating prayers into prayer, and the necessary ingredient in the translation is the faith of the one who prays.[15]

This faith is communicated in many ways: the way one walks, the way one speaks, the way one gestures, or even does nothing at all. We call it presence, or reverence, or conviction. We know when it is there and when it is not. Yet it remains elusive, like the sincerity of a handshake, or the genuineness of an embrace, like that unspoken "something" that tells you a person can be trusted and counted on. Nonetheless, for the ministry of presider it is the *sine qua non* of success in the task which the church assigns. No one can lead a community in prayer who does not pray publicly. It is as simple and as profound as that.

Beyond the functional lies the image of a person who is publicly vulnerable, doing in the purview of others what one normally does only in private or with very close friends. But this is the ministry: to embody the mystery of Christ, to be icon of the mystery of Christ. It is to illustrate the behavior of a human person before God and to invite others into the communion that is publicly displayed. It is to be with one who is beloved in the public forum, in voice, in body, in total presence, so that others may see and be summoned into that same intimacy themselves.

This view of the ministry of presider at prayer moves quite

easily into the second heading under which the commission of the church to the ordained may be named, that is, to act *in persona Christi*. It is a term that calls for some care, for it can be and has been easily misinterpreted.

In Persona Christi

Let me first give two interpretations which, although they surface in the Christian imagination from time to time, must be judged as inadequate and improper interpretations of *in persona Christi*. The first is an almost literal identification of the priest with Christ which sees the priest's own humanity displaced and superseded by the person of Christ. This is the kind of interpretation that makes the priest a stand-in for Christ, and imagines the priest as over against the assembled church. It tends to invest the priest with a dignity, an authority, and a power that far exceeds the claims of ordination and the limits of a human life. The consecration and transformation that go with the sacrament of orders do not perform any such marvelous alchemy.

But if this first interpretation overstates the transformation of ordination, the second drastically understates it. This second interpretation, which seems to be coming back into vogue, reduces the priest to the level of mere function, wanting to deny any transformation at all beyond that associated with baptism. Liturgical leadership is a task to be performed which finally does not require ordination to perform it. In the role of the liturgical leader the priest may represent Christ, but only in a weak sense. In this second interpretation the ordained are not seen to embody in any distinctive way the loving reality and saving mystery who is Jesus Christ.

Anyone familiar with the intricacies of eucharistic theology will recognize in these two interpretations parallels with the two positions on the real presence of Christ which were systematically rejected by the Catholic theological tradition: the crass identification of consecrated bread and wine with Jesus versus the mere representational presence of a Christ who is in fact elsewhere. Catholic theology has urged a position in between, insisting that, while bread and wine still look and act like bread and wine after consecration (retain the appearances of), something from their depth (substance) is radically transformed into Christ. Now I do not want to go off on a long tangent here with regard to "transubstantiation," nor do I even want to borrow that language to interpret the *in persona Christi* reality. I do think, however, that the insight captured by transubstantiation holds the key. *In persona Christi*, when it is applied to the ordained person, speaks of a reality deep within that person. Appearances, if you will, remain unchanged.

Let me draw the parallel out a bit. Just as bread and wine still look like and act like bread and wine after consecration, so ordained human beings still look and act like human beings after the consecration prayer has been prayed. Moreover, just as bread and wine *must* be food for that particular mode of Christ's presence to accomplish its (his) purpose, the ordained person must be a human being for yet another mode of Christ's presence to achieve its distinctive and intended purpose. Here I think is the final paradox of that noble insight called transubstantiation: to be something it is not, it must be precisely what it is. When consecrated bread and wine cease being food, they cease to be the body and blood of Christ. When a priest ceases to be a human being, he cannot be the presence of Christ envisioned by the phrase *in persona Christi*. In order to be something he is not, namely, the *persona Christi*, the priest must be precisely what he is, a human being.

In persona Christi is both a statement of fact (real effect) and a statement of mission (realized effect). It identifies something deep within ordained people which is proper to them as human beings, and which, when humanly enacted, is embraced by Christ as his own. The fact has the guarantee of the church's faith expressed in the invocation of the Holy Spirit and the laying on of hands; the mission demands that the priest live and act in accordance with that faith, and place his life and person at the disposal of that abiding Spirit.

It is this something from human depth which allows the Christ to be embodied and so to touch human hearts. It is this something from human depth which, precisely because it is embraced by Christ as his own, enables the ordained to fulfill the ministry which the church assigns. What this something is, however, is difficult to describe, because the metaphysical categories of the Scholastics (substance) do not easily translate into phenomenological modes of thought. Nevertheless, let me suggest two realities which are rooted in the depth of the human person, and which certainly serve the ministry of Christ in liturgical action: the priest's affections, and the priest's fidelity to his own human life.

First, affections. A handy dictionary distinguishes between affection and affectation. This latter is given as "an attitude or mode of behavior assumed by a person in an effort to impress others." Pretended behavior is not what the church has in mind by *in persona Christi*. Affection, on the other hand, is given simply as "tender attachment." I would suggest that the term *affection* does identify the ministry of *in persona Christi*.

The Jesus who is revealed in the New Testament is certainly a Jesus tenderly attached to his God. He called him Abba, Father. Likewise, this Abba is revealed as tenderly attached to Jesus: "You are my beloved Son" (Mk 1:11). Certainly, the God of the prophets is shown to be attached to his people, even as Jesus himself calls his followers not servants, but friends. At least as well as anything else, affection is the relationship between Jesus and his God, and between Jesus and his friends. And perhaps more than anything else, this affection, when genuinely embodied in a human being, makes this Jesus present to us.

The ministry of *in persona Christi* is a ministry to this network of relationships: Christ and his Father, Christ and his friends. It spells itself out in a welcome, in a healing, in forgiveness. It manifests itself in a word, a glance, a touch. It is spoken in a loving stance, in reverence, in ease and comfort before the Holy One. The Christ who abides with us is the Christ tenderly attached to his God and to his people, and one who would fulfill the ministry *in persona Christi* for us can only do so in tender attachment, that is, by a genuine affection for God and for people. "It [the liturgy] involves the presentation of man's sanctification under the guise of signs perceptible by the senses, and its accomplishment in ways appropriate to each of these signs" (SC 7). In assigning the ministry of *in persona Christi*, the church asks the priest to make his own human affections available to Christ and to his church, for it is these human affections which touch the human heart and invite people into prayer.

Secondly, fidelity to one's own human life. It is rightly said of Jesus that he was faithful to the mission God entrusted to him, a mission that was nothing less than the incarnation of the Son of God. As a human person, Jesus had a name, a temperament, a place in space and time, and a network of friends. As a human person, he had to choose his life, to claim it and shape it.[16] His many choices, however different they looked in their specifics, were all really the same choice: to be the Jesus God summoned him to be, or to be the Jesus others wanted him to be. To say that Jesus was faithful (obedient) is to say that he said *yes* to the unique person God revealed and called him to be, and did not seek to be either the Jesus of his own expectations or the Jesus which others would have preferred him to be.

This fidelity of Jesus to his own human life, as it was revealed by God, is the fidelity to which each human being is called. None of us is called to be Jesus of Nazareth. We are each called to become the unique person who bears our name. And each of us, though we are faced with many choices as we claim and shape our human life with and before God, has but one choice to make over and over again: to say *yes* to the unique person God reveals us to be, or to reject that in favor of the person either our own expectations or the expectations of others would have us be. One with Christ, and in his footsteps, we are summoned to be faithful (obedient) to our own unique journey.

It is not always an easy choice, particularly when we are faced with our brokenness and our sinfulness, with events that jolt and disappoint, with that unpleasant side which each of us would rather sweep under the rug. Yet, in Jesus Christ, God has said *yes* precisely to the unique human being each of us is, and the unique human journey that is our life. Jesus reveals and is God's eternal *yes* to us.

Among the liturgical actions currently reserved to the ordained is the proclamation of God's *yes* to us. Such is the nature of absolution and anointing, and indeed consecration in all its liturgical forms. This proclamation is critical, for, as Metz has put it so poignantly, it is "God's fidelity to man . . . [that] gives man the courage to be true to himself."[17] Christ alone reveals God's fidelity to us, and while it is true that finally it is the fidelity of the church, and not that of an individual minister, that is the effective proclamation of God's fidelity (*ex opere operato*), it is also true that the ordained minister most faithfully serves that proclamation to the extent that he embodies and exhibits by his own fidelity the revealing fidelity of Jesus Christ. In turn, it is by embracing the human fidelity of the minister as his own that Christ enables that fidelity to reveal and proclaim the faithfulness of God.

* * * * * *

At the beginning of these reflections I set as goal some understanding of the ordained based on the *lex orandi*, that is, on what the church *does* when it ordains and on what the church *asks* of the ordained. If these reflections yield a common heading under which this specific ministry for the church may be named, it is this: servant of the mystery of Christ. It is the mystery of Christ that is to be served, a mystery whose primary manifestation is the church, and especially the church assembled for liturgical prayer. It is always in the context of the priesthood of the church that the priesthood of the ordained is to be understood, as this ministerial priesthood is established to activate and to illustrate the priesthood that belongs to all. It is sacrament. Those who fulfill this ministry in the current church order, and those who may fulfill it in some future church order all share in a common goal: that the priesthood of Christ, which is the priesthood of the church, continue to be activated for the worship of God and the service of the world.

Notes

1. *Lex credendi* is used here to identify that articulation of the church's faith given in doctrinal formularies: *lex orandi*, that same faith expressed in liturgical action. These two expressions of faith ought not be in opposition (*ut legem credendi lex statuit supplicandi*, Denz 246), but rather serve as mutually corrective. Reflection on the *lex credendi* can critique and alter the *lex orandi*: reflection on the *lex orandi* can critique and alter the *lex credendi*.

2. The appearance of officially appointed lectors and eucharistic ministers is familiar. Such ritual appointments, often made by the local bishop in liturgical assembly, are far from the informal, ad hoc designations that are properly called "extraordinary." See David N.

Power, *Gifts That Differ: Lay Ministries Established and Unestablished* (New York: Pueblo Publishing Co., 1980).

3. Bernard Cooke, *Ministry to Word and Sacrament* (Philadelphia: Fortress Press, 1976); and Edward Schillebeeckx, *Ministry Leadership in the Community of Jesus Christ* (New York: Crossroad, 1981).

4. The Vatican II reform has made it clear that deacons, presbyters, and bishops all partake of the sacrament of orders, though the actual differences and relationship remain somewhat undeveloped. The nature of the current diaconate is most obscure of all. In spite of the disclaimer that deacons are not ordained to priesthood but to service (the cited *Constitutions of the Church Order of Egypt* III, 2 actually reads ". . . to service of the bishop"), ambiguity remains. The ordination ritual for deacons names them as assisting priest and bishop in the ministry of word and sacrament, which is not identical with the third-century deacon. Also, the technical term, "the laying on of hands which comes to us from the apostles," which in the episcopal rite is cited as the agent through which priesthood in its fullness is given, is likewise explicitly employed in the ordination of deacons (see bishop's instruction).

5. See J. Mohler, *The Origin and Evolution of the Priesthood* (New York: Alba House, 1969) esp. 51-108; also E. Kilmartin, *Church, Eucharist, and Priesthood* (New York: Paulist Press, 1981) 18-22.

6. The first was conferred at the presentation of the bread and cup after the consecration prayer; the second accompanied a second laying on of hands toward the end of the ordination liturgy. For the force of these in the *lex credendi*, see Denz 1771.

7. Declaration on the Question of Admission of Women to the Ministerial Priesthood, issued by the Sacred Congregation for the Doctrine of the Faith, 15 October 1976, section 6.

8. G. Diekmann, *Come, Let Us Worship* (Baltimore: Helicon Press, 1961); J. Jungmann, *The Place of Christ in Liturgical Prayer* (New York: Alba House, 1965).

9. The Apostolic Constitution promulgating the revised ordination rites cites these three, each taken from the respective consecration prayer, as the form required for validity.

10. The deacon is asked to "believe what you read, teach what you believe" when he is appointed herald of the Gospel; the presbyter is asked to "know what you are doing, and imitate the mystery you celebrate" when presented with the gifts to be offered to God; the bishop is instructed to "encourage the faithful to work with you" and to "listen willingly to what they have to say."

11. See my "Liturgy and Pluriformity," *The Way* (April 1980) 97-107.

12. The period of evangelization and precatechumenate, which is also called a period of inquiry, images someone drawn to learn the way of faith and prayer of the church by being drawn into a specific local church whose faith and prayer attracts them.

13. For a thorough study of this neglected dimension of scholastic theology, see J.F. Gallagher, *Significandi Causant: A Study of Sacramental Efficiency* (Freibourg: Freibourg University Press, 1965).

14. See General Instruction of the Roman Missal, nos. 1-6; see also T. Richstatter, *Liturgical Law: New Style, New Spirit* (Chicago: Franciscan Herald Press, 1977) 164-165.

15. See R. Hovda, *Strong, Loving and Wise: Presiding in Liturgy* (Washington, D.C.: The Liturgical Conference, 1977) esp. 14-15.

16. See J. Metz, *Poverty of Spirit* (New York: Paulist Press, 1968) 5-9.

17. Ibid. 19.

Sacraments:
Personal and Communal
Prayer

9

Liturgy, Prayer,
and Christian Spirituality

IN THIS THIRD SECTION I'D LIKE TO TURN OUR ATTENTION TO ISSUES
of prayer and spirituality. In the three chapters that follow I
will explore the ways of Christian prayer as this is shaped and
guided by the eucharist and the process of Christian initiation.
In this chapter I would like to address two more general questions: the nature of liturgical prayer and the relationship between the church's liturgy and more personal forms of Christian spirituality. The first is really two questions: how is it that
what we do in liturgy is in fact prayer, and what might happen to us if we celebrate the church's liturgy often enough and
long enough? The second is a question of intersection: can
Christian liturgy and Christian spirituality influence each other, and are both of them impoverished if they do not?

LITURGICAL PRAYER AND SPIRITUAL GROWTH

The title of this section embraces the two questions raised
above: how is liturgy prayer, and what might happen to us if
we celebrate the liturgy regularly over a period of time. These
questions are addressed to a whole range of activities, namely,
all that the Christian people do in liturgical assembly. This includes certainly the many rites that comprise Christian initiation and, of course, the Lord's Supper or eucharist. It includes

too the blessings and consecrations of married love and ordained ministry as well as the outreach in pastoral care for the sick and in reconciliation for the sinner. But it also includes simple attentiveness of God's word in silence or in shared reflection. It includes the gathering of our needs in urgent intercession. It includes the unselfconscious hymns and songs of *doxa*, that is, of praise and blessing upon the Lord.

Let me speak first of liturgical prayer, and then of patterns of growth to which liturgical prayer might lead.

Liturgical Prayer

A helpful way to begin exploring liturgy as prayer is to contrast the term "prayer" with the term "product." Many years ago John Gallen raised the contrast in an article entitled "Liturgical Reform: Product or Prayer?"[1] He used the term "product" to critique the language and imagery which had been used for centuries to address the church's liturgy. He posed the following challenge which still has poignancy almost twenty years later: "What the contemporary reform of the church's liturgy needs most in this moment in its history is the discovery of liturgy as prayer."[2]

We image liturgy as product when we speak of the eucharist and the other sacraments as signs that give grace. It is a *quid pro quo* image: do this and something else will be given to you. We image liturgy as product when we speak for or against the sacrifice of the Mass in objective terms, saying that *this* wins us a share in the merits of Christ, or that *this* only gives praise to God. And we image liturgy as product when we speak of a good liturgy or a bad liturgy with the distanced eye of a critic, or when in very subtle ways we think of sacraments as existing somewhere apart from the people who enact them. We "go to" a baptism, for example, "receive" the eucharist, "attend" a wedding or ordination—subtle language that keeps alive the image of liturgy as product.

If we are to speak of liturgy as prayer, we need to abandon all traces of the product image. We have to begin to image the liturgy primarily as a gathering of people who, in their gathering, do some distinct and definite things together. They listen to Scripture, call on God in prayer and song, and they select sometimes people and sometimes things that are the stuff of life, and set them apart. Then with sign and word and gesture they behave in a distinct way towards the people set apart, the material things chosen, and, of course, each other. There is no such thing as a kiss without two people kissing; there is no eucharist without a people giving thanks; there can be no *leitourgia*, liturgy, activity of the people, without a people performing the activity that is properly theirs.

If we are to begin to speak of liturgy as prayer, a second thing we must do is to examine carefully what Christians do in their various assemblies. It is surely not enough to do as traditional theology has done and simply lift out bread and wine or water and oil, and notice only the bare minimum of words that surround them. We have to look at everything and begin to see each bit of this everything as revealing moments in a profound dialogue of the heart: the approach of God, in all the wondrous ways God can and does approach us, and the response of the people, in the myriad ways God's gracious approach calls forth and gives shape to response. If liturgy is to be prayer, and not merely a time for prayer, we must learn to see the contours of this dialogue with God within the diverse moods and movements of liturgical action.

If we are to begin to speak of liturgy as prayer, finally, we not only have to look at all that the people do, but we have to inquire what the doing might do to them. The second question follows from the first. Human activity always has an effect on the people who carry it out. This is true of expressions of love and friendship; it is equally true of expressions of fraud and deceit. We may or may not become what we eat; we certainly become what we do. In the doing, something happens, and if the doing is truly prayer, what happens will be the visible and tangible side, the descriptive side, if you will, of such otherwise elusive terms as grace, merit, justification, salvation, and the like. Until we learn to get inside the *leitourgia* and see there a complex and pluriform dialogue between God and God's people, and until we learn all the inner ways of that dialogue, we will still be trapped in the lingering image of liturgy as "product," and not yet in full grasp of the liturgy as "prayer."

There are many things that have contributed to the awakening of this new task or challenge, but let me single out just two: the publication of Edward Schillebeeckx's well-known

Christ the Sacament of the Encounter with God,[3] and the promulgation of the Constitution on the Sacred Liturgy in 1963.

What Schillebeeckx did was to introduce a shift in the paradigm into the discussions of sacramental theology. The earlier paradigm, forged by scholastic theology and maintained well into this century, viewed sacraments as though they were physical objects. Schillebeeckx spoke instead of an encounter with God, thus inviting both questions and images of an interpersonal, dialogical nature. The person of Christ is present to manifest a personal God, and this Christ is made manifest as people interact with each other. This shift to the personal and interpersonal demands that the image of prayer, of a people at prayer, enter into any working definition of sacrament we might devise.

The Constitution on the Sacred Liturgy restored the importance of the total liturgical action, and of all the signs of faith that comprise it. The Constitution spoke, moreover, of the intrinsic purpose of the rites, and of the need to respect that inner purpose and allow it to be achieved, convinced that what God was doing on the level of faith was revealed and accomplished according to the inner ways and inner purpose of these rites. The liturgy does not exist on paper; it is a people in action, and the Constitution set as the highest principle of reform the full and active participation of all the people.

The Constitution also introduced a new metaphor, which Ignatius Loyola used in his compendium of prayer known as the *Spiritual Exercises.*[4] "It is through the liturgy, especially the divine Eucharistic Sacrifice, that the 'work of our redemption is exercised' (*exercetur*)" (SC 2).[5] It is a striking metaphor, one which allows us to see an older sacramental tradition in a new key. The phrase *ex opere operato* has had its share of troubles. It sounded much like magic. Do what the church intends, which simply meant do the ritual correctly, and grace will be given to those who put no obstacle in the way. Yet now, when coupled with concern for the inner dynamics of the total ritual action, and with stress on full and active participation in those dynamics, the image of redemption-exercise easily takes that tradition well into the realm of faith and prayer. With physical exercise the doing of it makes one strong and healthy provided one simply allows the exercise itself to do its thing. In the liturgy, which is an exercise of faith and interpersonal dynamic, the doing of it advances one along the path of redemption provided one enters the doing deliberately and lets the doing do its thing. It is not, however, an amorphous faith, but faith with a definite and deliberate shape. It is a faith embodied in the dynamics of the liturgical ritual which, as Vatican II put it, expresses, nourishes, and strengthens that faith (SC 59).

This metaphor of *exercise* clearly calls for a close look at what we do in liturgy and how the doing affects us, both to understand God's ways with us and indeed to be able to notice these ways of God actually unfolding in recognizable human form. Gone is the sense of grace or salvation as a hidden, behind the scenes metaphysical activity that takes no truck with human patterns of life and interaction. Attend to what you are doing, look and listen and feel beyond the surface to the depth of what you are doing, until the heart is awakened to the One who is present in the doing, and until the only word that can properly form in the heart and on the lips is "Amen"—so be it, let it happen.

Schillebeeckx's paradigm of *encounter* and the Vatican II metaphor of *exercise* together spell the path from liturgy as product to liturgy as prayer. And together they provide images far more successful than their static forebears to depict the way human people enter into and engage the *Mystery* that finally is the stuff of all liturgical action. Even as it introduced the exercise metaphor, the constitution continued: "It is through the liturgy, especially that the faithful are enabled to express in their lives and manifest to others the mystery of Christ and the real nature of the true Church" (SC 2). The path from product to prayer is likewise a path to the threshold of *Mystery* where God, Christ, church, and human people move beyond the confines of understanding and control into the realm of freedom, of becoming, and of fusion, human with divine, divine with human, human with human, a fusion which is alone worthy of the name communion.

From Liturgy as Product to Liturgy as Prayer

Before we move on to the question of spiritual growth, let me take the reality that is God, Christ, church, and human person to see how each fares in the transit from product to prayer.

The God of product is a possessing God who quite simply has what we need, and who gives it to us as long as we fulfill the conditions of his giving. Such a God is not usually imaged as being enriched when he gives. The God of prayer, on the other hand, is a becoming God who gives, not possessions, but himself. It is a gift that can only be received by those who give of themselves, for the gift is a kind of union where to receive of God and to give of oneself are but two sides of a single human act. The God of prayer is certainly enriched in the giving even as we are in the gift. The God of product must be a distant, or at least transcendent God, who is free to deal his possessions, graces, as he will, and who is unmoved and unaffected by human ploy. The God of prayer is himself the author of human ploy and his otherness is not a distance or a separation but a destiny, a not yet accomplished future which summons us and all creation toward completion. The God of product became incarnate once, and the man Jesus shone forth divine. The God of prayer continues incarnate until the final incarnation of God is complete in the final divinization of all he has made.[6]

In the world of product, Christ is for Christians the author of it all, the one who in death has swayed the God of product to look kindly on us, and who in victory over death now serves as mediator, intercessor, go-between in the dealing of gifts between God and human folk. The *Christos* is Jesus in the afterlife who awaits the appointed day when he will judge the living and the dead, presumably insofar as we have observed the conditions of God. In the world of product, the church is custodian, the keeper, if not of God, at least of the vehicles of God's grace. At its most insecure, the church can only tell the story and hold out the promise of gift; at its most bold the church assumes to set conditions of its own, convinced that the God of product will abide by them. As for us, in the world of product, we are the eternal beggars, who will receive if we ask and find doors opened when we knock. We must, of course, ask and knock. The gifts are what we need to pass the judgment test and win the final gift, life everlasting.

All these images shift drastically in the passage from product to prayer. For in the world of prayer, Christ, church, and human person are all in the process of *becoming*. The Christ is but the first-born, inseperably wed to the second-born, the third-born, the fourth-born, and so forth. He is the one who gathers, and who is himself incomplete as long as there is one who is not yet gathered. He is vine with growing branches, the head that needs legs to walk, hands to touch, lungs to take in air, and a stomach to take in food. He is the one who in victory draws all to himself, whose very victory is being accomplished in the drawing. The mystery of Christ is not simply Jesus in the afterlife awaiting a day of judgment, but a growing community of persons that even now yearns for completion. The church too is the becoming one, the body in formation, the clan being gathered, the yearning seeking fulfillment. We are so often blinded by our institutional images of the church that we fail to notice the pulsations. We are so often consumed with our own perceptions of the church that we forget that the reason it must be *semper reformanda* (always reformed) is that it is *semper facienda*, always in the making. In the world of prayer the mystery of church and the mystery of Christ are but two sides of a single mystery, the same reality, with the same dynamic, and the same destiny. And what of us? In the world of prayer, we too are unfinished human persons, who will never be finished in isolation, no matter how many treasures, spiritual or material, we hoard up for ourselves. We will never be complete as consumers before a product God. We can only be completed in the gathering, in communion, when the last wall of division is torn away, and when we are united to the God who gives of himself, to the Christ who gathers to himself, and to men and women whose own path to completion converges upon our own.

What is exercised in the prayer of liturgy is the becoming of God, the becoming of Christ, the becoming of church, and the becoming of human persons. The becoming of God is really the proper sense of *worship*; the becoming of Christ, the proper sense of salvation; the becoming of the church is really incarnation; and the becoming of persons, really the shining forth of the divine. In the prayer of liturgy, these four—worship, salvation, incarnation, divinization—are one and the same.

Spiritual Growth

Which brings me now to the question of how liturgical prayers leads to spiritual growth. The combined images of encounter, exercise, and becoming make it clear that we ought not to speak of the effectiveness of sacraments and liturgical prayer in terms of instantaneous accomplishment, but need to see this effectiveness in terms of process, something which gradually unfolds in human life and consciousness. Tradition has it that the sacraments achieve their effect *by signifying*,[7] and the liturgical task, as we have seen, is to make sure the ritual action signifies well. But the passage from signification to effect follows its own rules and takes its own time, and it is this passage which spells out the process of spiritual growth. Let me illustrate the kind of spiritual growth I am looking at, and then offer some reflections.

I once had the opportunity to preach an impossible homily. It was a week before a group of young children were to partake of their first communion, and the homily was given to the parents and the children at a special Mass at their school. I wanted to include the children at communion time, even though the bread and wine would not be given to them. I also wanted to tie the event in with their baptism. I preached two-thirds of the homily at the regular time, speaking of two gifts of God which were given to them in the baptismal water and the postbaptismal anointing: friendship with Jesus and loving acceptance by God. I told them I had to wait before I could speak of the third gift, the eucharist, and that I would need their parents to help me.

When communion time came, I invited the children up first. I touched them each on the head, and reminded them of the first two gifts: God loves you very much, and Jesus is your friend. I asked them then to stand around the altar in a circle. The parents then came up to partake of the bread and wine, and, when they did, they went to stand with their children around the altar. I then continued the homily, and told them about the third gift.

I told them about a friend of my sister whom I did not like very much, who used to come every Friday night to our home for dinner. I told them how I hated to sit there week after week looking at and listening to this girl I really didn't like. Then I told them how something started to happen just because I had to eat with her every week; I began to think, well, maybe she isn't so bad, and later, well, she's okay. The gift of the meal was helping me slowly to see this girl in a different way, which never would have happened if I hadn't sat with her at the same table week after week.

I made up the story to show the children and the parents the meaning and power of the gift of the eucharist, the power of sitting at the same table with someone, the power that in time can tear barriers down and draw people into communion. And I tell the story now to give but one small example of what I mean when I ask, "What are people doing, and how does the doing affect them?"

Each of the things we do in liturgical assembly, and there is a wide range of things that we do, has the power to tug at our behavior, our values, and our working images of life, of people, of God, of ourselves. On the one hand, there is our instinctive way, unchallenged and usually rooted in self-concern and self-preservation. It is sometimes known as the way of sin. On the other hand, there is the Way revealed by God in Jesus Christ, and acted out *per modum sacramenti*, in sacrament, in our liturgical assembly. Together we exercise ourselves in that Way of the Lord hoping and expecting that his way will gradually become ours. We know that it is not magic, and we know that it does not happen all at once. There would be no need for exercise, no need for liturgy, if it did. But because it does take time, there is the need to exercise every facet of the Way of the Lord, and be led by his power to embrace it as our very own.

A phrase of Parker Palmer from *The Promise of Paradox* comes to mind as exactly the point I am making here. "You don't think your way into a new kind of living; you live your way into a new kind of thinking."[8] If there is reason to engage in liturgical prayer of any kind, it is right here. To exercise ourselves in the ways of God in Christ, which finally is all that liturgy is about, is to set ourselves on a path of transformation, where our images, our affections, and finally our behavior are all made over. We don't think our way there first, and then concern ourselves with liturgy. We gather with our sisters and brothers and do the things which alone will take us there. We allow ourselves to be addressed by God, and then set in motion every conceivable human response to that address.

Of course, I am not thinking now of a single liturgical event.

No single event can tell the whole story, and no single event can embody the full range of response. That is why we have a liturgical year, a sequence of readings, a series of festal occasions. That is why we have a range of activities, which some call sacraments, which others call ordinances or covenants, and which still others prefer to leave unnamed. It is why we have silence and testimony, incense and pageantry, greetings of peace and prayers for the whole world. No single event can hold before us the destiny of God, of Christ, of the church, of ourselves. And no single event can lead us closer and closer along the path to that destiny. The theological purist might be tempted to see the eucharist as such an event, but only if the eucharist is abstracted from the Ethiopian dances, the Byzantine icon screen, the Coptic processions, and the Antiochene *maranatha*, and equated with the chaste simplicity of the Western forms of prayer. As a matter of fact, the tragedy of the current separations in the church is that we have, all of us, picked and chosen the exercises we will do, so that some have developed very strong ears, some a strong nose, some magnificent knees, and some very acute eyes. The ecumenical invitation, if we heed the summons of liturgical prayer, is to begin to understand each other's exercise along with our own, and by expanding the range of our prayer expand the possibilities for our redemption.

I asked what might happen to us if we do this thing called liturgy often enough and long enough. What I am suggesting here, as a first response, is that the answer will depend on the range of activities we are willing to take part in. If we only listen to the word, we may never know how much that word actually empowers us to do. If, on the other hand, we never listen to the word, we may not realize that what we do is not of our own power, and we may tend to think and act as if it were. If we never sense the yearning of a *maranatha*, our capacity to hope will surely dwindle; and if we never dance before the ark, our *alleluias* are doomed to be very dull. If I am speaking of the transformation of image, of affection, and of behavior as the path of liturgical prayer, certainly the first sense of spiritual growth as we enlarge the patterns of our prayer will be to enlarge our images of God, of Christ, of the church, and of ourselves; to allow and to experience perhaps untapped affections toward God, toward Christ, toward the church—that is each other—and toward ourselves; and to let those affections take shape in the way we behave. And if we are drawn from narrow images to ever larger ones, we might finally come to see that worship is indeed the becoming of God, salvation indeed the becoming of the Christ, incarnation indeed the becoming of the church, and divinization indeed the goal of all human life, and of all creation as well.

It would be nice if we could map out ten or twenty steps or stages along the path of spiritual growth which liturgical prayer opens up to us. A theologian would be sorely tempted to do so; a saint would know better. But being trapped somewhere between the two, let me venture to sketch two modest sample mappings. I have drawn the first from the inner dynamic of the eucharistic action, and the second from patterns that unfold both in the rites of Christian initiation and in the seasonal passage from Ash Wednesday to Pentecost Sunday.

In the eucharistic action we are first addressed by the word of God. This is more than a liturgical *part one*; it is a fundamental fact of the Christian life. It stands in tension with our own desire for autonomy to confess that what we do as Christians always does, or at least should, originate in God. One could spend many years of life struggling with that truth before the response *Amen*, so be it, suggests itself. That could be one stage on a mapping, one level of spiritual growth. The eucharistic action, however, calls forth some specfic exercises: the giving of ourselves over to God with this Jesus whom we remember, the surrender to the decision of God to unleash his power upon and within us, and the commitment to be for each other breakers of the same bread and sharers of the same cup with all that this involves. We call them "three parts of the Mass": offertory, consecration, and communion. And, in the world of the product, I guess that is all they were. But in the world of prayer they are much more. They are movements in the dialogue with God, and stages of transformation, life steps toward our final destiny. Paul named them from the depths of his own transformation. "None of us lives to himself, and none of us dies to himself. If we live, we live to the Lord; if we die, we die to the Lord" (Rom 14:7-8). To be *to the Lord* is truly the meaning of *offertorium*. In his Letter to the Ephesians he speaks of "the immeasurable greatness of his power in us who believe" (Eph 1:19), which the *Good News* translation calls "the same as the mighty strength which he used when he raised Christ from death." What is this if it is not the meaning of *consecration*? And finally, he offers the full sense of *communion* when he writes to the Colossians: "Put on then, as God's chosen ones, holy and beloved, compassion, kindness, lowliness, meekness, and patience, forbearing one another and, if one has a complaint against another, forgive each other; as the Lord has forgiven you, so you also must forgive. Above all these put on love, which binds everything together in perfect harmony. Let the peace of Christ rule in your hearts, to which indeed you were called in the one body" (Col 3:12-15).

It is surely to trivialize what Paul is naming here if we do not see these as stages in a life that is being transformed, each with its own struggle and resistance, each taking time and grace, and each bringing us closer to that for which we were made and that for which we believe Christ died.

That is one possible mapping of part of the journey; the second involves a slightly different set of transformations. It comes, as I said, from the rites of Christian initiation, and from the time of year when that initiation is most aptly enacted. The rites of initiation involve an intense period under the word, heightened in the purifications of Lent, and leading to the threefold sacramental enactment of baptism, chrismation or confirmation, and eucharist. After Easter it envisions what I call "party time" when the new Christians and the old share together in common witness what happened and who they are in the happening. The final time is devoted to the sending of the church to bear witness to the world until he comes again. Holding this together with the Lenten prayer texts, I have drawn out four dimensions of the Christian mystery which can equally be seen as four stages of spiritual growth. There is the personal following of Jesus, as one who is presented with images of people being involved in one's relationship with the Lord, and of oneself needing to attend to others as part of that following. The third takes seriously the incorporation imagery of baptism, where entrance into the water is at once entrance into church and Christ. One is no longer on the outside of Christ relating to him as other; one becomes the within of

Christ, seeing the world, God, and others through his eyes. Following this sacramental transformation, there are the Ascension and Pentecost images of Spirit, witness, and mission, images of the church sent forth to take the message to the world and give it the flesh and blood of their own lives. Personal, relational, sacramental, missionary. Each of these is more than a theological slogan; each is a way of living. And each marks a stage in transformation on the road to final communion with God and the final divinization of all creation.

These two possible mappings are admittedly hasty, and they are offered only as samples of how the journey of spiritual growth from liturgical prayer might unfold. The final word will not be spoken until the eschatological banquet itself, if even then. My aim here has been simply to explore the challenge to discover liturgy as prayer and the growth in the Spirit that such discovery might involve. Theologians can examine it; saints can be amused by it; the rest of us can slowly set out to see if it holds any promise. We can gather in assembly and do the things that Christians have discovered make sense for Christians to do. And we can seek there an appeal to our flesh and blood and to our heart and mind, an appeal which slowly but surely may draw us along the path of groaning to the freedom of the children of God.

LITURGY AND SPIRITUALITY:
A QUESTION OF INTERSECTION

Let me turn now to the second general question posed at the beginning of this chapter, namely, the relationship between the church's liturgy and more personal forms of Christian spirituality. My concern is to bring together two areas of Christian life that have long neglected each other, or at least held each other *as other*, but which are invited to discover each other anew when liturgy is rediscovered as prayer. Years ago Walter Burghardt, addressing the newly formed North American Academy of Liturgy, lamented the loss to theology when it did not take the liturgy of the church seriously and the corresponding loss to liturgical studies when so few liturgists were themselves profound theologians.[9] A parallel lament gives shape to the reflections to follow: the loss to Christian spirituality when it does not take into account the public prayer of the church and the loss to liturgy when professional liturgists do not bring to their professional task a profound awareness of the mystery of God. Let me explore the possible truth to each lament with an eye to the following thesis: that there is a spiritual depth to all study and practice of Christian liturgy and a liturgical face to any spirituality worthy of the name Christian.

Spirituality

Let me talk first of *spirituality*. Spirituality is a large term and quite elusive. It is always hard to pin down just what it means to those who use it. It is definitely an "in" word. Put *spirituality* in your brochure, and you are bound to attract a crowd. All sorts of people are into "spiritual direction." All sorts of ministry students want to go into "spirituality." Yet I am never quite sure what it is they want to "go into." After being a spiritual director myself for a number of seminary students, I have to confess that I am not quite sure I know what spiritual direction is either, and I find myself somewhat skeptical of those who are convinced that they do.

Let me play the skeptic's role for a moment and explore the issue as I see it with, I hope, at least a healthy sense of skepticism. My concern is that spirituality can too easily be read through the lens of a psychological paradigm and become quasi-therapy rather than true spiritual growth.

Meaning of the Term. At the very least, one can say that Christian spirituality should have something to do with Christian life, with prayer, and with the profound human journey into the mystery of God which is at the same time the mystery of God made human and the mystery of human life transformed into the divine. Spiritualities are frequently associated with people whose own life journey and the language they used to describe it become a guide for the journeys of others.

We can speak, for example, of a Pauline spirituality where Paul urges a life "worthy of our calling," speaks boldly of the mystery of God made manifest in Jesus Christ and of the human journey to walk the same path that Christ himself walked before us, even though it takes us through death to resurrection. Paul speaks of what he has seen. We can speak of a Johannine spirituality, that mystical view of the God made flesh that has so deeply influenced Byzantine liturgy and prayer. John had eyes that could gaze upon the torture of the cross and see there the glory of God and the final hope of all human life. John also had such a profound view of the union of people with Christ that he crafted some of the most powerful metaphors in Christian literature: the bread of life, the vine and the branches, the water and the blood from Christ's own side. John, too, speaks about what he has seen.

We can also speak of a spirituality rooted in the vision of some of our greatest saints—Theresa, John of the Cross, Francis, Clare, and, if I may plug my own spiritual family roots, Ignatius of Loyola. All these men and women have engaged the mystery of God, journeyed deeply into the God made flesh, and discovered that God of mystery deep within the contours of their own human life. They have spoken eloquently of that journey, guiding others into the mystery they had seen and touched and tasted. To embrace a spirituality rooted in such heroes and heroines is to be a disciple, a learner from these women and men, and to choose a life journey into the mystery of God guided by them and inspired by the vision that they have set forth.

We can also speak of "vocation" spirituality, though this tends to be more nebulous without the life witness and vision of heroes and heroines that have given it flesh. It is possible, for example, though much more difficult, to weave a life journey for married persons out of the doctrinal stance that marriage bears witness to the union of Christ and his church. It is possible—and I'm afraid potentially quite dangerous—to weave a life journey for ordained priests out of the doctrinal stance that the priest stands in the place of Christ. It is possible, though I fear it yields very slender guidance, to weave a life journey for laymen and laywomen on the basis that their vocation is to bring the Gospel into the secular world. It has been done, though the witness is not as rich as that which carries the names of our great heroines and heroes.

The point to note is this. Whether we speak of a spirituality associated with persons or of one associated with vocation—however rich or slender—the content of the term always has something to do with Christian life, with prayer, and with the profound human journey into the mystery of God which is at the same time the mystery of God made flesh and the mystery of human life transformed into the divine. Anything short of that is short of true Christian spirituality.

Current Distortions. Here is where my skepticism enters in. When I listen to some of the current gurus of spirituality, I hear a language very different from that used by Ignatius or Theresa or Paul. I hear much more the language of personal growth and fulfillment, of recognition and affirmation, of "feeling good about one's self," than I do of companionship with God born of contemplation, of life transformed through suffering and injustice freely embraced, of death to oneself in order that others may live.

I weep when the Enneagram or the Myers-Briggs analysis replaces the almost erotic intimacy with Christ described by John of the Cross in his "Dark night of the soul," or the stunning challenge to discipleship and companionship presented in some of the great Ignatian meditations on the mystery of Christ. The psychological tools are fun and even helpful, but they create a fascination with oneself and in the end leave us alone with that fascination. I grow very sad when the paradoxical wisdom of our heroines and heroes is replaced by the strategies and stages of psychological paradigm. A language that was once very large and awesomely beautiful has been transformed into a language that is very self-centered and very small.

The same thing happens when I engage in spiritual direction myself and ask my directees what it is they are looking for. Esentially they are looking for what the gurus promise: personal growth and fulfillment, recognition and affirmation, a good feeling about one's self. They all know their Myers-Briggs letters, and most know their Enneagram numbers. But very few know the language of companionship with God both of contemplation or transformation of life born of suffering and injustice freely embraced. Very few speak of dying to themselves that others might live. I once remarked to a friend in Cambridge that I was astonished at how much time these ministry students spent watching themselves grow.

May I be allowed one case study as a single example. On the eve of his ordination, after I had heard his confession, I asked a brother Jesuit what spiritually he wanted most to hear from God. He answered, "That God loves me and accepts me." I looked at him and said, "That's easy, but I think God wants to say much more to you. I think God wants to speak of the people you are going to serve, of the compassion God wants you to bring to them, of the vision God wants to awaken in them through you. I think God has greater desires of you and wants you to have larger desires than you do."

The spirituality of Ignatius, as is commonly known, involves a journey that has as a *first* phase the freedom of living as a loved sinner. But that is just its first phase. The *second* one is the passion to serve the redemption of the world with Christ who is its redeemer. The *third* phase is the compassion which allows the crucifixion itself to unfold within one's own life. And the *fourth* phase is the true freedom to embrace the world and all that is in it through the eyes and with the affections of the risen Christ. How sadly small it is for a Jesuit, on the eve of his ordination, to seek only to be loved and accepted by God.

The liturgy of the church does not allow us self-doubts that much of the contemporary spirituality seems to make its stock in trade. The liturgy of the church assumes that we are sinners who belong in the presence of God. "We thank you for counting us worthy to stand in your presence and serve you" (Eucharistic Prayer II). It does not allow us, unless we ourselves distort the text, to be self-centered, self-conscious, self-concerned. The liturgy of the church stretches us to be for others—not for ourselves—from the liturgy of initiation where even our own renewal of baptismal promises is not done for ourselves but to be the context for the baptism of others, right through to the liturgy of Christian burial where the proclamation of resurrection is boldly made that we may, in Paul's words, "comfort one another."

The liturgy of the church, with all its many moods and rhythms—some of which make us feel good, some which do not—takes the human journey where the psychological paradigm cannot take it. It takes us beyond letters and beyond numbers, beyond self-fascination and beyond self-fulfillment into the mystery of God where the God-become-flesh is the center and where human life, yours and mine, is transformed into the divine.

Liturgy

Let me turn to the second lament, the loss to liturgy when its ministers, practitioners, and theologians do not bring spiritual depth to the task.

Goal: The Renewal of Christian Life. The renewal called for by Vatican II was, as we all know, only in a first phase the reform of liturgical texts. That part of the task can be easily dispatched. It has, in large measure, already been accomplished. The deeper renewal envisioned by the council was a renewal of faith or, in the council's own words, "an ever increasing vigor to the Christian life of the faithful" (SC 1). The aim, as I have come to describe it, was to recapture the richest expressions of our faith lodged in the heritage of the church universal, East and West, and unleash that richness upon the people of today.

For example, it was deemed urgent to open up the riches of Scripture rather than content our prayer with only a meager collection of biblical texts. It was considered important, too, to recapture the language of the Spirit of God as agent in transforming the human heart and in particular the primary concern of the Spirit "that all of us who share in the body and blood of Christ may be brought together in unity" (Eucharistic Prayer II). It was considered essential that our symbols speak lavishly, not gingerly: that bodies be immersed in water; that oil be lavishly spread; that food look and act like food. Finally, it was held to be the highest goal that people engage the mystery of God by actively participating in the signs and symbols, the words and the prayers, the songs and the gestures that constitute our liturgical prayer. "In the restoration and promotion of the sacred liturgy, the full and active participation by all the people is the aim to be considered before all else" (SC 14).

If there is a single sentence in the constitution that has captured my own heart and mind in regard to the spiritual depth of the church's prayer, it is this: "It is through the liturgy, especially, that the faithful are enabled to express in their lives and manifest to others the mystery of Christ and the real nature of the true Church" (SC 2). To bring to expression the reality of Jesus Christ, his stance before the God he names *Abba*, and his stance before the people he names "not servants but friends": this is the true depth of the church's prayer. It is the true depth into which the church's prayer invites all who pray.

Now let me play the skeptic once again. If spirituality, without the corrective of the public prayer of the church, is in danger of yielding to a psychological paradigm, my experience tells me that liturgy, without the corrective of a true and solid spirituality, can all too easily be taken over by the dynamics of a political paradigm.

Primacy of Unity. Let me focus my skepticism in one place only, on what I take to be one of the most remarkable recoveries in the reformed eucharistic liturgy of Vatican II—the request for unity among those who partake of the body and blood of Christ. It is quite explicit in all of the new eucharistic prayers of the Roman Sacramentary and in most of those employed by the other churches of the West in their own liturgical reforms. Judging from the earliest eucharistic texts we have, that of the *Didache* and the anaphora of Hippolytus, unity was the first desire of the church to be expressed in eucharistic prayer. It was only later replaced by desire for personal benefit and still later by prayer for the conversion of bread and wine.

With the restoration comes a truer sense of communion, not so much Jesus coming to *me* as Jesus in our midst setting us in relation to each other. This prayer restores the eucharist as the primary sacrament of reconciliation, the primary place where Paul's plea to the Corinthians is to be realized: "that there be no dissensions among you" (1 Cor 1:10). Eucharist is the sacrament that heals division, not the one that causes it.

The good news is that the eucharistic liturgy has become a lot more fun for people. People enjoy coming together in a way that was not in great evidence before Vatican II. The kiss of peace has taken hold, sometimes to orgy proportions. People talk in church before, after, and sometimes even during the eucharistic celebration. There is a friendliness in evidence that is a refreshing change from the days when "sister" and "father" hovered over us making sure that we behaved. Visitors and strangers are introduced and welcomed. A new ministry of hospitality has arisen in many places. And Roman Catholic priests are joining their Reformation colleagues in standing outside the church after the liturgy to greet the people and be greeted by them. "Loved your sermon, Father."

But there is bad news as well. In many places, so my own

experience tells me, liturgy has become a divisive force, not a unitive force. There are many hands seeking to control its ways rather than to liberate us to enter its ways fully and freely. I fear that liturgy can become at times a political tool, making points and negotiating issues, rather than a profound journey into the mystery of Christ or a transformation of the human heart into the ways of God.

Witness bishops insisting that the people kneel during the eucharistic prayer, even during the Easter time when classically kneeling is forbidden, in order to preserve the distinction between the ordained and unordained. They don't seem to have realized that you cannot pray *doxology* or sing a great *Amen* on your knees. It doesn't work. The body won't let it work.

Witness that the insistence on a variety of ministers working together has yielded new battles over turf. God help the presider who steals a one-liner from the deacon, or the lay reader who presumes to read the gospel.

Witness the fate, in some places at least, of the genuine and good concern that the liturgy use inclusive, not exclusive, language. It becomes almost an obsession with men and women both guarding the language so strenuously that all hell breaks loose should a presider or reader or anyone else simply slip up.

Control: A Subversion of Unity. Now all of the above difficulties began with a good idea. It is important for our prayer that the presider in some way stand out and not simply be "one of the crowd." It is important that the many ministries be on display. It is important that the language we use draw both women and men into the prayer of the church and not leave anyone deliberately alienated from that prayer. Yet when the good idea gets drawn into the political paradigm and hands seek to control the liturgy rather than invite people into its gracious ways, it no longer serves the church at prayer. It begins to tear us apart instead.

It is at this point that we need to hear the wisdom of our heroines and heroes, and with force. Our heroes and heroines of the spiritual life never imagined themselves in control of the ways of God. They were always vulnerable to God's gracious approach. The liturgy, too—if it will serve God's ways among us—must find us vulnerable to its power. It is not a tool in our hands to serve our own issues and demands, whatever they be. It is, or should be, God's gracious approach to us, a gift to unify us beyond the divisions that are caused by our issues and demands. If I may adapt a phrase of one of my intellectual heroes, Paul Ricoeur, liturgy will heal, but it must humble us first.

I must take exception to a remark by my esteemed colleague Aidan Kavanagh, who once asserted that liturgy was rite, not prayer. It is my deepest conviction that, if liturgy is *not* prayer, it is not worth doing, and it may well be a dangerous weapon in the hands of those who control it. But if it *is* prayer, the price we will be asked to pay for successful liturgy is high. It will be nothing less than the journey which the liturgy itself enacts, the journey into the mystery of God made flesh, the transformation of human life into the divine, and the death of oneself and all one's issues and concerns in order that others may live. Liturgy will heal us, but it must humble us first.

A LITURGICAL SIDE TO CHRISTIAN SPIRITUALITY

Let us now go to the intersection of liturgy and spirituality and ask first of all how liturgy might protect spirituality from yielding itself to the psychological paradigm. There are many points I'd like to explore, but I will content myself with just two theses.

The first is that *the language of all authentic Christian spiritualities is public language and cannot be privatized without doing it violence*. Public language belongs to a community of people. It maps the public vision of that community and shapes both its public life and the prayer of its members. It is large language, large enough to allow a diversity of people to hold their lives together in a common vision and a common task. The language of Christian spiritualities is, in fact, itself liturgical or at least quasi-liturgical in both the way it behaves and the purpose it serves. Because of this, the liturgy of the church, which is *the* public language of the church and which likewise cannot be privatized without violence to itself, can serve as a model for all more specific spiritualities within the church.

My second thesis is less a question of modelling and more one of direct interaction. I propose that *every spirituality can and should intersect with the liturgy of the church*, each on its own terms, and if it cannot, there is something inauthentic—and perhaps dangerous—about the spirituality in question.

Spirituality as Public Language

Let me explore the first thesis, spirituality as public language, from personal history with a focus on the Spiritual Exercises of St. Ignatius. These Exercises, which belong to the church and not just to the Jesuits, contain the life-blood of Jesuit or Ignatian spirituality.

When I entered the Society of Jesus in 1956, the accepted means of employing these Exercises was the preached retreat. A few of these retreats were brilliant. Many more went from mediocre to "okay." Some were disasters. But all employed the same common structure, the same common patterns, the same common language. Even when all they did was give us something to joke about later on, we had a common language in which to appreciate the humor.

As public language, the Exercises shaped our vision, inspired our dreams, motivated our choices; the vision they set forth allowed us to see a great diversity of lifestyles and apostolates born of the same source and reflecting the same passion for the "greater glory of God." The teacher, the politician, the scientist, the theologian, and the giver of retreats all had in their grasp the language to hold their ideals together: service of the kingdom, in the footsteps of the crucified savior, toward the transformation of human life and human history seen through the eyes of the risen Christ.

About halfway through my life as a Jesuit, a different medium to employ these Exercises was recaptured: the directed retreat. It was hailed as good news, and rightly so. The directed retreat provided for individual guidance through these Exercises and unleashed the power of Spirit discernment, which is the stuff of individual choice and decision, in a way and to an extent undreamed of in the preached retreat. The shift from preached retreat to directed retreat was rapid and total.

The shift, however, had a dark side to it which some of us are only now beginning to notice. As the once-public medium of the Exercises went private, the once-public language went private as well. We lost the Exercises as a language of common discourse. They no longer served to shape our common vision or to forge our common dreams. Without the corrective of public discourse, even the great meditations of the Exercises became functions of personal growth and no longer the language to shape dreams and visions.

I began to notice this when what I call "weasel words" from our congregation documents began to serve for our younger Jesuits what the Exercises once served for us. Service of faith and justice became the "in" phrase, and unless we were serving faith and justice as those who most adopted the phrase proposed, there was something suspect about our life as Jesuit. A shrinkage was taking place.

I am not against service of faith and justice. The phrase just pales so pitifully next to "service of the kingdom under the banner of Christ." Service of faith and justice is a "cause," service of Christ and his kingdom is a "mission." The service of faith and justice turns my gaze to the poor and oppressed and to those without faith, but all it gives me with which to respond is my own meager compassion and my own very small project. That is a more subtle form of self-centeredness. Service of Christ and his kingdom turns my gaze to the poor and oppressed and those without faith as well, and to many, many more. But it gives me more than my own compassion; it gives me *companionship*, and it gives me the vision of Christ and the passion of Christ to challenge and shape my own. Service of faith and justice may or may not lead me to the worship of God. Service of Christ and his kingdom is the worship of God.

The practical end may, and possibly should be, the same. The path to that end, however, is quite different. The language of congregation documents is simply no substitute for the large language of spiritual vision.

There is, as I say, something liturgical about the public language of any spirituality. It is public. It shapes and becomes the work of the people. It belongs to the community and cannot be usurped or distorted by any individual without the community rightly raising critical voices. Its vision is large, large enough to encompass many styles of living it out. And because it engages people not merely in an apostolic task but even more in the mission and journey of Jesus Christ, it involves these same people in the worship of God and the sanctification of human life and human history. The challenge of the church's liturgy to any spirituality is to keep its language public, to keep its vision large, and to remind it that its full and final task is the worship of God and the transformation of humanity. Liturgy will keep spirituality from becoming self-centered and small.

Interaction of Spirituality and Liturgy

I can explore the second point, the interaction of spirituality and liturgy, more briefly, this time using personal observation as well as personal history. Forgive me if I stay with the Spiritual Exercises of Ignatius which is the world I know best.

From time to time, directors of retreats find the liturgy of the church embarrassing, awkward, and even intrusive. A director is taking someone through meditations on her or his own sinfulness, and along comes a resurrection reading or a joyful feast. Or a director is guiding a retreatant through a meditation on generous service, and the Scriptures for the day are full of gloom and foreboding. The director decides to suppress a feast or change a reading to fit the retreatant.

I have long felt that such tampering with the liturgy during a retreat shows great ignorance of both the retreat dynamic and the liturgy. There is something wrong when the church's prayer is seen to interfere with the prayer of one of its members. It also betrays a false understanding of role on the part of the director, as though the director had to control the environment of prayer for those who were engaging the mystery of God in their own lives.

During my own tertianship retreat when I was struggling through the second week and a woman religious was entering the third week, along came a liturgical feast with a fourth-week resurrection reading. It was as though the church did not even care that we were making the Spiritual Exercises of Ignatius. But really it didn't matter. For me, and I hope for her, God found two different voices by which to speak in our hearts, and it was after all God, and not the "topic of the retreat," who was important.

The liturgy of the church, left alone, may clash with the designs of the director; it cannot clash with the designs of God. And it reminds the director, or any other weaver of the language of a specific spirituality, that all such exercises and all such language are at the service of a mystery which no one can control. Direct interaction of the liturgy of the church with any spirituality keeps that spirituality honest and free to be a language which directs us into the mystery of God.

A SPIRITUAL SIDE TO CHRISTIAN LITURGY

What of the other question: a spiritual side to the liturgy? If liturgy can help save spirituality from the psychological paradigm by keeping its language public and its dynamic not only one of human growth but of growth into the mystery of God, how shall spirituality in turn save liturgy from its own temptation to yield itself to the political paradigm?

I propose that the liturgy itself can reveal the answer if we allow it to reveal to us the proper approach we must take to it. Liturgy will reveal itself to be prayer and show us the kind of prayer it is, if we listen carefully. Vatican II says that the liturgy expresses the mystery of Christ, that in the liturgy *we* express the mystery of Christ, and we cannot express that mystery in our own flesh and blood without being drawn into its dynamic and its depth.

All liturgy begins with the liturgy of the word, the proclamation of God's agenda, God speaking God's own agenda in the person of Jesus Christ. All liturgy begins in the presence of God who sets forth *the* Word made flesh. And word calls forth response.

Just to hear the word requires a humility that sets aside all other agenda that might stand in its way. Liturgy heals, but it must humble us first. It demands that we put on what we hear, make it our own, give it our own flesh and blood. All that follows the word proclamation is response: our response, God's response, our surrender to what God's response makes of us. Proper response to the word takes us into the agenda of God where God, not we ourselves, determines the outcome. The classic eucharistic pieces of offertory, consecration, and communion, which have their counterparts in each of our sacraments, are neither more nor less than this: our response, God's response, our surrender to what God's response makes of us.

Whatever issue, concern, or agenda we bring, which in the

political paradigm is the task to be accomplished, needs to be set into the word proclaimed in order to find there its proper definition. Our task is not to accomplish but to surrender to the accomplishment of God, which is never a *fait accompli* which we passively accept but an ongoing action which we are invited to co-act with God. Our task is to allow our own small agenda to be enlarged, redefined, and transformed into God's agenda which we will in freedom take to be our own.

We are all familiar with the newly rediscovered definition of liturgy as the work of the people. It is certainly an advance over an understanding of liturgy that sees it only as the work of a few. But that definition of liturgy—as the work of the people—has a fatal flaw, and it is that flaw which renders it vulnerable to the political paradigm. It tends to put *us*, and not the mystery of God, in control.

If we listen to the liturgy itself, it does not name itself as the work of the people but as the work of God in the midst of and within the people. God names the agenda. God draws us into God's agenda; God transforms us for the task of God's agenda and redefines that task in a way, and to an extent, that we ourselves could not dream or imagine. If we listen to the liturgy itself, it will show itself to be about that same journey of human transformation of which the mystics speak so eloquently.

If the challenge of liturgy at the intersection of liturgy and spirituality is to keep the language of spirituality public and honest, the challenge of spirituality at that same intersection is to keep liturgy humble and true. We are humbled when we realize that—our newly rediscovered definition of liturgy notwithstanding—liturgy is not the work of the people; it is first and foremost the *work of God in the people* transforming them, us, and all human life into God's own glory. Those of us engaged in the liturgy of the church as practitioners, ministers, or theologians need the wisdom and insight of true spirituality to illuminate that transformation and to instruct us in its ways.

Notes

1. *Worship* 47 (1973) 580-591.
2. Ibid. 587.

3. E. Schillebeeckx, *Christ the Sacrament of the Encounter with God* (New York: Sheed and Ward, 1963).

4. "This expression "Spiritual Exercises," embraces every method of examination of conscience, of meditation, of contemplation, of vocal and mental prayer . . . For just as strolling, walking, and running are bodily exercises, so spiritual exercises are methods of preparing and disposing the soul to free itself of all inordinate attachments, and after accomplishing this, of seeking and discovering the Divine Will regarding the disposition of one's life . . ." See *The Spiritual Exercises of Saint Ignatius*, trans., A. Mottola (New York: Image, 1964) 37.

5. The word "exercise" translated the Latin *exercetur* in *The Documents of Vatican II*, ed., W. Abbott (New York: Guild, America, Association, 1966). This same word is given as "accomplished" in *Vatican Council II: The Conciliar and Post-Conciliar Documents*, ed., A. Flannery (Collegeville: The Liturgical Press, 1975). Though the Flannery text is the edition most usually cited throughout this volume, the Abbott text is here employed precisely because of the metaphor of "exercise" which captures an element of the process of redemption which the more static term "accomplished" does not.

6. *Incarnation* and *divinization* are complementary perceptions of the continuing action of God as indwelling Spirit. Incarnation images that action as entrance into flesh; divinization images it as emergence from and transformation of the within. Here the insights of Christian East and West converge to speak of a single act of God-with-us.

7. See J. Gallagher, *Significando Causant: A Study of Sacramental Efficiency* (Fribourg: University Press, 1965).

8. P. Palmer, *The Promise of Paradox* (Notre Dame: Ave Maria Press, 1980) 60.

9. This double lament subsequently appeared in Walter Burghardt's "A Theologian's Challenge to Liturgy," *Theological Studies* 35:2 (June 1974) 233-248.

10

Public and Private Moments in Christian Prayer

SEVERAL YEARS AGO, I SAT IN DISCUSSION WITH SEVERAL YOUNG JES-
uits who had recently completed their novitiate. The topic was
liturgical prayer. After a while, one of them remarked how
odd it was that, in the two years of novitiate, no one had ever
spoken of liturgy as prayer. There were indeed liturgical
events: daily eucharist, occasional reconciliation services, even
morning and evening prayer services from the liturgy of the
hours. Though these indeed may have been prayerful times,
and were certainly considered an important ingredient in
one's spiritual life, they were seldom named or explored as activities of prayer. Rather, the term prayer was used and developed almost exclusively for one's private meditation and contemplation.

I use this example, which is by no means an isolated inci-
dent, as a way into the topic I would like to reflect on in this
chapter. The topic is the shape of Christian prayer. In particular, I would like to look at the two forms which Christian
prayer may take: the communal, public form, on the one hand,
and the private, personal form, on the other. In ordinary par-
lance, liturgy is taken to belong to the former, while devotions
and private meditations are placed in the latter. Moreover, as
in the above example, these two forms of prayer are all too frequently held to be in opposition or conflict.

The opposition may be voiced as when, for example, liturgical ministers insist that the full and active participation called for by Vatican II does not allow someone to remain withdrawn in the private space of personal need and concern during the assembly's liturgical actions. It is assumed that such personal needs and concerns should be "dealt with" elsewhere, that during a specific liturgical action all attention should be given to the liturgical action itself. The opposition is likewise voiced when retreat directors feel the need to reshape the liturgy of the day so that it "fits in" with the meditation themes that are being offered to the retreatants. The opposition may be unvoiced, but be very much in operation, as when we give subtle priority to one form over the other, or simply refrain from one of the two altogether. To pray the office, for example, and neglect the personal journey inward, would be one example of this kind of choice. To acknowledge one's sinfulness before God in private, and ignore the community's forms of sacramental reconciliation would be another, though the opposite of the first.

I have chosen to hold the two together in the title of this chapter, naming the personal and the communal, the private and the public, to be *moments* in the one act of Christian prayer. By this I want to make clear from the beginning the path I wish to follow, namely, to see what is all too often the source of imagined conflict as complementary and necessarily related within the unity of Christian prayer. The prayer of Christ and the prayer of the eucharist, which is at once the prayer of Christ *and* the prayer of the Christian people, will be our guide. But first, let us look at three faces of the alleged conflict.

CONFLICT BETWEEN PRIVATE AND PUBLIC PRAYER

One of the most frequently heard cries as the new liturgy was unleashed upon the people of the church was the lament, "I can't pray anymore." Rosaries, novena books, and even personal copies of the *Missale Romanum* were suddenly taken away, and in place of the cherished quiet which those tokens secured, came the busy-ness of standing and sitting, reciting and singing, fumbling with paper leaflets, and worst of all, a round of handshaking to instill chaos just when everything was supposed to quiet down for communion.

Purists, of course, were quick to point out that the people were praying the wrong way, or at least in the wrong place, or maybe at the wrong time. And the purists must have been right, for the complaint is seldom heard anymore. As we rightly rejoice in what has been gained liturgically since Vatican II, we might well wonder for a moment what has been lost. A sense of mystery and awe. A strong *mythos* to capture the imagination and evoke deep human response. A sense of quiet that allows us to dwell personally with the Holy One who dwells incarnately among us and within us. And we can compound the wonder when we realize that even the sense of loss has been lost, though the praying capacity of most liturgical assemblies does not seem particularly noteworthy. A waggish remark is attributed to G.K. Chesterton, that biblical scholarship has probably made Scripture more clear; it has certainly made it more dull. At times I feel the same waggish impulse in regard to our new liturgical forms.

A second case of conflict. Jesuits, more than any other retreat directors, have a rigid program of meditations to guide retreatants along their spiritual journey. When the liturgy was enacted in the preconciliar fashion, there was no difficulty to be found with Ignatius' directive that one meditation take place during the time of Mass. For people in the pews there were few distractions coming from the altar. The postconciliar liturgy, however, has tended to send Jesuit retreat directors, and many others, into a tailspin. What if a retreatant is occupied with meditations on the passion, and the church is inconsiderate enough to come along with readings on the incarnation, or the healing ministry of Jesus, or even the resurrection? Surely these would be a distraction from the dynamic of the retreat if they are given much attention. I've known retreat directors who prohibit priest retreatants from preaching during their retreat because of the attention the day's liturgy of the word would then demand. Some simply abandon the church's calendar if it offers conflictual texts and symbols. One director suggested that no liturgy be celebrated at all until the last day of the retreat, with the retreat itself serving as a long liturgy of the word. Others have celebrated Holy Week in October, or Christmas in March. One has the sense that there must be something wrong with our theology if these kinds of things can happen.

Just one more point of conflict. The new rite for the sacrament of reconciliation continues to bewilder and frustrate pastors and ministers. The introduction to the new rites intermingles language about new beginnings and personal integrity, language, that is, that belongs to the personal form of prayer, with references to the community celebrating its faith, and the community serving in the ministry of reconciliation, language of the communal form. The rites themselves share this ambiguity. There is the common form (Rite III) which cannot be freely used, in spite of the council's admonition that common forms of the sacraments are to be preferred to private forms. There is the private form (Rite I) which is not being used, at least not by large numbers of people, and, in spite of urgings from on high in the church, there is little likelihood that this form will ever again enjoy the popularity it once had. Finally, there is the "hybrid" (Rite II), which tries to combine both the private and the communal dimensions of the sacrament, but which in fact robs both of the best they have to offer.

These are but three instances of conflict and awkwardness which may arise when the personal and the communal moments of Christian prayer are confused or held to be in opposition. The problem with all of them is that they are based on a false distinction *and* a false prejudice. Private forms of prayer are taken to be the only prayer that takes one into one's own concerns, one's own needs, one's own depth. Liturgical prayer is about community and interrelationship. Moreover, and here is the prejudice that especially inflicts the sacrament of reconciliation, the public nature of ritual prayer, and the pace which that prayer must follow, makes it "too easy." It does not permit honest confrontation with oneself and, in particular, with one's sinfulness. The prejudice in each case would demand that some kind of intense personal experience be required for the prayer to be truly prayer.

Communal prayer, on the other hand, is communal action, which takes people out of themselves into care and concern for others. Personal concerns and needs and desires are considered an escape, a withdrawal from the true dynamics of communal prayer. The call to *koinonia*, community interaction, is a very noble thing. But the prejudice lurks that this outgoing thrust, however noble and good, is something other than true prayer.

The distinction, I say, is false, because all Christian prayer, whatever form it may take, involves people of necessity *both* with their own personal depth *and* with the depth of relationship with others to which Christians are summoned. "By this shall all know that you are my disciples, that you love one another" (Jn 13:35). "The one who does not love does not know God; for God is love" (1 Jn 4:8). "If you say, 'I love God,' and hate your brother or sister, you are a liar; for if you do not love your brother or sister whom you have seen, you cannot love God whom you have not seen" (1 Jn 4:20). If personal and communal forms of prayer are held to be in opposition, it must be said that neither of them is by itself Christian prayer.

True Christian prayer understands that there is always a communal dimension to one's personal journey, and, at the same time, that a depth of personal prayer is essential to the *koinonia* into which our public prayer calls and fashions us. True Christian prayer relates the two dimensions in an integrity that is found both at the heart of Christ's own prayer and in the eucharist itself, that action-prayer by which we continue to bring the prayer of Christ to living expression in our lives.

THE PRAYER OF CHRIST

Let us look first at the prayer of Christ. Christ's own prayer is the privileged prayer that shapes and guides all Christian prayer. The starting point for the prayer of Christ is found, not in any particular form of prayer, whether it be private contemplation or temple worship, but rather in the proclamation that identifies his life, his mission, his relationship to God. As recorded in the Gospel of Mark: "The time is fulfilled, and the kingdom of God is at hand . . ." (Mk 1:15).

The kingdom of God, as is commonly known, is not a place nor even a time. It refers to the reign of God, the Godship of God, the order of reality where God is all in all. And this kingdom is not simply a statement of fact announced by the words which Jesus spoke. It is proclaimed and indeed located within everything Jesus is and does. The reign of God is the relationship between Jesus and Abba, a relationship which is pressed out as motive and manifestation in all Jesus' actions, be they actions with others or acts of withdrawal from others into his own human journey.

The well-known hymn in the Letter to the Philippians proclaims the counterside of the reign of God when it says of Jesus that he "was obedient unto death" (Phil 2:8). His obedience, his attentive listening to the claim and direction of Abba, was itself the living expression of the proclamation he spoke. It guided his solitude, the personal form of his journey, and his intimacy, which is the communal, relational, public side of his life. In his proclamation of the reign of God, the personal and communal moments of his life find their unity and interrelation. And since his whole life was a living relationship with Abba, both the personal and communal moments of his life are necessarily interrelated moments of his prayer.

There are at least three events recorded in the Gospels that can illuminate the personal side of Jesus' prayer and its necessary ordering toward the communal: (1) the temptations in the desert, where he must struggle with the truth of his own identity and mission; (2) the garden and the cross, where he must choose that mission in a definitive and final way; and (3) those moments in between where all we are told is that he "went up to the mountain to pray."

The whole venture into the desert is for Jesus a withdrawal in response to a revelation about who he is. "You are my beloved Son; with you I am well pleased" (Mk 1:11). It is given as a new revelation about his own identity as a person, and he needed time to dwell with the implications of that revelation for his life and mission. The familiar temptations portray Jesus as naming his own truth in the face of illusory promises and alternatives, but it is precisely a truth for his public life and mission that is chosen. His desert prayer is not separated from the business of life, not a time to attend to "personal things" in some kind of guarded isolation. His desert prayer is prayer about his life, about how to conduct his life. Mark has Jesus *immediately* on the scene again, preaching the God who had claimed him, and inaugurating the mission which his experience of Abba revealed to him.

This same truth is claimed and chosen once again both in the garden and on the cross. In both, there is an intense journey into the depth of his own solitude, a solitude which is even more pronounced in the experience of abandonment by Abba. Yet in both it is a journey for public action, for the action of his death, for that action which has stood for two thousand years as public testimony to the truth of his own inward journey. The cross is at one and the same time Jesus' definitive *yes* to his own personal journey and to the God revealed in that personal journey, *and* the definitive action of Jesus for others. "In this is love, not that we loved God but that God loved us and sent his Son to be the expiation for our sins . . ." (1 Jn 4:9-10).

Finally, and with much less drama, there is the "mountain prayer." It has been pointed out by many a commentator, and I am sure by many a homilist and retreat director, that Jesus never did anything of significance without first withdrawing to pray. This includes the selection of the disciples, several healing and miracle actions, and indeed the final decisive choice to "go to Jerusalem," which was the fruit of his mountain transfiguration.

The point of all this is that Jesus' solitude, his own personal prayer, was never divorced from the activities of his life, but was rather ordered to them. And the truth which was claimed, or rather which claimed him, in those moments of withdrawal was expressed, brought forward, enfleshed in the actions which emerged from it. What followed was not something that was separate from his prayer, an overflow, perhaps, but really an essentially different activity. Those actions that followed *continued* his prayer, bringing forth the public side of his personal journey inward. To capture this in a distinction that will be very helpful when we turn to our own Christian prayer: the public life and action of Jesus was always the *context* of his inward journey, and his journey inward became the *content* of all that he said and did.

Let us turn this around and look a bit at Jesus in public. The Gospels do not give much attention to Jesus' liturgical life, though we can call three events into focus. The first is his preaching in the synagogue, where he reads from the text of Isaiah about the anointing and mission of God's servant. The opening words of his homily are indeed jolting: "Today this scripture has been fulfilled in your hearing" (Lk 4:21). The second is the cleansing of the temple, recorded differently by

John and the synoptics, but showing Jesus in each case, not only departing from the accepted temple but severely challenging them. And the third, the actions of Jesus in what is recorded as a Passover meal, "on the night he was betrayed."

In none of these do we have the liturgical equivalent of simply "going to Mass," or "singing the office." There is an entrance into the event that involves assurance, self-possession, even boldness. He does not simply acquiesce in "what is usually done here." He does not simply yield to liturgical rubrics. Neither the synagogue ritual, the temple customs, nor the supper patterns are treated as sacred realities that cannot be touched. He approaches in each case as one in touch with God, as one who brings forth into the public arena actions that speak and embody his intense relationship with Abba. It is that relationship and its demands for public action that stand above ritual, customs, and pattern. "It is I of whom the scripture speaks." Your customs make of my Father's house a den of thieves." "I shall not drink of the fruit of the vine until the kingdom of God comes."

We could also look at some of the relational events in Jesus' life, such as his healing actions, his words of forgiveness, his admonitions and behavior in various meal situations. These would not be properly considered "liturgical" situations in the Jewish sense. They are, however, the stuff of Christian sacraments, and therefore can serve to illuminate the ways of Christian liturgical prayer. In these also, without looking in any detail, we can see in Jesus a freedom, a self-assurance, and a knowledge of what he was about that is pressed forth in what he says and does. "If you will, you can make me clean . . . I will; be clean" (Mk 1:40-41). "That you may know that the Son of man has authority on earth to forgive sins . . . I say to you, rise, take up your pallet, and go home" (Mk 2:10-11). "Why do you eat and drink with tax collectors and sinners? . . . I have not come to call the righteous, but sinners to repentance" (Lk 5:30-32). Nowhere is Jesus presented in an action that does not reveal the depth of his personal journey into Abba. His actions bring forth that personal depth even as they arise from that personal depth.

It is this integrity of public and private, of personal and relational, that is characteristic of the life and the prayer of Jesus.

When he is in private, his thoughts go to those with whom he is related, to whom he is sent. When he is acting in public, his very actions unveil a depth, indeed a power, that displays his personal journey into Abba. Once again, the public, communal form of his prayer is the *context* of the personal form, and the personal form is the *content* of the communal.

The prayer of Christ, the integration of the personal and the communal, the intertwining of solitude and intimacy, is the model for true Christian prayer. His prayer is both the *context* and the *content* of ours. To bring this now to our lives as Christians, let us turn to the eucharist, which is the intimate wedding of Christ's prayer with our own.

THE PRAYER OF THE EUCHARIST

We might at first blush be tempted to consider the eucharist as public and communal prayer pure and simple. After all, it is our *liturgy*, the public work of the assembly. Aidan Kavanagh, in his *Shape of Baptism*, even speaks of the "public business" of the assembly to name the eucharistic action and the task of Christian initiation. It is true that one way of naming the shift brought about by the postconciliar liturgical reforms is to see it as a move away from the Mass as a time for private prayer to the eucharist as the community's action, from the form of the personal to the form of the communal. Nevertheless, I think that a closer look at the eucharistic action, especially its inner dynamics, will disclose the fallacy of such a naming.

The inner dynamics of the total eucharistic action reveal the same integrity, and the same inner relationship between the form of the personal and the form of the communal which we saw as characteristic of the prayer of Christ. There is a movement between the two that captures the relationship between them. The action begins with *assembly*, the calling together of people from disparate activities into public relationship. It certainly begins with the form of the communal. This, however, is only a beginning. It is by no means yet the true *koinonia* into which the eucharistic action calls and fashions us. Immediately the assembly is summoned before the word of God, a place which, if we attend to it correctly, belongs not to the form of the communal, but rather to the form of the personal. This personal nature of the liturgy of the word needs carefully to be understood.

Each of us in assembly is addressed by the word of God *alone*. It is a word which only makes sense and has true power if it touches down somewhere in unique human lives. It is not classroom instruction, a "message" meant for the masses. It is not an event of information at all. The true dynamic of the word of God is for Christ, and the God he reveals, to address each person in the same way that God, Abba, addressed Jesus. That is, in his own personal depth. So many homilies fail to recognize that. So many preachers, content to offer "message" and explanation, remain in the form of the communal, neither speaking *from* their own personal depth nor speaking *to* the personal depth of others. Needless to say that preaching which neither comes from nor goes to the form of the personal is simply not preaching at all. It is so much less, and a serious disservice to the word of God and to the people who have assembled to hear it.

The liturgy of the word belongs to the form of the personal and its aim is to feed, nourish, challenge, and support the personal journey of each person assembled. It aims further, if we let the prayer of Christ guide our understanding, to bring about an act of obedience, of attentive listening, that may call forth a personal response from each of the listeners.

The first response to the word of God in our liturgical prayer is *offertorium*, whether that offering is made of food (eucharist), or sinfulness (reconciliation), of sickness (anointing), of service (orders), or of human love (matrimony). *Offertorium* brings forth our baptismal truth: a human life placed within the life and prayer of Christ. Acts of *offertorium* will be genuine to the extent that they express personal gift, personal choice, personal commitment, and personal entrustment to the *Other* who has in Christ spoken to us. Within the eucharistic celebration the actions of *offertorium* are many: creed, petitions, collection, the presentation of bread and wine. What these actions serve to do is begin to bring forward into the form of the communal what has happened in the form of the personal.

This movement is, as I say, gradual. It is not a case of leaving one and instantly passing over into the other. The dynamic of *offertorium* is only indirectly relational. We are not yet looking *at* each other, but rather *with* each other to the One who is met in the personal form. This remains our stance throughout the eucharistic prayer of consecration, which is as much a prayer of entrustment as it is of thanksgiving, a prayer of surrender—the great *Amen*—as it is of transformation. If the word thrusts us in assembly into the form of the personal, the eucharistic prayer takes us together to the limit of the personal where everything is handed over in trust to the God whom Jesus reveals to be completely faithful. "Not my will, but yours be done . . . into your hands I entrust my spirit . . . through Christ our Lord through whom you give us all that is good . . . Amen, Amen, Amen."

Consecratio, as the transforming act of God, is the limit of the personal. It is only at that limit that the One who receives our Amen, our surrender of obedience, takes the form of the personal and transforms it into the form of the communal. "May all of us who share in the body and blood of Christ be brought together in unity by the Holy Spirit" (Eucharistic Prayer II). At that point we greet each other in peace. At that point we sit down at table together. At that point we acknowledge and proclaim the relationship in which the Lord sets us by addressing God as "our" Father. From that point on we can move from the assembly to action and life beyond the assembly, from table relationship to those areas of life where that same relationship is yet to be established.

Yet, in the paradox of it all, the form of the communal never ceases to be, and *at the same time*, the form of the personal, for our capacity to be in relation, to be of service, to be Christ "actors" to others will always be a function of, and a manifestation of, the personal workings of God within us. True entrance into the communal form will draw on, and draw out, the depth of our personal journey. And, like it or not, it will send us back into that personal journey, at times to find rest, or strength, or wisdom, or faith, or hope, or new freedom to live even more deeply. The communal form of our prayer retains within it the form of the personal, for it needs the depth which the personal supplies. And it continues to shape the form of the personal to greater and greater depth. Again, to recall the relationship established earlier, the communal form is the *con-*

text of our Christian prayer, and the personal is its *content* and its depth.

I hope it is clear by now that the prayer of the eucharist does not allow a neat packaging of Christian prayer into the private, personal form, on the one hand, over against the public, communal form, on the other. Rather, it reveals and embodies the necessary and true relationship that must exist between them. As in the life and the prayer of Christ, so also in our own life and prayer, the two flow one into the other. The personal journey is not, and cannot be, an isolated journey, however withdrawn from the form of the communal it may at times take us. We make it always side by side, and always in the context of our *koinonia*. At its limit, where the God of Jesus is met in all his faithfulness, and with all his unrelenting demands, this God who calls us to his ways turns us to each other, and to all men and women, saying, "Be now for each other sister and brother." And this call to *koinonia, communio*, which is the communal form of Christian prayer, demands the full depth of our personal journeys into God.

It is important to grasp that we turn toward each other and outward to all people, not by abandoning the personal journey, but *precisely as part of it*. The turning outward and the relationship itself are the fruition and proper completion of the personal form of prayer. For the communal form is neither more nor less than many personal journeys pressed out into relationship and mutual interaction. Both the personal and communal are conducted before God whom Jesus reveals, and both are empowered by the action of God. They are, in short, two faces of our relationship with God, and therefore of our prayer.

PRIVATE PRAYER AND PUBLIC PRAYER

Let us look at now what we commonly call "private" prayer and its relationship to "public," liturgical prayer. I have called the first the form of the personal because no Christian prayer can be truly private. It begins with the word of God, which is community property, and does not belong to any individual. The final test of its authenticity is a discernment process which likewise implies a role of the community in one's personal prayer. Likewise, I have called the second the form of the communal because no Christian prayer can be simply public act without some personal investment on the part of the "actors" in what they do, and without personal vulnerability to what they do. In short, I have used the terms personal and communal in order to move away from any false opposition that may be imagined between these two related moments in Christian prayer.

What is at stake here is not meditation versus Mass, or private devotions versus the liturgy of the hours. At stake are two component moments in a human life that is claimed by the God revealed in Jesus Christ. These are the moment of solitude and the moment of intimacy, neither of which can succeed without the other. Solitude without intimacy becomes selfish, isolated from the real order of human life, and, one might add, extremely lonely. The same can be said of personal prayer that loses its proper communal context. Intimacy, on the other hand, that is without solitude runs the risk of becoming empty, shallow, and at times destructively manipulative. The same is true of communal forms of prayer. One cannot recognize the God of love in solitude who does not know the ways of love. One cannot grow in the ways of love who does not know the ways of love. One cannot grow in the ways of love who does not respect the unique human journey and freedom of oneself and others. Solitude and intimacy, and the relationship between them, give the true shape to Christian prayer.

Solitude, by which I mean the personal journey into one's own human depth, is likewise the journey into the mystery of God, where God claims obedience from each person and sets us all in relationship. It is God who establishes for us the form of the communal. Intimacy, on the other hand, which is the journey into human relationship, is likewise the journey into God, where we learn, as Dorothy Sayers once remarked, the renunciation of God when he made us free. In human relationship we meet each other, forgive and heal each other, and know in such interactions the ways, the summons, and hence the presence of God. To divorce either the personal or the communal from the pursuit and discovery of God is to remove them both from the realm of Christian prayer.

We cannot simply say that meditation and devotions are "private" prayer, for without a communal reference as the proper *context* of our meditation and devotions they cannot be Christian prayer at all. They may be solipsistic musings. They may be pscyhological self-analysis. They may be flights of pure fancy or simply blissful rest. But they are not Christian prayer. At the same time, if there is no personal investment when the community gathers in assembly, if there is no personal depth that comes from one's journey into the God within each of us, then neither the eucharist, nor the sacraments, nor the liturgy of the hours can be considered true prayer either. To the extent that liturgical prayer *can* be considered to be the form of the communal, it must include within itself the personal prayer of those assembled. To the extent that meditation and devotions can be considered the form of the personal, they must include within themselves the *koinonia* established and desired by God, which is their fruit and their proper expression.

THE CONFLICT REEXAMINED

My main hope in these reflections has been to illustrate the relationship between personal and communal prayer, and to lay aside any opposition which consciously or subconsciously we might want to give them. By way of conclusion, let me return to the opening three instances of confusion and conflict, and examine them in light of the relationship which the prayer of Christ and the eucharist establish.

The first is the complaint, "I can't pray anymore," and the prohibition of any private devotional space for individuals in the assembly on the grounds that "the full and active participation by all the people is the aim to be considered above all else" (SC 14). Let me speak first in favor of this impulse. If the stress on active participation has served to pull people away from purely solipsistic prayer that sought to unite them with God, yet left them painfully isolated from those in assembly with them, it has served a good purpose. It is good for people to become aware that a greeting of peace, for example, is not an intrusion on their preparation for communion, but an important step in that preparation. It is healthy for people to be pulled away from prayer forms that are overly self-conscious, filled with endless apology, and which in the end block the prayer off from the Good News of Jesus Christ. And it is important to have dispelled certain fantastic images of Christ, such as Christ lonely and seeking companionship, or fragile and needing our protection, or terribly needy and claiming us exclusively for himself. The form of the personal had to be brought into the form of the communal. It had to recover its proper communal context.

Nonetheless, the complaint remains well taken, and ought to be resurrected if indeed it has been lost. Whatever the gain, it is not good if all of us, all the time, are forced to stand and sit and sing and recite and move about on cue with no regard to who we are, or where we are in our own personal life. That would seem to me to be a flagrant violation of the principle of adaptation. It certainly precludes the personal form from achieving its proper place in the liturgy, and thereby condemns it to being a very shallow experience. It is not good, for example, when the presider "performs" correctly, but is not at all transparent or vulnerable to the words said or the actions done. Nor is it good when men and women simply carry out the dictates of the ritual with little or no faith, hope, or genuine love in evidence. It is definitely true that the personal form needs to be attended to in a variety of ways outside of the liturgical assembly. It needs, however, to be attended to in ritual action as well.

Take the extreme example of a person who needs simply to be "left alone" so that the ritual act might gently make its impact felt. In principle, if true *koinonia* is the aim, and not some narrow kind of conformity or manipulation, this ought to be both possible and allowed. A not so extreme instance of this is the grieving immediate family of someone who has died. Most frequently the personal form is all that they can bring to the assembly, and this must be respected. But back off from the extreme to more ordinary folk and more ordinary occasions. There ought to be ways in which, for all of us, the ritual invites entrance beyond the surface. There ought to be, but so many parish "celebrations" seem not to have discovered them. A proper respect for the rhythms of the ritual would certainly help, allowing silence where silence is called for, assuring that key elements of ritual (e.g., the eucharistic prayer) are not rendered drab by drab recitation, or overshadowed by the attention given to trivial acts (e.g., the washing of the hands). Also crucial is a deep sense of personal presence on the part of the liturgical ministers, especially the presider and homilist. Helpful too would be a strong recovery of the aesthetic dimension of ritual prayer—in sight and sound and smell—to evoke those human affections that are the truest language of the personal form. Matter of fact ritual begets matter of fact experience, and matter of fact experience is not a personal experience at all.

Any attempt to imagine Christian liturgy without this deep personal dimension is simple nonsense and bad pastoral strategy. This much is evident: only when we can guide people to enter ritual prayer with the same personal depth as once they entered their private devotional space "while Mass went on," with the same personal depth where the real issues of their lives are being struggled out, only then will we have reached the true aim of the liturgical reform. Moreover, any thought that ritual prayer precludes the possibility of personal space where people can dwell with the needs and desires and deep realities of their own personal journeys simply ignores the inner rhythms and dynamics of Christian ritual prayer, and the needs of people who themselves make liturgy out of ritual text. Entrance into liturgy to that extant is the fullness of the "full and active participation" called for by Vatican II.

If people discover by doing our new liturgy that they can indeed pray again, then we will have succeeded in the task. If, on the other hand, they simply forget that prayer remains what our liturgy is about, so much the worse for us all. To return to the remark of Chesterton, now that we have made our liturgy more clear, there is need to recover its vitality and its depth.

The second example, retreat directors threatened by liturgical texts and symbols. I guess the first thing that can be said in their favor is that such directors rightly suspect that the liturgy of the word belongs to the personal form. It is here that the supposed conflict arises. Two things, however, need to be examined before the conflict can be resolved, and with a resolution that would allow the church's liturgy simply to be itself, even with an assembly of people who just happen to be intensely engaged in the personal form of prayer.

The first is a proper understanding of the personal form. Recall that the personal form is always a journey of an individual person into the mystery of his or her own human life, guided by, and summoned by the word which God speaks. Any ministry to that journey, whether it be homily, reading, or direction, remains rooted in this personal form, that is, it must speak from personal depth to personal depth, and this in service of both God's and the person's freedom. The readings do not provide a message to be grasped. Nor does the retreat handbook provide an objective path that must be followed. When we remember that it is the freedom of God to touch people when and where God chooses to touch that is the prime reality being ministered to, any conflict between the retreat symbols and the symbols of the liturgy disappears. Even if objectively resurrection readings seem to clash with incarnation readings, and both with readings on Christ's passion, in the personal form people will hear and receive from both what is appropriate to their own unique place on the journey. The word of God cannot be a distraction to the word of God.

The second thing that needs to be examined is the attitude of the retreat director toward his or her task. I have the sense that directors who find the church's liturgy awkward during directed retreats are really uncomfortable with the freedom of God to touch people where God chooses, and feel the need to control rather than guide the Spirit's action in their directees. It is in some ways the same confusion of the personal form with the communal form that homilists who think that the "message is all" fall victim to. Such confusion is not good homiletics; it is not good direction either.

At the same time, we must remember that the intense personal journey undertaken on retreat is only distanced from the relational realities of Christian *koinonia*, never separated from them, and that the reason for the journey at all remains always and everywhere Christian life and mission in the church, that is, God's *koinonia*. Not only is the church's liturgy not in conflict with the retreat journey, it serves to keep that journey solidly rooted in real Christian life.

Finally, the awkwardness of sacramental reconciliation. This is of course a very complex issue which cannot be resolved in a few concluding remarks. In part, it is a function of the consciousness of sin, which seems to be reshaping itself among Christian people. Sin must be seen as a true fraction of *koinonia* before reconciliation can be anything more than a new name for absolution. In part, also, it demands a deeper understanding of the patterns and processes of forgiveness and healing of rupture within persons, between persons, and among larger social groups. Both of these lie beyond the scope of this chapter.

One thing that these reflections can illuminate is the need for at least two forms of sacramental reconciliation, one which properly serves the personal form, and one which properly serves the communal form. It would seem that this need is addressed in the new rites for the sacrament, but this is in fact not the case. For *proper* service, the personal form must lead to the communal as its own true expression and completion, and the communal must draw out the personal as its own deepest content.

Rite I does indeed address the personal journey, and in the personal interaction between penitent and confessor it does allow the time and the care that one's personal journey demands. It attempts to serve what the introduction calls "new beginnings" and that dimension of ongoing Christian initiation which Aidan Kavanagh (*Shape of Baptism*) calls "conversion therapy." The rite's principal problem, however, is that it images itself to be complete in itself, and in no way opens out onto the communal form. Thus it is aborted at the very point where reconciliation is possible.

Rite III, on the other hand, suffers from not having within itself sufficient call on the personal. It jumps too quickly into the communal form. General admission of sinfulness accompanied by a distant voice giving distant forgiveness is probably not able to bring people to the limit of the personal where God transforms personal forgiveness into reconciliation among people. If the first does not bring forgiveness to proper reconciliation, this third tries to draw reconciliation out of something less than personal forgiveness.

Rite II holds the key to both, provided it is taken as guide and not as a successful rite in itself, which it is not. As guide it reminds us that a communal context is always necessary for the personal form of forgiveness, and that reconciliation with the community arises out of a serious experience of forgiveness.

One way of beginning to move forward toward adequate rituals of forgiveness and reconciliation is to examine carefully the personal need and, in an initial step at least, keep this separate from the communal need. In other words, do not ask a personal form to achieve a communal need, nor a communal form to achieve a personal need. The personal journey, which involves new beginnings, honest presentation of oneself before God (sacramental integrity), and radical conversion in one's life, must necessarily follow a time line different from that of the communal need, which is the community's celebration of its faith that in Christ sin is overcome. I say "as an initial step," however, because the two cannot remain permanently isolated. The personal must still lead to the communal, and the communal must still draw out the personal.

Let me start with the communal form, which is, according to the Constitution on the Sacred Liturgy, the proper form for celebrating any of the sacraments. We must question the current prohibition against celebrating this sacrament within a eucharistic context, a prohibition that fears a confusion of sacraments. The eucharist is itself the sacrament of reconciliation, intimately related to both baptism and penance which are "for the forgiveness of sins." Just as the initiation process leads one into eucharistic communion, the reconciliation process restores and deepens that eucharistic communion. Penance is the path to eucharist that sinners follow. It is no more a "confusion of sacraments" to enact reconciliation within a eucharistic celebration than it is to baptize and confirm.

We must also question the current insistence that anyone who partakes of "general absolution" must confess privately as soon as possible. It would seem that the reverse would better assure the proper movement from personal into communal, namely, that one who receives private absolution ought to bring this to the communal form when this is possible. At any rate, this communal form ought to allow some personal interaction of sinner with presider, even if it be only a generic admission of sinfulness coupled with a laying on of hands and prayer in response. Whatever form it would take, however, the communal form is not a substitute for the personal, but rather stands as its outcome and completion, whether that personal form be included in some minimal fashion in the com-

munal ritual form, or be conducted in more intense ways outside of the assembly and only later brought forward for full
reconciliation.

The personal form ought to follow personal norms and patterns. Perhaps the spiritual direction model, which lies at the
heart of the penitential practice inherited from the Celtic
church, remains the best process for personal forgiveness. In
that case, however, a single ritual would probably not be sufficient. Rather, the sacrament would most likely need to unfold
over several sessions or longer before achieving adequate response to the personal need. The personal form, however,
should never be seen as complete in itself. It should be ordered from the very beginning to an experience of forgiveness
which then is brought to the assembly for completion in reconciliation. A festive eucharist, or a communal celebration in the
context of eucharist, would be its proper conclusion.

In each of these examples, a problem was set by either imagining the personal and the communal forms of prayer as opposed or in conflict, or by giving preference to one of them to
the exclusion of the other. The relationship between the personal and the communal developed throughout this chapter,
in which the communal form is recognized as the *context* of
the personal, and the personal, the *content* of the communal,
offers some resolution to the conflict. It also, it is hoped, serves
to illustrate for other questions as well the inner dynamic that
is the shape of all Christian prayer.

11

Living the Sacrifice
of Christ

THIS CHAPTER FOLLOWS CLOSELY UPON THE PREVIOUS, AND IS A CON-
tinuation of the exploration begun there into the ways of
Christian prayer as this is shaped and guided by the eucharist
and the process of Christian initiation. There I proposed that
the personal form of prayer is not opposed to, nor independent of, the communal form of prayer. Rather, the personal always flows into the communal as its own proper completion.
Personal and communal are related as content and context: the
communal provides the *context* of all Christian prayer; the personal provides its *content*. This necessary relationship between
personal and communal continues to be maintained here.
However, for the sake of exploring the personal in greater
depth, I am going to bracket the communal until the journey
of the personal itself calls it forth. In the previous chapter I
said that it is only at the limit of the personal form that God
transforms the personal into the communal. In this exploration
I want to take a closer look at the personal form and at that
limit where God does the transformation.

To give the overall plan, I want first to look at the eucharist
in the context of Christian initiation, and specifically at the
light which has been shed on the eucharist by its inclusion in
the Rite of Christian Initiation of Adults (RCIA). Then I will
look at Jesus' own initiation, that is, the shaping of his own

185

human life in obedience to Abba. This initiation of Jesus is the heart of his own *sacrificium*, and, consequently, the heart of the eucharistic sacrifice which brings all the baptized into his sacrificial journey. It is that choice to which the eucharist guides us, in which the eucharist shapes us, and for which the eucharist empowers us. Thus the eucharist will emerge, not so much as a single action, but as a path, a passage, a personal journey of faith and hope. Thus, too, it will emerge as our living of the sacrifice of Christ. The brackets on the communal will be removed only in the next chapter at that level of the journey where God sets men and women in relation.

THE EUCHARIST AS INITIATION

Among the many things which the RCIA has restored to Christian understanding is that the eucharist is not only a special moment in the initiation process, and not only the proper term of baptism and confirmation. In the pattern given by RCIA, the eucharist is *itself* the sacrament of ongoing Christian initiation. Christian initiation, which is begun at the first whispers of faith in the human heart, or, in the case of infants, at the gracious presentation of a child to the church by his or her parents, is by no means totally contained in or concluded by a single movement through water and oil to the table. It continues to move forward each time any one of us takes our place at the table, that is, each time we fully take part in the full eucharistic action.

With the relationship between the three sacraments of initiation restored, after long centuries of both ritual and conceptual separation, it is possible to recognize that all of the baptismal imagery given in the New Testament about new life, inner transformation, a grafting onto Christ in his death and resurrection, is *at the same time* imagery for the eucharist as well. It is possible to recognize that the very same dynamics of union with Christ and the transforming anointing of God which are pressed out (expressed) in the ritual forms of baptism and confirmation are likewise pressed out in different ritual forms whenever the church in community enacts the eucharist. It is these dynamics, pressed out again and again, that make of the eucharist, as Augustine so aptly named it, "the repeatable sacrament of initiation."

There is a clear parallel between the task of the catechumenate and the liturgy of the word. The opening instruction given to the catechumens gives the task succinctly: "Now the way of the Gospel opens before you, inviting you to make a new beginning by acknowledging the living God who speaks his words of truth to us. You are called to walk by the light of Christ and to trust in his wisdom. He asks you to submit yourself to him more and more and to believe in him with all your heart. This is the way of faith on which Christ will lovingly guide you to eternal life" (RCIA 76). To walk by the light of Christ, to trust in and follow the ways revealed by Christ: this is the purpose of the catechumenate. It is the purpose of the liturgy of the word as well.

The same parallel can be drawn for the other movements of initiation. The true meaning of the "plunging" of baptism as the placing of a human life *into* the life reality of Jesus Christ is likewise the meaning of what we do at *offertorium*, whether the ritual form of *offertorium* be the prayers of intercession, the creed, a solemn procession of gifts, or a simple setting of the eucharistic table. And the anointing of confirmation, which is God's claim and consecration of the life which is placed with God's Son, whether it be done by presbyter or bishop, in infancy or at some other time of imagined Christian maturity, enacts for the first time what eucharistic consecration enacts again and again, namely, God's transforming action on all that is placed into Christ. Baptism and confirmation are not themselves repeated for they sign each of us with a decision of God which will not be withdrawn. For our sake, however, what is done in these sacramental actions can be and must be repeated until our lives are formed into that decision of God. In eucharist God's covenant in Christ is proclaimed again and again *pro nobis*, that is, for our transformation.

The invitation given by RCIA to understand the eucharist within the process of Christian initiation challenges the more episodic approach to the eucharist which we are accustomed to take. It seems to me, at least, that our usual approach is to speak as though each eucharist were complete in itself, with no necessary relationship to any other eucharist. We say, for example, "that was a good one, that one was okay, that was really bad," as though such assessments were really important. And when one is over, whatever the assessment, we move on to the next as though to a totally new experience. What we have not had in our spiritual language is the mechanism to connect one eucharist with another, and to know that in the connection, in the flow of one eucharist into another, what is really important is to be found.

It is very telling that people in religious formation are far more concerned with how often someone "goes to Mass" than they are with what might be happening to people when, over a period of time, they do "go to Mass." It is as though frequency alone had something to do with sanctity. It is all the more curious when these same religious people recognize that, in the arena of personal prayer, no single meditation means very much at all. In that arena the concern is with patterns that develop over a period of time, patterns of stagnation, of struggle, of growth. It would seem appropriate to recognize that no one eucharist means all that much either, and that the same pursuit of patterns over a period of time is likewise possible, necessary, and in fact more important with regard to our eucharistic praying as well. But, as I say, there has not been the mechanism to trace or even speak of the ongoing inner transformation that should be happening in the continued experience of eucharistic celebration.

The RCIA and the language of Christian initiation give us that mechanism, and urge upon us the task of learning how to use it. If the eucharist is restored as the repeatable sacrament of initiation, the sacrament of ongoing initiation, then the way becomes open to see the connection between the various eucharists we celebrate. The way is open to locate our eucharistic praying within the transformation process of Christian initiation. The way is open to explore and name the path of transformation along which the eucharist may take and guide us.

There is a metaphor used in an early translation of the Constitution on the Sacred Liturgy which has intrigued me, and has guided much of my reflection in this regard. It too provides help to examine the movement from one eucharist to another. It is, to be sure, a playful metaphor. It is also a powerful metaphor. Citing the prayer over the gifts for what was once called the ninth Sunday after Pentecost (before we discovered the high poetry of "Ordinary Time"), the constitution says that "through the liturgy, especially the divine Eucharistic Sacrifice, 'the work of our redemption is exercised'" (SC 2).[1] The Latin word is *exercetur*. It is translated as "accomplished" in the later Flannery edition of the text, a choice which loses the dynamic of the metaphor employed in the earlier translation. The Flannery text makes redemption sound finished, which it may be on God's part, but surely is not on ours. The more dynamic word employed by the earlier text recaptures the process of God's redemption happening *pro nobis*. Redemption is "exercised" in the eucharist, and by being exercised it is being accomplished for us.

The metaphor of "exercise" gives us, along with RCIA, yet another mechanism to explore the process of Christian initiation. It gives a way to examine and understand the path along which the eucharist can take us. Redemption has to do with transformation, with conversion, with ongoing growth and development. It has to do, moreover, with something deep in the human heart. In celebrating the eucharist we are being redeemed, converted, transformed. Something happens to us that can be traced and described. Something happens that can be guided and nurtured.

In addition to the process of initiation and the metaphor of "exercise," a third gain for understanding the ways of eucharistic praying is the once forgotten and only lately remembered scholastic adage that *sacramenta significando efficiunt*, that sacraments achieve their effect by signifying. They place an image in our consciousness which takes its place alongside of other images, sometimes even conflicting images, of the same reality. It may be an image of who we are before God, or in ourselves, or with each other. The images which sacraments introduce to our consciousness are privileged images, for they are rooted in the revelation of Jesus Christ. By our partaking of our sacraments, we allow those images to be planted in our consciousness in the deep hope that they will become the only, or at least the primary, operational images for our life. We allow them to be planted so that they can compete with all the other images that are not rooted in Christ's revelation, but which owe their origin rather to the realm of human sinfulness. The planting is the beginning of conversion, a seeding for the transformation which God wishes to work in us.

And what follows the seeding? Consider that every image calls forth its own affections. If I image you as a threat, I shall fear you. If I image you as an exploiter, I shall be very cautious and guarded with you. If I image you as kind and loving, I shall be drawn to you, open to you, trusting of you. And if I image you as dull and insignificant, I shall pay you no notice, or worse, overpower and exploit you. Evey image calls forth specific affections, and these affections in turn give shape to human behavior. Like it or not, we do what we want to do, and it is the affections that determine the wanting.

This is the process that is set in motion in our ritual prayer, for there we not only plant an image, but act out, however briefly, the proper behavior which the image calls for. At eucharist, for example, I not only image you as sister or brother, but I extend my hand in a greeting of peace. And in the process, one set of affections is set over against all counter-affections which may otherwise hold sway in my life. Apart from the table where I do greet you in peace I may not in fact be treating you as brother or sister. The battle between sin and grace is really a battle of affections, and the victory of grace over sin will only be achieved in the conversion of the heart, when the affections of Christ conquer the affections of sin, and as a result empower me to change the way I behave toward God, toward others, toward myself.

Redemption exercise is then not only a transformation of consciousness, the gradual overcoming of all other images by the images revealed by Christ. It is likewise, and more importantly, a transformation of affections and behavior. It takes time. It takes frequent doing ("exercise"). It takes openness and a deep vulnerability to the doing. And the transformation can be measured, guided, and observed.

The point of this reflection so far is that the eucharist can and needs to be seen within the process of Christian initiation, a process which has something to do with human life, human growth, and human transformation. It is not something we merely attend or even participate in. Eucharist is something we do, and something which deeply affects us in the doing by changing our images, our affections, and our behavior. Initiation and redemption are of a piece, names for the transformation of the human heart, and the key to our own transformation into Christ lies in exercising ourselves in his own affections so that they gradually become our own. This is the work of our *anamnesis* (remembering).

It is essential to recognize that the prime arena of struggle, conversion, and growth is the arena of the human heart. And it is essential to recognize that, if we will be guided by Christ along the way, it is to the growth and shaping of his own affections that we must look. And so we now turn to the initiation of Christ.

THE INITIATION OF CHRIST

The affections of Christ, as all human affections, can be clustered under the two main headings of solitude and intimacy, that is, the journey inward into the mystery of God within and the journey outward into the mystery of other people. The one cluster gathers his affections toward Abba, whom he met deep within himself. The other gathers his affections toward his disciples and friends, and all others to whom Abba sent him. Since the present focus is the personal journey, we will look here only at the affections shaped in Jesus' solitude, and at the God who engaged him along the way.

In a small yet powerful work entitled *Poverty of Spirit*[2] Johannes Metz looks at the personal journey of Jesus through the lens of poverty or dependence on God. He traces Jesus' growth in this dependence, not as a given received with ease and without struggle, but as a free choice born of struggle and claimed as his own in the face of enormous inner resistance. Metz insists that Jesus' life, no different from any other human life, is a mandate from God, and that the scope of the mandate is for Jesus to become a fully human person. This "involves more than conception and birth. It is a mandate and a mission, a command and a decision."[3]

Metz's work is a reminder that the human life of Jesus had no foreordained pattern known in advance that had to be followed. Some strands of popular piety notwithstanding, Jesus did not have the security of knowing what the next step would be, nor was he in full control of the outcome. Rather, the life of Jesus, like every other human life, had to be shaped in the living. It was filled with people and events, insights and discoveries, each of which constituted a new revelation about his own human life. And each demanded of him a choice: who shall he be, what shall he say, what will he do. Many of the choices came easily, a natural flow from the depth of the person he had already become. Some drove him back to the source of that depth, namely, the God-Abba within, where the choice had to be born of struggle, and where the struggle itself took him deeper into the mystery of his own human life and into the mystery of his God. The struggle revealed a life to which he must be faithful. In the choices which he made, faithfulness and unfaithfulness stood before him as the terms of the choice.

Metz reflects on the temptations in the desert as a paradigm of all the choices which Jesus had to make in his life. In the desert the terms of faithfulness and unfaithfulness became clear. On the one hand, there is the voice of the tempter, which carries the illusions of his own expectations and the expectations of others. "If you are the son of God . . .," then let me tell you how the son of God should act. On the other hand, there was the voice within, the voice which was from Abba, the voice of his own human conscience and human integrity. This voice held before him the one choice which, precisely because it does not come from outside himself, but from within, is the one choice that will keep him faithful both to his own life and to his God. "I am the son of God . . .," but God alone will tell me what that shall mean. Faithfulness is born of listening to God within. Faithfulness is obedience to the voice that is heard within.

It is difficult in our own day, when autonomy and self-actualization hold our imaginations as important values to be pursued, for us to be comfortable with the complete dependence of Jesus on Abba and the full obedience of Jesus to Abba. His life did not originate from himself; it was given to him and was guided by the design of Another. He was always free, but never autonomous. It is even more difficult for us to be comfortable with this because we have lived so long with images that have stressed the divinity of Christ and which have played down or romanticized away his total dependence on Abba. Nonetheless, however difficult it may be for us to receive the truth of Jesus' dependence on Abba, it is absolutely necessary that we do so, because such dependence on God is, at its deepest, our truth also.

The dependence of Jesus on Abba, his "poverty," as Metz names it, is finally the truth of the sinless one to which he was obedient unto death. Underneath all the choices that went into the shaping of his own life, whether they are seen through the lens of poverty, dependence, faithfulness, or obedience, there is, finally, but one choice: *yes* or *no*. Yes to this new revelation, this new demand, this new movement in his life which he knew to be *his* life, or simply *no*. In the movie version of *Jesus Christ, Superstar* a song at the end has the disciples pleading: "Can we start again, please?" A lovely song, but a united voice from without pleading with Jesus to say *no*. And we know, of course, from the outcome of the story that the answer was not *no* but *yes*. There was no starting over: Jesus would be faithful to the end.

The question we must ask is this: what affections shape a life of such obedience and fidelity? What affections allow one consistently to set aside all other voices and to choose what one hears from one's own true depth, from Abba, the God within? Certainly the affection of generous giving and certainly the affection of profound trust. Without these the only choice that a "sensible" person will make in the face of costly demands is *no*. Yet the problem with both generous giving and profound trust is that neither of them is easy to come by. Both can only be born and nurtured from struggle in the inner depth of the human heart. They do not come easy; they are always the fruit of a sometimes very painful victory. And they cannot be born at all unless Another resides deep within to call forth the generous gift and invite profound trust. The place of their birth is and must be the journey of human solitude where the God of Jesus is to be found.

Neither generous giving nor profound trust are well perceived if we lift them too quickly out of the realm of solitude and read them through a romantic lens of intimacy. The language of risk, very appealing to the noble soul in the face of one or very few relationships, speaks a very different challenge in the depth of one's solitude. We must never forget that for Jesus the final choice of obedient surrender was not a romantic choice. It was made in the painful experience of abandonment even by Abba. It was made in what Metz calls "the dregs of poverty: worship."[4]

The school of Jesus' solitude, in which he learned to listen by listening, to obey by obeying, to trust by trusting, is the school in which he learned to be, and chose to be, the human person God destined him to be. In his faithfulness he showed himself to be the Sinless One. It is the school in which he learned to say *yes* to his destiny, whether it be the pleasant task of choosing disciples or the frightening choice of crucifixion. It is the school in which he found within him a God who demanded a very definite shape to his human life. And it is the school in which this same Jesus teaches us the truth about our own human life.

But obedience is not the only lesson which the school has to offer. For in his solitude Jesus discovered not only a demanding God but, far more importantly, a God who promised to be faithful. A faithful God. Here is the key to Jesus' faithfulness, and the key which he offers for our own. Metz gives it as the true secret of all human poverty: "God's fidelity to man is what gives man the courage to be true to himself."[5] If the first—listening, obeying, and giving over—is the shape of Jesus' *faith*, this second, the faithfulness of God, is the source of Jesus' *hope*. And Jesus did need hope. Though we might live in the era when Jesus' own faithfulness has been vindicated in the resurrection, he did not. He had to face the cost of his faithfulness with no other resource than a profound trust in the God of the covenant, the God who promised to be faithful. Jesus could only trust that he would be vindicated, and not ultimately destroyed.

This view of Jesus' life—a faith pressed out in surrender, a faith that deepened as each choice of his life was made, and each *yes* to that life given, whatever the circumstances or the cost, and a hope which brought him closer and closer to a God who seemed further and further away, and who lingered finally only as a name to be cried out in anguish and a remembered promise to be trusted—presents the human journey that *is his sacrifice*, and proclaims to us all that the sacrifice of Christ unfolds only and always in the depth of the human journey itself. This takes us from the journey of Christ to ourselves and our own initiation into him.

OUR INITIATION INTO THE WAY OF CHRIST

Our lives as Christians are shaped by the way of Christ. As disciples we walk in his footsteps. As the baptized we live his own sacrificial journey. As a people born of the new covenant we are claimed by the same God of promise who shaped and guided Jesus' own faith and hope. In sacrament we express this each time we initiate someone into the church and each time we celebrate our eucharist. If the initiation of Jesus demanded that his affections of faith and hope, of generous giving and profound trust, be trained and exercised in order that he be faithful to the unique life that was given to him, the intiation of each Christian likewise demands that faith and hope, generous giving and trust, be trained and exercised if those who follow Christ will be faithful to the unique life given to each of them. The choice of faithfulness or unfaithfulness remains for each of us.

Christ can reveal, as indeed he has revealed, that God is faithful to any human life that is shaped and chosen as Jesus' own was shaped and chosen, that is, according to the inner voice of conscience, integrity, Abba. He can reveal himself to be companion to us in our solitude where our choice of faithfulness must be made. What he does not do and cannot do is take away from us the task of choosing for ourselves. He can empower us to say *yes* to our own human life; he cannot say *yes* in our stead.

In the Gospel of John there is a metaphor which can shed light on our own initiation journey, on what Christ can do for us and on what he cannot do. It appears in the dialogue of Jesus with the Samaritan woman at the well of Jacob (Jn 4:5-42) where Jesus asks the woman for water and then suggests that she ask him for water which would quench her thirst forever. Let me explore this metaphor a bit.

The metaphor of water and thirst does not speak a surface relationship with Christ. It calls us, rather, into Christ's presence on a very deep level. It asks us to bring our yearnings, our deepest desires, and with them our fears, our frustrations, our uncertainties. It is very much a metaphor of our own solitude. It asks us to come before Christ where we are most vulnerable. It asks us to find in Christ someone who can fill those yearnings and desires, someone who can ease our fears, soften our frustrations, give meaning and motivation to go forward even where we have no certainty of the outcome. It is a powerful metaphor, but one which must be treated very delicately.

Part of the delicacy is to realize that Christ never offers us an escape from human life. He always invites us more deeply into human life, into our human life and his. There are times when we would all like to find in the Gospel the kind of instant cure that so many television advertisements pretend to offer. Or maybe a dream vacation to a fantasy island where the sun always shines, the water is always seventy-two degrees, and where our every wish could come true. But Christ does not offer such cure or fantasy. If we let him be God's word to us in our solitude, he can only take us more deeply into everything we want to escape from.

In order to understand how this metaphor of thirst and quenching is a profound description of our initiation journey, it is necessary to take an honest look at the deepest yearnings of our heart which are our thirst. For some it could be a loneliness that yearns for a relationship it never seems able to find, or a failure in relationship that has hurt or destroyed another. For others it could be confusion about life, an uncertainty about the future, and a deep desire for a security which is always just over the next hill. For still others it could be a sickness that radically alters one's life, and yearns for a healing that cannot be. The faces of our thirst are as many as we, and to each Christ offers a drink that can quench and satisfy.

But I repeat, he does not offer an escape from human life. That is not the thirst-quenching he has to give. And it cannot be, for that is not the path he himself traveled. If his path was to take each moment of human life, struggle with it if it had to be struggled with, and then in full faithfulness say *yes* to that life once again, that must be the true path of our initiation also. That must be the path we follow in his footsteps. That must be the only quenching he can give to our thirst.

This choice of *yes* or *no* to life is a very basic choice for us as much as it was for Jesus. It is for us too the choice of faithfulness or unfaithfulness, of salvation or sin. And it underlies all the choices we must make in our lives. When life goes well, when all is happy and at peace, it is easy to say *yes*, or so it seems. When life does not go well, however, at those moments when our thirst is very pronounced, it is much easier and more common to want to say *no*. Anger is a form of saying *no* from which a *yes* must be wrested. So is our common malady known as "the poor me's." "Why doesn't the other person change?" is another way to say *no*. "Why does it have to happen to me" is yet another. Whatever the ways of saying *no*, and they are legion, in that refusal life comes to a standstill and turns in on itself. We cannot go forward where we say *no* to life.

At the well Jesus tells the woman that the time is coming when we will worship God in spirit and in truth. The time is at hand when we will not need a temple or a church to offer our gifts to God, but only a life that is lived and deep yearnings of the heart. This word of God announces that the very struggles which make up each human life are the stuff of true worship, and faithfulness its primary ritual act. If we allow a personal address to us in those struggles, Jesus says to us: "Journey inward with me; I want you to find Abba too. Journey inward with me; I will teach you worship in spirit and in truth. Journey inward; I will take you to the One who gives power to say *yes*."

The woman at the well took Jesus to be offering a way out of her thirst, and a way out of the need to come to the well at all. She was wrong, as we are wrong any time we seek to escape from the struggles of human life. What Jesus offers her, and us, in the face of our deepest yearnings is a way *into* those struggles, not a way out. He offers us the power and the freedom to say *yes* to those yearnings and even to the pain which those yearnings bring us. He offers, in other words, the victory of his *sacrificium*. He does so by naming that the real thirst is not the yearnings themselves, but the *no* we give to our life in the face of those yearnings. That is the thirst he can quench if we let him empower us to say *yes*.

And how may he do that? Only by leading us again and again to the place of generous offering. Only by leading us again and again to the place where we too can exercise profound trust in the God he has come to reveal to us. Only by joining us to himself as the apprentice joins to the artist where with him we can exercise his affections of faith and of hope.

The place of water and oil, and the table set with food. The place of his *offertorium* and God's *consecratio* where the victory over sin calls us from isolation and frees us for *koinonia*.

THE SACRAMENT OF SACRIFICE: EUCHARIST

It appears then that our initiation journey presents us with the same fundamental choice for our life that the incarnation mandate presented Jesus for his own: *yes* or *no* to our own human life, with *yes* being the choice Christ urges and empowers us to make. As the sacrament of his own *sacrificium*, the eucharist is the place where our initiation journey blends with his, and where the journey of our own solitude comes to term in the same place where his came to term, namely, Abba, God of covenant, God who is faithful. Let me bring these reflections to a close by looking at the eucharist again as the place where our affections of faith and hope are formed, and where the power to say *yes* is offered to us.

Certainly the liturgy of the word is the place to begin. It is in the word proclaimed in all its many moods and movements that the affections of Christ are revealed to us. It is in the word proclaimed, moreover, that the faithfulness of God is set firmly before us. And it is in the word proclaimed that Christ is given to us as companion for our own personal journeys in faith and in hope.

But for the word to be truly effective, it must not only be proclaimed. It must also be heard, and heard in such a way that the affections of Christ which it portrays be called forth as our own. The word invites and demands response, and in the eucharist the response is threefold. Clasically we name it offertory, consecration, and communion, and it is the first two that are of concern here.

The term *offertory* has had an odd history which has served to obscure rather than identify the true *offertorium* of the eucharist. Since the Middle Ages it has named something that the presiding priest did for everyone else, and led the church to think of the power to offer as belonging to the priest alone in virtue of his ordination. It has also been taken to name a "part of the Mass," a sequence of prayers and gestures from the unveiling of the chalice to the beginning of the eucharistic prayer. Changing the name of offertory to the presentation of gifts has only covered over, not corrected, this obscurity.

With the postconciliar stress on full and active participation of all the people in the liturgical action, *offertorium* is restored as an act belonging to all. And as we begin to understand that active participation goes much deeper than standing, sitting, singing, and reciting prayers, *offertorium* can be recovered as the very thing Paul was naming in his Letter to the Romans when he said: "I appeal to you, brethren, by the mercies of God, to present your bodies as a living sacrifice, holy and acceptable to God, which is your spiritual worship" (Rom 12:1-2).

Offertorium is an expression of affection, the very affection of generous giving which shaped the obedient life of Christ, and which is in its expression our entrance into his obedient life. I say expression. In the ritual of the eucharist it has many expressions, but most especially the intercessions and the presentation of gifts. But these expressions are true *offertorium* only to the extent that they indeed express an affection of the heart, a true offering of one's own human life. If the affection is absent, the gesture is empty of all but theoretical meaning.

Offertorium is likewise the first response to the word in our other sacramental acts. In reconciliation we offer our sins and sinfulness; in anointing our sickness; in marriage the love of two people; and in orders the service of ministry to the church. Each is an act of generous giving or giving over, of obedient surrender of certain aspects of human life, done always in the context of the eucharist and Christian initiation where all human life is placed with Christ to Abba. Whatever the ritual action, in *offertorium* Christ exercises us in his obedient surrender to God, the first step in the possibility of saying *yes* to life in all of its many choices.

Consecration has had an even odder history that has even more forcefully obscured the true *consecratio* of the eucharist. For most of its history the focus has been exclusively on bread and wine, losing sight of the people who are consecrated by eating the bread and drinking the wine. "Send your Spirit upon *us* and our gifts . . .," the ancient prayer prays. It is the "us" through the gifts to whom consecration is given.

Consecration is the act of God transforming with faithful love everything that is placed with Jesus Christ. Everything

and everyone. If we do not lose consecration in images of alchemy, with exclusive focus on "things-to-be-changed," and
if, instead, we hold consecration in the personal sphere, where
a personal God communicates in act with a community of persons, then the true consecration of the eucharist is recovered
as a place of meeting. It is the place where we who have given
generously with Christ meet Abba and his promise to be faithful. Whatever we proclaim as "happening" in consecration
happens because the obedience of Christ has been vindicated,
and in Christ God has made covenant with all men and wom-
en. Consecration is a word of election, and the transformation
it refers to is a transformation of love. Language which has
long kept consecration in the realm of the material must yield
once again to the fuller, and theologically more accurate, form
of the personal.

In the realm of the personal, the consecration of the eucharist is and must be for us the place of hope, the place where we
are drawn beyond what is seen to the One who is not seen.
Whether we name the consecration to be the *verba Jesu*, or the
invocation of the Spirit, or the whole eucharistic prayer, is
quite secondary to the exercise of hope which is true consecration—quite secondary to the human meeting with God who in
Christ lingers for us as a word of promise to be trusted. "This
cup is the new covenant in my blood. Do this, as often as you
drink it, in remembrance of me" (1 Cor 11:25).

The gift of saying *yes* to our life can only be given in this
meeting, and can only be born of this act of trust. Whatever the
vehicle that holds the promise before us, be it absolution, or
anointing, or nuptial blessing, or prayer of consecration, it is
the promise, and the One who makes the promise, that alone
can evoke our *yes* when everything conspires to have us say *no*.

The point of promise, and the meeting with Abba, is the
limit of the personal journey. At that point, *and not before*, we
are set in communion with each other. At that point the personal yields the communal as the continued act of obedience
and trust. We have explored here the generous giving of *offertorium* and the profound trust of *consecratio* as the necessary
conditions for *yes* to be possible. What remains for the next
chapter is the full embodiment of that *yes*, namely, the *koino-
nia-communion* in which the God of Jesus sets us.

Notes

1. The early translation is from *The Documents of Vatican II*, ed., W. Abbott (New York: Guild, America, Association, 1966).

2. Johannes Metz, *Poverty of Spirit*, trans., J. Drury (New York: Paulist Press, 1968).

3. Ibid. 5.

4. Ibid. 49.

5. Ibid. 19.

12

The Challenge
of God's "Koinonia"

THE REFLECTIONS IN THIS CHAPTER BELONG WITH THOSE IN THE PRE-
vious two chapters and conclude a three-part exploration into
the nature and shape of Christian prayer as it is guided by and
expressed in the eucharist. The first drew out the relationship
between the private, personal dimension of prayer and its
completion in the arena of relationship and communal action.
The second put brackets on the communal in order to explore
in depth the personal journey which the eucharist invites all
Christians to take. Essential to the second essay was the need
to go to the limits of the personal journey before those brackets on the communal could be removed, because it is at those
limits, and only at those limits, that God sets us in relation to
each other. In this final essay, the brackets are removed so that
a similar close look can be given to the communal dimension
of Christian prayer.

There is a point that must be made at the very beginning,
one which was carefully prepared for, though always held in
the background, in the earlier two chapters. The point itself is
fairly commonplace, though its implications are less commonly drawn out and attended to. It is that the relationship or *koinonia* which we enjoy as Christians, and which we enact and
are led to each time the eucharist is celebrated, is a relation-

ship that is *established by God*. It does not arise from us. Even
where we can say it has been already achieved to some extent
in a local community or in the larger church, even there it continues to be established and maintained by God and not ourselves. This point is foundational to any consideration of the
communal dimensions of Christian prayer.

There are two reasons for stressing this at the very beginning of this chapter. The first is that if we forget that *koinonia*
is both God's mandate and God's gift to us, and become se-
duced into thinking it arises somehow from our own good
will and determination, we will fail to notice that the communion we do enjoy is itself quite limited, and the source of
limitation is nothing less than the limits of our own good will.
We will fail to notice, moreover, that *at those limits* we are ourselves agents of division and opposition far more than we are
of communion and reconciliation. The second reason has to do
with the quality of relationship to which God calls us. As
drawn out clearly in the previous chapter, God's *koinonia* is established precisely at that point where each of us is empowered to say *yes* to our own human lives in all their uniqueness
and unfinished fragility. God's *koinonia* demands that we say
yes not only to ourselves but to each other, and under exactly
the same terms. If we do not remember that God sets us in relation at the point of freedom from all external demands and
expectations, all that we will establish for ourselves is a network of relationships where we try to level expectations and
demands on one another. And whatever we may call that, it is
not the *koinonia* which God desires to establish among us.

God's *koinonia* determines the communal dimension of
Christian prayer. What I would like to do in this third essay is
to explore the challenge of that *koinonia*, especially as it is expressed and made manifest in the eucharist. I'd like to consider that challenge as it is issued to any local assembly whenever that assembly enacts the eucharist. I'd like to explore the
implications of the challenge as it moves beyond any one assembly and strives to forge a universal church from the communion of local churches. And I'd like to follow the challenge
still further as it urges the church itself always beyond its own
imagined boundaries into human history, human society, and
that particular human future which we call the kingdom of
God.

In order to do this, I am going to sketch a collage of three pieces, each of which will contribute to the task more by suggestion than by hard logic. The first will draw on Scripture for an initial glimpse of the scope and range of this *koinonia* of God. The second will tap a neglected strand of eucharistic faith, namely, the eschatological thrust of the eucharist identified in Christian hymnody as *pignus futurae gloriae*, the pledge of future glory. The third will be a collection of tools drawn from several sources: from ritual studies on the rites of passage,[1] from an examination of the Christian imagination by William Lynch in his *Christ and Prometheus*,[2] and from a work that has already influenced these reflections so far, *Persons in Relation*, by John Macmurray.[3] From the collage will come some common threads to take us more deeply into the third response to the word of God proclaimed in eucharist, that response which emerges only after and out of *offertorium* and *consecratio*, namely, the communion of God's people in Christ.

A BIBLICAL VIEW OF GOD'S "KOINONIA"

The baptism of Jesus, explored in the previous chapter on the personal journey, needs to be revisited here. It contains and embodies the three movements of offertory, consecration, and communion which, together with the word, constitute the essential structure of the eucharist and of all prayer which the eucharist shapes. The baptism itself expressed Jesus' own determination to be about the work of Abba. It was an external act at the beginning of his public life to bring forth his inner affections of obedience and generous giving. It is the same inner affections which the author of Hebrews identifies as at the heart of Jesus' whole life. Remember its use of Psalm 40 (vv. 6-8) for Jesus:

> Sacrifices and offerings you have not desired,
> but a body you have prepared for me;
> in burnt offerings and sin offerings you have
>   taken no pleasure.
> Then I said, "Behold I have come to do your will,
>   O God." (Heb 10:5-7)

Immediately upon this *offertorium* of Jesus' baptism comes his *consecratio* by God, which, in the realm of the personal, is always an action of a personal God upon a person.[4] God's words are words of true consecration: "You are my beloved Son; with you I am well pleased" (Mk 1:11). And after his time in the desert, the time which took Jesus along his own personal journey to the point of saying *yes* to his own unique life, identity, and mission, we find the beginning of *koinonia*: his preaching and his gathering of disciples to himself.

Thus at the very beginning of his public life a dynamic is set in motion, a dynamic of *gathering to himself*, which continues throughout his own life, and which, after his death and resurrection, still continues in the life and mission of the church. A *gathering*. A gathering for which there are no limits. A gathering whose terms are set in Paul's magnificent recapitulation in Romans 8, and in the more concise declaration of Jesus in the Gospel of John: "and I, when I am lifted up from the earth, will draw all to myself" (12:32). To fully grasp the true nature of God's *koinonia* as revealed in Jesus Christ, this dynamic of gathering and its unlimited scope needs to be held on to.

Earlier in this volume I discussed the significance of the meal in Christianity. In the section on the biblical witness, I called attention to several "meal story" texts that illustrate various aspects of the meal that are of significance to Christian life and prayer. Without repeating those reflections in full here, let me nonetheless call on them again as stories that further identify this *koinonia* which is established by God. As "meal stories" they not only serve to describe the relationship in which God sets us to each other; they do so by naming a series of challenges which belong to a people whose essential identity and mission is established and celebrated in the eucharistic meal.

The text cited from Matthew (9:10-13) where Jesus was critiqued for eating with publicans and sinners, recalled that the meal is the place where sinners are welcome, the place where mercy is given and reconciliation is brought about. A second text cited from Matthew, the multiplication of bread and fish (14:14-20), called attention, not only to the welcome that was to be given to all, but to the task which is assigned to the disciples to serve and feed those who are assembled. And the Pauline texts from 1 Corinthians (8:9-12; 10:16-17; 11:27,33) set forth a triple mandate: not to harm any member of the Body;

to show care and respect for one another; and, to uphold the unity of the Body which is Christ's own Body. At the point where we say *yes* to ourselves in all our unfinished fragility, there we must likewise say *yes* to one another. At the place where unity is established, there we must observe the demands of unity lest the Lord himself be violated and we be condemned.

More texts of Scripture could be called on to further enrich our picture of God's *koinonia*, such as the advice for living with each other which Paul gives in abundance, and the forceful statements of John equating true love for God with love for the brethren, but this is enough for the suggestive nature of the collage. I am not trying to give an exhaustive picture or a well-honed argument. My aim is to invite the reader's imagination into a familiar world of biblical proclamation and to let that familiar world speak once again.

What I do want to call attention to, however, is the unqualified picture which the New Testament gives, and to call before us how easy it is for us to qualify it. How easy it is to enjoy the loveliness of the picture and to see it as quite possible, provided the people involved are nice people like ourselves, who share our values and our doctrine, and who look and act very much like ourselves. It is very easy to romanticize God's *koinonia* down to the level of our own good will, and to enjoy these pictures at the center where our good will is strong. It is easy simply to block out the severe judgment these same pictures impose on us as we move out from the center to the periphery of our relationships where good will is not so evident. Yet the picture and the challenge which God's *koinonia* offers remains unqualified, at the center, at the periphery, and beyond the periphery in that vast arena where relationships do not yet exist at all.

The journey thus far has been a pleasant journey, and it was meant to be. One hope is that it summon forth the actual experiences of communion which we do already enjoy. We need to hold on to the real *koinonia* of our experience, for that must always be the starting point for any further call into relationship. A second hope, however, is that it make us feel a bit uneasy about the limits we impose on our own *koinonia*. It is important and necessary to wander out to the edges a bit and let the very *koinonia* which we do enjoy challenge us where it has not yet been achieved. Community is both a gift and a challenge. It becomes a gift where we meet the challenge. It remains a challenge where we do not.

ESCHATOLOGICAL DIMENSION
OF EUCHARISTIC FAITH

Let me turn to the second piece of the collage, drawing on the eschatological dimension of eucharistic faith. Eschatology has been an "in" thing in theology ever since the existential theology of the sixties passed the torch in the seventies to the theology of hope. Nonetheless, the eschatological dimension of the eucharist has not been very well developed. For most people in the pews, and for many in the sanctuary as well, it remains clouded in vague images of a banquet somewhere that is somehow prefigured in what we now do. I have the sense that the most alien phrase in the revised eucharistic text, one which least captures our attention and imagination, is the phrase within the embolism of the Lord's Prayer: "we wait in joyful hope for the coming of our Savior, Jesus Christ."

There is a very powerful working definition of eschatology in the second volume of Karl Rahner's *Sacramentum Mundi*[5] which can help us dig out some of the richness of this "waiting in hope," and some of the truth of the eucharist which is our pledge of future glory. He says, first of all, that eschatology is not an advance report of events that are going to happen later. It is a simple enough starting point, except that it jettisons what little sense of eschatology most people live with. In Rahner's view eschatology does not offer us a view of tomorrow, a picture of something that is going to happen if we wait long enough. It certainly does not offer us an escape from the here and now realities of our lives.

Quite the opposite. True eschatology leads us to look at and to embrace the here and now as a people who must make decisions about and in that here and now. Rahner goes on to describe eschatology as a forward look which is necessary for us for our spiritual decisions in freedom. Eschatology gives us a way of looking at the here and now, whether that "here and now" be events personal to one's own life or events that affect many people together. It locates events within the context of what we call "saving history," that is, history as it is deter-mined by the Christ event. But in the process, it fixes our gaze on the concrete human situations of our lives and tries to un-veil within these situations a longing for fulfillment. The aim is to see within each human situation a purpose and a destiny that is established by God and revealed in the event of Jesus Christ, and this to enable us to come to a decision in light of that purpose and destiny. The bottom line for Rahner is that we accept each situation, whatever it be, and enter it creative-ly, so that our choices will bring forth from it a realization of God's possibility for the world.

Let me try an example. The husband of a family dies. That is the human situation, and for everyone involved, wife, family, friends, it is a time of decision and choice. What meaning, what value, what response will be given? There are many pos-sibilities within the event. One can succumb to grief and con-fusion and choose to stay there. One can choose to be angry with God, and reject any word of God's mercy and goodness. One can close up in oneself, unwilling in one's own grief to support and comfort others. These are all real options which can be chosen in the face of death. None of them, however, represents either the choice toward God which is worship or the choice toward others which is God's *koinonia*. This latter represents yet another option for choice within the same hu-man event. What eschatology tries to do is open the event, to help us see beyond the grief and the confusion, beyond the an-ger and self-centeredness to another possibility which can make of the death both an act of worship and an act of love for others. This is not an imposition from without. It too is a real possibility in the event. What Christian faith proclaims is that it is in fact the option which Jesus Christ makes possible and urges us to choose. It is God's possibility for the event placed alongside of other possibilities, yet placed in such a way that we are urged to choose God's possibility above all other possi-bilities. This is the appeal of eschatology: an appeal for choice in the present. "Behold I set before you life and death . . . therefore choose life" (Dt 30:19).

There are two points here that need to be stressed. The first is the accent on the present. The eschatological projection of Christian future is no more an escape into the future than the remembrance of Christian past is an escape into the past. The reason to remember is for choice in the present. The reason to look forward is for choice in the present. Every choice needs a motive, and the motive which Christian eschatology offers us comes in the form of a destiny which we can bring about if we choose correctly. It comes in the form of a possibility to transform the present beyond its own capabilities precisely by revealing within the present a future which would not otherwise be known. It comes in the form of an invitation to reach into the here and now and bring forth from it God's own desired future.

The second point that needs to be stressed is the accent on free decision. Eschatology is an appeal to human freedom. It does not yield a future that will come about willy-nilly, automatically, without the need for human agency. The human person, by his or her decision and choice, is a necessary part of the process of bringing God's future into history. By naming God's future as the truth of the present and by choosing that future above all other possibilities for the same human event, we join God in bringing about God's future.

The appeal of God's future is certainly necessary for the personal journey of each individual, for it provides an essential motive for saying *yes* to one's own life. Such affirmation recognizes and acknowledges that God's future for any human life is the deepest truth and the deepest integrity of that life. The appeal of God's future, however, is not limited to the personal alone. Its dominant images, in fact, are communal, and the appeal which they give to our personal choices and decisions is always toward *koinonia*. If indeed the appeal of eschatology were limited to the personal journey alone, there would be little more to be said than has already been said in the previous chapter. But the appeal goes beyond the personal to the communal identifying the *koinonia* we already enjoy *as God's future*, and inviting us to expand that *koinonia* without limit. It goes to the periphery of our communal life where the relationship of sister and brother is yet only a possibility still to be realized. If there are in fact no bounds to the *koinonia* to which God summons us, and if the appeal of eschatology is always towards *koinonia*, then true eschatology is the voice of challenge, of invitation, of urgent appeal at whatever point short of that *koinonia* where we do set up boundaries of our own making.

There is some homework we will have to do if we are going to open up eschatology to the possibility of making its proper appeal to us. We have to abandon some inherited images, and call on some earlier ones that have been forgotten. We have to abandon, for example, Augustine's static image of the *visio Dei*, an image of God simply "there," awaiting the faithful as a reward for their faithful lives. In its place we have to recapture the dynamic sense of the *reign of God*, which names God's activity even now wedded to our own bringing forth into history God's own kingdom. We have to abandon, for another example, the twelfth-century distinction between the church militant and the church triumphant, where a radical distinction is made between *them*, the saints who "made it," and *us*, those struggling to get there. In its place we need to recover the vital and vibrant communion of saints, all of us, striving together for the completion of what has begun in the life of the first-born.[6] "And I, when I am lifted up, will gather all to myself."

The proper affection of true Christian eschatology is "yearning," an "urgent longing," a restlessness. This is the thrust of our "waiting in joyful hope," and it needs to be recovered. Popular images of the *eschaton* have sadly been deprived of this vitality and vibrancy. They do not tap into our yearnings, our longings, our deep restlessness, and as a result they fail us where they are needed most. There is no doubt that our faith, our life, and the truth of God's revelation will be much better served if, in place of static images of reward and rest, we can regain images of yearning and restlessness. If we remember that the saints in heaven are not "at rest," but rather are yearning for us and with us as they themselves appeal and pray on our behalf. If we remember that the Spirit is not at rest, but is, as the Greeks say, *dynamis*, an active force within us drawing us with Christ to Abba and into relationship, *koinonia*, with one another. True images of eschatology do not give us a picture of a kingdom that is to come. They show us rather that kingdom in the process of becoming, and include within themselves a whole cast of characters, even ourselves, who are actively involved in the task of bringing the kingdom into being here and now.

There is a final point on eschatology that we need for this piece of the collage. It is a delicate one, for it is not always immediately clear what the demands of God's *koinonia* might be. I sometimes joke about the Bronx-Irish-American piety of my youth that insisted "if it hurts, it's got to be good!" Those days spoke of a God who was pleased with more and more suffering. It stands in contrast to today where we are more likely to adopt a Walt Disney approach, looking for the magic wand or the political clout to make all suffering and negativity better. Today's image of God is that of a "nice God," who surely is affronted by all human negativity. The first tended romantically to glorify the crucifixion; the second tends blithely to overlook the crucifixion.

The truth is there is truth in both, and the trick is to know which is which. On the one hand, there is the fact that in times past Christians have found in their faith resources to endure suffering, discrimination, poverty, and other negativities by subsuming them under the symbol "the cross." At its worst, of course, such assessment is simply not Christian, denying the world and human history in the face of a "pie in the sky" promise. At its best, however, sufferings have been seen to be "birth pangs," the bringing forth of new and mysterious forms of life. This experience, borne witness to by countless Christians before us, cannot be abandoned or ignored. On the other hand, our current sensitivities call for sharing of blessing, for breaking of real bread beyond the ritual moment, and suggest that it is inauthentic for us to do eucharist if we do not include somehow in our prayer and action the hungry, the poor, the outcast, the despised. At their worst, our current sensibilities take us dangerously close to Pelagian ideology. At their best, however, they urge us to be honest and to take our proper responsibility for each other and for God's kingdom which we are involved in bringing forth. This voice too, borne witness to by countless numbers, cannot be abandoned or ignored.

There is always the temptation to simplify things by opting for one or the other, either pushing ourselves totally to the task or pushing the task entirely into the hands of God. But the choice is not one of either/or, and things simply are not so simple. After Vatican II the Dutch Bishop Becker made the remark: "We mustn't give people holy water when ordinary water will do." This is true. At the same time, the counter-remark also needs to be made: "We mustn't offer people only ordinary water when it is holy water they desire and need." My own sense is that the true appeal of Christian eschatology needs to embrace both affirmations and to accomplish two things that cannot and ought not be confused or conflated. It must urge us to the limits of our own possibilities and not allow us to escape our responsibility where we can in fact act and accomplish. And it needs to instruct us what to say and choose *at those limits.* Even in powerlessness we must choose. Even powerlessness contains God's future as one of its inner possibilities. While it is truly irresponsible to claim powerlessness to avoid doing what in fact we can do, it is a futile illusion to think that all things are possible, and a serious mistake to abandon the deepest wisdom of a crucified Christ.

There is a parallel here with the personal journey that affects that communal journey as well. In both we speak of limits. In both, the closer we get to those limits, the deeper we taste our own poverty and helplessness. In both we are drawn in poverty to the One who not only brings forth his kingdom among us, but who wishes to be worshiped along the way. If, in the words of Johannes Metz, worship is born from the dregs of poverty,[7] the same must be true of the church as for each member of the church as it was for him whose disciples we are.

The eucharist is our eschatological meal. It is our "pledge of future glory." It brings us together in a faith-filled human situation which should, if we let it, stir our yearnings and our longings. The eucharist projects a future where all men and women will live in fact as sisters and brothers, and in so projecting it urges us to choose that pattern of relationship in the here and now of our own human lives. "May all of us who share in the body and blood of Christ be brought together in unity by the Holy Spirit" (Eucharistic Prayer II). It is a commitment to choose such relationships where such in fact can be chosen, and a silent prayer of hope where such relationships lie yet beyond our reach. Both, though in different ways, bring forth the kingdom of God.

The eucharist remains a journey even after God sets us in relation to each other. And the path of the journey remains the same, namely, handing over every human situation and event of life to God in obedience and trust (offertory), allowing God to speak and name his own future within that situation or event (consecration), and following the mandate of that consecration to deeper and further relationship (communion) in Christ with others. The handing over is not an escape from responsibility. It is done to help us choose wisely. God's mandate remains to bring forth his truth from within every human event. God's mandate remains into *koinonia*. It may be chosen within the realm of what we can do, and manifest itself in some positive action. It may be chosen at the limits of our possibilities, and be instead a silent witness to hope. But it is our choice to make, and the handing over or entrustment to God is the necessary condition for the choice to be properly responsible and responsibly proper.

The eucharist continues to place this truth before us. It continues to lead us through many conversions long after we say *yes* to ourselves. It continues to proclaim in *consecratio* God's firm commitment and fidelity to us. And it continues to challenge us to say *yes* to each other, beyond all the boundaries we seek to establish, and under the same conditions with which we say *yes* to ourselves. The challenge of the eucharist to say *yes* to each other can never go away as long as one *no*, one refusal, remains spoken upon the earth.

SOME TOOLS FOR FURTHER UNDERSTANDING

Let me look briefly now at the third part of the collage. As mentioned in the introduction, this is a sort of tool kit, a collection of insights and methods which will further enlighten us for the task of hearing and responding to the challenge of God's *koinonia*. These too are merely suggestive, offered to give a deeper sense of what is involved in choosing God's kingdom into history.

The first is drawn from studies in primitive rites of passage which divide the passage into three distinct stages. Stage one, the time of separation, sees the mother give her child over to the agents of the passage, namely, the special group of "initiators" who will lead the child into adulthood. Stage two, called the time of liminality, is the time spent with these initiators.

Stage three is the return, the reaggregation of the child-now-adult into the life of the family and community.

The dynamic of separation is easy enough to understand. It is the act of giving over, of letting go. The dynamic of liminality is a bit more elusive. In fact, one does nothing at all. What happens in this stage happens on the edge of the community life, and lies in the hands of others. It is therefore out of everyone's control. Yet it nonetheless calls for and demands a new way of acting when the period of liminality is at an end. The child returns, looking still very much like the child who left only a short time before. Yet, as a result of the passage, to both mother and tribe the child is no more. What returns to be reaggregated is now an adult to be respected and treated as such. There is little evidence to motivate the new ways of behavior. There is only the conviction of a transformation that took place. It is a choice to treat the child as an adult, and in that choice lies the completion of the passage and the authentication of the transformation.

This is the point for our own reflections on God's *koinonia*. Since there is nothing obvious that has happened in the passage to force the new ways of acting, these new ways remain an act to be chosen. Trust in the period of liminality (consecration) is motive for the choice. And the choice to behave in new ways (communion) authenticates that choice.

The second tool comes from William Lynch's *Christ and Prometheus* in which he seeks to understand the relationship between the religious imagination and the secular imagination. Lynch notes the classic opposition between the two, and blames the opposition on the religious imagination and its demand that the secular be converted to the religious. Noting that the only yield of this classic opposition is further opposition and alienation, he seeks an alternative to bring them closer together. His suggestion is that it is the religious imagination, and not the secular, that is in need of conversion. The religious imagination needs to understand itself, not in opposition to the secular, but within the secular, as the secular's primary resource for success in its own project. The secular aims to humanize society. Lynch points out that it cannot succeed in its task without the contribution of the religious imagination. He also points out that the religious imagination can

only succeed in serving the secular if it yields its own demands and enters the secular on its own terms.

What Lynch outlines for the religious imagination is truly a
choice that involves self-abnegation and a form of death. It reminds one of the kind of thing Peter had to go through when
God called him to set aside the restrictions and prohibitions of
his Jewish past and enter the Gentile world on its own terms.
"What God has made clean, do not call unclean" (Acts 10:15).
It serves our own reflections as a paradigm for overcoming
opposition and resistance and moving toward God's *koinonia*.
To say *yes* to the other is to enter the other's life on the other's
terms, to be converted to the other and not demand that the
other be converted to oneself. God's *koinonia* demands self-
abnegation and a form of death. There is no other way.

The third source of insight comes from Macmurray's *Persons in Relation* where he speaks of a certain paradox involved
in all human relationship. While it is obvious that relationships are formed positively between people, what is less obvious is that they are at the same time formed negatively in opposition to all others who do not share in the relationship. The
intimacy of marriage or friendship, for example, is the positive
side of a relationship which at the same time excludes others
from that same intimate circle. The same is true of church bodies and relationships among religious peoples. Catholics, for
example, define others as non-Catholics. Christians speak of
non-Christians. Religious people claim something for themselves which non-religious people do not have. Theists are opposed to atheists. And so it goes.

The problem with this is that negative definition builds
walls around whatever relationship is under consideration,
and is one of the boundaries we set on God's *koinonia*. In the
irony of human relationship, the negative is necessary, and yet
contains the potential to destroy the very relationship it constitutes. Sooner or later, especially if the walls are taken to be absolute and no move is made to expand relationship beyond
them, the relationship which they contain will falter. As Macmurray puts it: "to be fully positive, the relationship must be
in principle inclusive, and without limits."[8] Realizing that he
is speaking of an ideal, he nonetheless argues that "the self-
realization of any individual person is only fully achieved if

he [or she] is positively motivated towards every other person with whom he [or she] is in relation."[9] As Christians we claim that only the sinless One lived this ideal, and our inability to achieve it for ourselves identifies the reality of sin in us which has not yet been overcome by Christ. It also identifies the point of our own lives where the appeal of the eucharist, enacted "for the forgiveness of sins," must be most forcefully attended to. Boundaries and sin must be overcome if God's *koinonia* is to be achieved.

Macmurray acknowledges that if this level of openness to others were achieved, the redemptive function of religion would be complete.[10] Indirectly he names the purpose of religion gradually to remove these negative exclusions from human relationship. It is not unlike the Pauline view of the *eschaton*, where there is neither Greek nor Jew, male nor female, slave nor free person, but all are one in Christ. Yet he reminds us that, even where the achievement remains far off, the only path to achievement is to continue to choose toward it, to continue to conquer the negative by choosing the positive over it.

If this were achieved, says Macmurray, "religion would then be simply the celebration of communion—of the fellowship of all things in God,"[11] which it is now only in hope and not in fact. In the meantime, on the way to this fulfillment, religion's primary purpose is to sustain the intention to achieve this degree of fellowship. This names for Christians one of the major reasons to enact the Lord's Supper until he comes.

A COMMON THREAD

So much for the collage. The biblical piece reminds us of the unqualified simplicity of God's *koinonia*, which it offers as the shape of all human relationships, between friends and lovers, among church assemblies and churches, between religious people and non-religious people, between nations and races, and finally within all creation itself. We can qualify it away, or let it be the motive and challenge and constant direction of all the choices we make. But its challenge stands without qualification. The eschatological piece reminds us that the emergence of God's *koinonia* is God's goal for all human history. It is a goal, however, which resides in each human situation as but one of its many possibilities and options. God's goal will be achieved only if we choose it, and this choice does not always come spontaneously to us. Yet, in God's design, nothing will happen unless and until we human people choose to make it happen. God does not violate creation, but urges it on to completion. Finally, the tools. Well, they too name the task as one of choice, but name it in such a way that the cost of the choice comes to surface. It involves choosing beyond the evidence, and acting accordingly. It demands dying to oneself, and seeing oneself within the life of the other, whether the two realities involved be persons, or churches, or nation, or races, whatever. And it demands the frightening risk of letting down the barriers that divide, of choosing the positive beyond the negative, of gradually letting exclusion become inclusion.

If there is a common thread that runs through them all, it is the accent on choice, and the realization that Christian initiation and transformation is not only the task of persons; it is likewise the task of churches, and nations, and races, and indeed all creation. For Christians the challenge is set forth each time they gather to do eucharist. It is the challenge, at the very point of saying *yes* to oneself, to say *yes* equally to the other, without demanding that the other change, fit one's rules, pass one's test. It makes no difference whether the "other" be another person, another local assembly, another Christian church, another religious group, another race, another nation. To place such demands is to violate the simple observation with which this chapter began, the profound truth that lies at the heart of our eucharistic faith, namely, it is God who sets us in relation and not we ourselves. The journey of obedience, of *offertorium*, will and must continue until the *koinonia* is achieved. In the meantime we have only the *consecratio*, the place where our own fragile obedience meets the Abba of Christ and the pledge of future glory that even now continues to summon us.

What shall it mean for people to let down barriers that divide them? For assemblies and churches to let down barriers that divide them? For religious peoples and nations and races to let down barriers that divide them? We have only to choose to find out. And it will certainly not happen unless and until we do choose.

* * * * * *

When I originally delivered this essay at St. Paul's Seminary, it bore the title "A Christian Shape to Church and Society." In its coming to be, I was tempted, for only a very few moments, to try to spin out some visionary structure which would live up to the title's promise. I quickly realized that such a vision might be brilliantly inspiring, but would have no more value than the forecasts of tea leaves and Tarot cards. In our own Christian storehouse we have already ample visions and images to guide us into relationship. We even have our constant exercise in the act of eucharist. I decided instead to do what the eucharist itself does, namely, make a simple appeal to human freedom and decision. Hence the structure of the collage. Just how simple it turned out, I am not sure.

At any rate, the biblical witness is just that, an appeal. It names one possibility among many possibilities for human history and human relation and asks us to choose this possibility above all others. Our eschatological faith also makes an appeal, especially at the periphery of our relationship where we are less likely to want to choose God's option. Yet it speaks God's option with force and urges us to choose. And the tools, offered to stimulate the imagination and name the terms of the choice, also make an appeal. And a challenge. They point out how costly the choice may be. They remind us that the choices for God's future will necessarily take us beyond the evidence and beyond our own need for a secure structural identity, and demand that we risk being overtaken where we are most vulnerable. Others could choose the negative and destroy us.

In the face of such an appeal, and such a costly challenge, we can only come back again and again to the place of God's word, God's promise, God's fidelity. We can only proclaim the death of the Lord until he comes. For in that promise and in that death God announces that the negatives, all negatives, whatever their threat, have been rendered finally without power.

The word God speaks remains Jesus Christ. The word God speaks becomes men and women gathered in relation about a table. The word God speaks, both Christ and us, is a word that yearns for completion. All we can do, and all we need to do, is listen, follow, trust, and choose. Thus will the church take Christian shape. Thus will society take Christian shape. Thus will history take Christian shape. And thus will come the *koinonia* of God.

Notes

1. See, for example, A. van Gennep, *Rites of Passage* (Chicago: University of Chicago Press, 1960).

2. William Lynch, *Christ and Prometheus: A New Image of the Secular* (Notre Dame: University of Notre Dame Press, 1970).

3. John Macmurray, *Persons in Relation* (1961; reprint Atlantic Highlands, NJ: Humanities Press, 1979). This work, along with its companion *The Self as Agent* (1957; reprint Humanities Press, 1978) contains the Gifford Lectures delivered by Macmurray in 1953-1954 under the title *The Form of the Personal*.

4. This point was developed in the previous chapter.

5. *Sacramentum Mundi*, ed., K. Rahner (New York: Herder and Herder, 1968) 2:244, s.v. "Eschatology" (article by K. Rahner).

6. This need is developed nicely by Robert Hoeffner in "A Pastoral Evaluation of Funerals," *Worship* 55 (1981) 487-490.

7. See Johannes Metz, *Poverty of Spirit*, trans., J. Drury (New York: Paulist Press, 1968). The final chapter in Metz' work is entitled "The Dregs of Poverty: Worship."

8. Macmurray, *Persons* 159.

9. Ibid.

10. Ibid. 165.

11. Ibid.

$3^{0\ 0}$ 8^{0}

$\$ 24,^{0\ 0\ 0}$